MW00337013

Movers and Stayers

Movers and Stayers

The Partisan Transformation of Twenty-First Century Southern Politics

IRWIN L. MORRIS

OXFORD

UNIVERSITY PRESS

OXFORD
UNIVERSITY PRESS

Oxford University Press is a department of the University of Oxford. It furthers
the University's objective of excellence in research, scholarship, and education
by publishing worldwide. Oxford is a registered trade mark of Oxford University
Press in the UK and certain other countries.

Published in the United States of America by Oxford University Press
198 Madison Avenue, New York, NY 10016, United States of America.

© Oxford University Press 2021

All rights reserved. No part of this publication may be reproduced, stored in
a retrieval system, or transmitted, in any form or by any means, without the
prior permission in writing of Oxford University Press, or as expressly permitted
by law, by license, or under terms agreed with the appropriate reproduction
rights organization. Inquiries concerning reproduction outside the scope of the
above should be sent to the Rights Department, Oxford University Press, at the
address above.

You must not circulate this work in any other form
and you must impose this same condition on any acquirer.

Library of Congress Cataloging-in-Publication Data
Names: Morris, Irwin L. (Irwin Lester), 1967– author.
Title: Movers and stayers : the partisan transformation of twenty-first
century Southern politics / Irwin L. Morris.
Description: New York, NY : Oxford University Press, [2021] |
Include bibliographical references and index.
Identifiers: LCCN 2020029870 (print) | LCCN 2020029871 (ebook) |
ISBN 9780190052898 (hardback) | ISBN 9780190052904 (paperback) |
ISBN 9780190052928 (epub)
Subjects: LCSH: Political parties–Southern States–History–21st century.
| Party affiliation–Southern States. | Political culture–Southern
States. | Demography–Political aspects–Southern States. | Migration,
Internal–Political aspects–Southern States. | Southern
States–Politics and government–21st century.
Classification: LCC JK2295.A13 M67 2020 (print) | LCC JK2295.A13 (ebook)
| DDC 324.2730975–dc23
LC record available at https://lccn.loc.gov/2020029870
LC ebook record available at https://lccn.loc.gov/2020029871

DOI: 10.1093/oso/9780190052898.001.0001

1 3 5 7 9 8 6 4 2

Paperback printed by LSC Communications, United States of America
Hardback printed by Bridgeport National Bindery, Inc., United States of America

For Chris, Maddie, and Cameron

Contents

Acknowledgments   ix

1. The Shifting South: Understanding Geographic Polarization
    and Partisan Change   1

2. Migration and Partisan Change: Movers and Stayers   21

3. Population Growth and Partisan Change in the South   47

4. Players in the Migration Game: Understanding the
    Distinctiveness of Movers   71

5. Migrant Magnets: How Movers Change the Politics of Their
    New Homes *and* the Places They Leave: The Case of Whites   107

6. Migrant Magnets: How Movers Change the Politics of Their
    New Homes *and* the Places They Leave: The Cases of
    People of Blacks and Latinos   133

7. The Special Case of Retirees: When the Elderly Move   161

8. Movers, Stayers, and the End of Southern Politics?   175

Notes   193
Bibliography   207
Index   215

Acknowledgments

Back in the South after two decades in Maryland, I'm reminded of one constant: summers sure are hot around here. A few years ago, wearing my political scientist hat, I would have been able to think of few more constants—or at least "consistents"—but as you'll be able to tell soon enough, my list of "consistents" has shortened quite a bit since I started work on the volume you have in your hand (or on your iPad or your phone or whatever).

I have been seriously interested in southern politics for about 25 years. I still blame Trey Hood for getting me hooked in the first place and Quentin Kidd for encouraging that failing. Collaborating with them while at Texas Tech, and after we all moved somewhere else, has been one of the most enlightening and enjoyable aspects of my career. So much of what I think about the South and its politics goes back to conversations with them.

I also want to acknowledge the role of the Biennial Citadel Symposium on Southern Politics in the maturation of my perspective on southern politics and my relationships with other students of southern politics. Regularly held in Charleston at almost the perfect time—early spring—I look forward to this meeting more than any other.

I have benefited greatly from the comments and suggestions on preliminary versions of pieces of this book from panelists at "The Nationalization of Politics: Evidence across Cities, Regions, and Nations" panel at the 2019 Annual Convention of the American Political Science Association and the most recent (2020) iteration of the Citadel Symposium. I am particularly indebted to Chuck Bullock, Thomas Ogorzalek, David Rohde, and Seth McKee for their helpful comments. Bryan Gervais, my co-author on *Reactionary Republicanism* (2018), has played an important role in the development of my perspective on the character of our political parties, particularly the Republican Party. Reviewers at two different stages of the development process at Oxford also made important contributions to the final manuscript.

Research and writing are tough work. It helps immeasurably to have a great research assistant. On this project, I have been lucky enough to work with two: Nick Miras at the University of Maryland and Kristina Bell at NC State University. Their efforts to gather, format, and display the data and related results were immeasurably helpful. They were fantastic, and I know they'll go far. I also want to acknowledge the resources made available to me through the William T. Kretzer Distinguished Professorship in Humanities. I might have finished the book without this support, but it certainly wouldn't have been done on this timeline.

Thanks so much to Dave McBride, my editor, who always believed in the idea and, finally, the manuscript, and all of the wonderful editorial and production staff at Oxford University Press. A first class operation.

Finally, thanks to my wife Chris and my kids, Maddie and Cameron. All stuck at home during the COVID-19 pandemic, they gave the "old man" a wide berth while he was writing.

Irwin L. Morris
June 6, 2020

1

The Shifting South

Understanding Geographic Polarization and Partisan Change

When V.O. Key (1949) wrote *Southern Politics in State and Nation*, the end of the Democrat-dominated Solid South sat beyond the conceptual horizon of all but the most prescient students of politics. Southern politics was Democratic politics.

Republicans had lived in the South since the Civil War, and they were the dominant party during Reconstruction. These Republicans—overwhelmingly African American—sent the first African Americans to the U.S. House of Representatives and the Senate, but when Reconstruction ended, and Jim Crow laws and the white primary systematically disenfranchised black voters, Republican fortunes plummeted. Starting in 1880, the first post-Reconstruction federal election, Democratic presidential candidates won every southern state in every election—with the exception of 1920 (when Warren G. Harding won Tennessee) and 1928 (when Herbert Hoover won all of the Rim South states except Arkansas)—until 1948.[1] And in 1948, it was Strom Thurmond, the Dixiecrat candidate, who took several southern states from Harry Truman. The Republican candidate, Thomas Dewey, failed to win a single southern state. During this era, no other region of the country was dominated by a single party. Even in the largely Republican New England states, every state but New Hampshire had split support between the parties' presidential candidates during the 1912–1940 time period.

This overall Democratic dominance obscured certain pockets of Republicanism throughout the South—pockets of Republicanism predominantly found in but not limited to the Rim South. Still, while there were Republicans in the South at that time, they were few in number. Even in areas where Republicans were most heavily concentrated—for example, the Appalachian mountains of southwest Virginia, upper East Tennessee, western North Carolina, and northern Georgia—electoral victories were rare, and maintaining localized political control proved exceedingly difficult.

It was at the presidential level that Republicans made their earliest sustainable inroads. Since 1952, Republicans have won a single southern state in every presidential election. In some (more recent) presidential elections, Republican candidates won all of the southern states. Though Republican success came earliest at the presidential level (Aistrup 1996), the same partisan shift, albeit admittedly delayed, has occurred in federal congressional elections, state elections, and local elections as well.

Jump forward a half-century, and it is the Republicans that dominate southern politics. The congressional elections of 1994, when the Republicans retook the House, are often seen as the realigning elections (Gaddie 2012).[2] Still, there were six more years of southern Democrat Bill Clinton's presidency. But in the 2000 and 2004 presidential elections, not a single southern state[3] went for the Democratic candidate (even though one, Al Gore, hailed from Tennessee) (Moreland and Steed 2012). By 2012, only two governor's mansions were home to Democrats. In advance of the 2016 elections, there were only three southern Democrats serving in the U.S. Senate. Following the election of 2014, not a single white southern Democrat held a House seat in the Deep South (Alabama, Georgia, Louisiana, Mississippi, South Carolina). And the percentage of Republicans in state houses—both upper and lower houses—has increased steadily over the course of the 21st century. Republicans did not enjoy the unfettered dominance Democrats exercised during the first half of the 20th century, but their level of control was trending in that direction.

Democrats have, however, begun to make inroads into what appears, at first glance, to be a Republican version of the "Solid South." Shut out in 2000 and 2004, both President Obama (in 2008 and 2012) and Secretary Clinton (in 2016) won at least one southern state; Obama won Florida, North Carolina, and Virginia in 2008 and Florida and Virginia in 2012. Clinton took Virginia in 2016 (and came close to winning Florida). Though Clinton underperformed Obama's 2012 results nationally, the magnitude of her underperformance was slightly less in the South, and in three of the largest—and fastest growing—southern states—Georgia, Texas, and Virginia—Clinton actually outperformed Obama's 2012 results. A similar, if equally subtle, partisan shift manifested in the congressional and gubernatorial elections. Democrats added a Senate seat (in Alabama) in a special election in 2017 and a win in North Carolina's gubernatorial election in 2016. In 2018, Democrats successfully defended every House seat they held in the South while Republican House members lost seats in Florida, Georgia, South Carolina, Texas, and Virginia. Most recently, Virginia Democrats took control of both houses of the state legislature for the first time in 25 years.

These recent election results suggest that voters' support for Democratic candidates is growing. Is there similar evidence of a shift in voters' partisan attachments? Using the Cumulative Common Content (2006–2018) file from the Cooperative Congressional Election Study (Kuriwaki 2018) to gauge southerners' partisan attachments over the recent past, there is evidence of a clear shift to the Democratic Party. From 2006–2010, Republican voters outnumbered Democrats in the southern states.[4] In certain individual years, the gap between Republicans and Democrats was substantial. In 2008 and 2010, Republicans enjoyed an advantage in excess of five percentage points. Since 2010, however, southern Democrats have increased their numbers at Republicans' expense. Over the last three years of the sample, the Democrats have built an average advantage in excess of half a dozen percentage points. Just as Democratic gerrymandering in the mid-to-late 20th century created a political environment in which the partisanship of representatives (particularly state representatives) lagged voters' partisan attachments, Republican gerrymanders have produced a gap between current voters' preferences and the partisanship of their state and federal legislators.

Slowly but surely, Democrats are gaining supporters (and representatives) in the South. However, Democratic support is not growing equally across the South. In fact, what we are seeing is an increase in geographic *polarization* in the South. While Democratic support grows in certain states and locales, it is declining in other areas.

Ironically, the places where this growth is most prevalent are the same places where Republicans had their earliest significant successes in the 1960s and 1970s, the places where students of southern politics who focused on economic growth and migration as the engines of southern partisan change found the fullest flowering of Republican support—the Rim South. (See Map 1.1.)

Map 1.1 depicts the change in the Democratic candidate's percentage of the two-party popular vote from the 2000 presidential election to the 2016 presidential election. The 2000 election is the obvious starting point for an analysis focusing on the current century, but it is also a reasonable analogue for the election of 2016. The incumbent president was not a candidate in either

Map 1.1. State-Level Partisan Shifts in Presidential Elections (2000 vs. 2016)

election. Both elections occurred at the tail end of two-term Democratic administrations, and in both cases the Democratic candidate won the popular vote and lost the vote in the Electoral College. While the Democratic candidate's advantage in the popular vote was larger in 2016, the Democratic candidate's disadvantage in the Electoral College was also larger in 2016. Given the relatively stable national results, any state-level partisan shifts over that timeframe would be significant.

The states in the darker shades of gray—Virginia, Texas, Georgia, North Carolina, and South Carolina—in Map 1.1, Hillary Clinton (the Democratic presidential candidate in 2016) outperformed Al Gore (the Democratic presidential candidate in 2000). The darker the color, the greater the increase in support for the Democratic presidential candidate from 2000 to 2016. In the lighter gray states, Gore outperformed Clinton. The lighter the color, the greater the *decrease* in support for the Democratic presidential candidate. According to class-based theories of partisan change, Republican growth has been (and should still be) greatest in the Rim South. That's not what we see in this map. We see Republican growth in both the Deep South (Alabama, Louisiana, and Mississippi) and the Rim South (Arkansas, Tennessee, and to a lesser extent, Florida). We also see Democratic growth in the Deep South (Georgia and South Carolina) and the Rim South (North Carolina, Texas and Virginia). With the important exception of Florida—an extremely competitive state for years—there is another key difference between the blue states and the red states: population growth in the dark gray states is much faster than population growth in the light gray states.

Democrats are gaining supporters (albeit slowly), and these partisan gains are coming in the faster-growing, more populous states. Republican losses in the House came in the largest southern states: Texas (1st in population), Florida (2nd), Georgia (3rd), Virginia (5th), and South Carolina (7th). It was in Virginia, one of the South's larger, faster-growing states, that the Democrats scored such a significant statewide victory in 2019. These big state gains reflect the geographic character of Clinton's performance in the 2016 presidential elections. Where Clinton outperformed Obama's 2012 results in the South, it was in the larger states. In the five largest southern states (Texas, Florida, Georgia, North Carolina, and Virginia), Clinton outperformed Obama 2012 by nearly 1.5 percentage points. In the rest of the South—the six smallest states—Clinton *underperformed* Obama 2012 by more than four percentage points. This is a six-point gap clearly associated with population size and growth.

At the national level, an increasingly popular explanation for the relationship between Democratic support and state population is the distinctive geographic locus of Democratic and Republican support. Simply put, rural voters tend to be more likely to support Republicans, and urban voters tend to be more likely to support Democrats (see Monnat and Brown 2017 for a description of the research on the rural–urban partisan divide in 2016).[5] Given this dynamic, one might reasonably conjecture that states with smaller populations have more extensive rural areas, and states with larger populations are relatively more urban (at least in the South). But the relationship between urbanization and state population size in the South is anything but straightforward. First, any urbanization ranking of southern states depends upon the specific measurement of urbanization. If the states are ranked in terms of the percentage of population living in an urban area, Tennessee is more urban than North Carolina (a significantly more populous state), and Florida is much more urban than Texas (also a more populous state). If the states are ranked in terms of the percentage of land area classified as urban, Texas is less urban than a majority of the other southern states.[6] No simple relationship between state size and urbanization exists, at least in the South.

Historically, the urban–rural partisan divide has not been an accurate characterization of southern partisan geography. During the Solid South era, there was obviously no significant partisan divide to speak of. In the late 20th century, the last strongholds of Democratic conservatism were found in the rural South, not the urban South, but these strongholds were disappearing. By the 1990s, Republicans were making significant gains in the rural South. Nationally, rural areas have long been more supportive of Republicans than urban areas. Monnat and Brown note that "Trump's rural advantage in the 2016 election did not signal a new trend. Republicans have long won larger rural vote shares, particularly in Appalachia, the Great Plains, and parts of the South [in addition to the southern Appalachians]" (2017:227). Today, to the extent there is regional variation in the partisan attachments of rural voters, rural voters in the South tend to be relatively more supportive of Republicans than rural voters in other regions (i.e., the Northeast) (McKee and Teigen 2009).

This rural–urban divide manifests most consistently among white voters. Though rural voters have generally been more supportive of Republicans since at least the late 1990s, people of color—particularly African Americans—in rural areas have long supported Democratic candidates. Significant portions of the rural South are heavily populated by minority voters, voters who are far more likely to identify as Democrats than white voters. A number of rural southern counties are majority minority, and these are certainly not bastions of Republicanism. The rural shift to the right is the result of an even more dramatic shift to the right by whites living in rural areas. But if a rural–urban divide now exists in the South, can it explain the recent trajectory of Democratic support? Obviously, a growing rural–urban divide driven primarily by the increasing conservatism of whites in rural areas can't explain the subtle (albeit growing) region-wide shift to the *left*.

Likewise, claims that the leftward shift of southern politics results from the transition of rural areas to suburbs or urban areas are difficult to reconcile with the demographic data. Rural areas simply have not transformed at a rate consistent with the leftward shift in partisan support. The transformation of rural areas to suburban areas or suburban areas to urban areas (or rural areas to urban areas) often takes decades. These recent partisan shifts are a product of the last 20 years—in some cases they are more recent than that.

This subtle leftward shift may well be ephemeral. This nascent shift in partisan attachments could be rolled back by future events. Predicting the future is a fool's errand, but it is especially so in the realm of southern politics. Still, this subtle shift might also signal the onset of partisan sea change in southern politics. Seventy years later, are we at the same type of crossroads that Key described in *Southern Politics*? Empirically, the answer obviously remains to be seen. But beyond that, what do our theories of partisan change lead us to expect? How much do these theories help us understand this historical moment and the political crossroads where we find ourselves? Let's start that discussion with a few thoughts about my hometown.

I grew up in a town of around a thousand residents in the heart of the Appalachian Mountains. The Kentucky, Tennessee, and West Virginia borders are within an hour's drive. My hometown was one of only five incorporated communities in the county. Significantly larger in 1980 than it is today, it was served by Republican Congressman William Wampler for all of my childhood. Wampler lost his seat to Democrat Rick Boucher in 1982—a year in which Reagan's Republicans lost more than two dozen seats in the House—and Boucher held the seat until the "Tea Party" elections in 2010. That seat, "the Fighting Ninth," has been held by a Republican ever since. An overwhelmingly (over 96%) white county, over 80% of the ballots cast in the 2016 presidential election were for President Trump. How well do extant theories of partisan change explain the recent political trajectory of my hometown? Not well.

Grand theories of southern politics view the region through the lens of *race* or through the lens of *class*. Often, culture plays an important role in our understanding of the region and its politics, but culturally oriented perspectives rest on a bedrock of race or (less often) class.[7] Race-based theories of southern politics go back to the creation of the sub-field with the publication of Key's (1949) *Southern Politics in State and Nation.*[8] Given that the economic transformation of the South has occurred much more recently, it should be no surprise that class-based theories of partisan change began to develop in (and still tend to focus on) the Reagan and post-Reagan eras.

Race-based theories of southern partisan change tie Republican growth to local racial context.[9] When it became clear by the mid-1960s that the Republican Party was to be the home for racial conservatives, Key's (1949) "black belt hypothesis" implied that the higher the proportion of African Americans in the local community, the more likely whites were to switch to the Republican Party.[10] Key (1949) himself makes the claim that whites in the black belt perceive a greater threat to their social and political positions because of their proximity to large numbers of African Americans. As they feel more threatened, they become more racially conservative. Over the course of the post-war era, as the Democratic Party becomes increasingly progressive on civil rights issues and as the Republican Party turns to the right on issues related to civil rights and race with the development and implementation of the "Southern Strategy," racially conservative whites shift into the Republican Party. Thus, as the relative size of the local African American population increases, so too does the white support for the Republican Party (Giles 1977; Giles and Buckner 1993; Giles and Hertz 1994; Glaser 1994). This logic plays an important role in much of the most prominent work on southern partisan change (see, e.g., Aistrup 1996; Black and Black 1987, 1992, 2002, and 2012; Browder 2009; Hood, Kidd, and Morris 2004 and 2008; Mathews and Prothro 1966; Glaser 1996; McKee 2012; Crespino 2007; Valentino and Sears 2005).

Hood, Kidd, and Morris (2012a) update and extend Key's logic to the post–Voting Rights Act (VRA) electoral environment in which whites reacted not to the relative size of the black population in their community but the relative size of the *politically mobilized* black population in their community. When Key was writing, blacks were effectively excluded from the suffrage, so the governance question faced by conservative whites was not "How do we compete effectively in the political arena?" but "How do we prevent blacks from entering the political arena?".

In the context of the second question, perceptions of threat were based on the relative size of the entire black population in the local community. However, following the passage of the VRA in 1965, the focus shifted to the prior question. In that context, black mobilization, and the relative prevalence of mobilized African Americans, played a much more important role in the realignment of conservative whites into the Republican Party. As African Americans mobilized, it became increasingly difficult for racially conservative whites to maintain control of the local and state-level Democratic Party apparatus. As conservative whites struggled to maintain control of the southern Democratic Party—a task which was always more difficult than it appeared (Caughey 2018)—they fled to the increasingly conservative (and increasingly white) Republican Party. Ironically, the shift of conservative whites out of the Democratic Party had a direct (positive) contextual effect on the subsequent mobilization of African Americans and their increasingly strong attachment to the Democratic Party (Hood, Kidd, and Morris 2012a).

Race-focused theories of southern partisan change drew critiques from proponents of class-based theories (see Nadeau et al. 2004; Shafer and Johnston 2001 and 2006; Stonecash 2000; Stonecash and Brewer 2001; Nadeau and Stanley 1993; Abramowitz 1994; Levendusky 2009). According to class-based perspectives on southern partisan change, income growth and greater wealth drove the increase in attachment to the Republican Party and support for its candidates. Those with the most conservative attitudes toward economic policy (including welfare policy) fled the Democratic Party from the Reagan years forward. Proponents of the class perspective argued that southerners were becoming more like residents of other regions, regions in which economic status played a large role in determining partisanship.[11] Lublin (2004) argues that it is southern attitudes on economic issues that drives white partisanship in the 1980s, and that even in the 1990s, when issues related to race and culture became more important, they did not supplant economic issues (Kimball, Owings, and Artime 2010). Some even concluded that the connection between class and partisanship in the South outstripped the class dynamic in other regions. Just after the turn of the 21st century, Nadeau et al. wrote, ". . . class-based partisanship is not only a reality in the South but . . . it is now considerably stronger than in the rest of the country" (2004).

Note that in-migration from other regions plays a key role in class-based theories of southern partisan change. As certain parts of the South began to experience significant economic growth, they drew population from across the South and from other regions. Those moving to these high-growth areas tended to be better educated and tended to earn higher incomes at a time when those demographic characteristics were associated with greater attachment to the Republican Party. Also, the job-seeking migrants from other regions were more likely to be Republicans than the native southerners, who were overwhelmingly Democrats (see Shafer and Johnston 2006).

Culturally oriented theories of southern partisan change offer an apparent counterpoint to theories focused on race or class. Religion has long played a key role in southern culture, and with the growth of movements such as the Moral Majority and the extensive Republican efforts at the state, regional, and national levels to attract Christian Evangelicals, scholars of religion and politics attribute the dramatic growth of support for the Republican Party in the South to the region's social conservatism (see Green, Kellstedt, Smidt, and Guth 2009; Kellstedt, Guth, Green, and Smidt 2007; Adams 1997; Layman 2001; Perlstein 2001; Rozell and Smith 2012; Hillygus and Shields 2008; and Williams 2011). As Rozell and Smith note, "While Key ([1949]1984) famously notes that the 'black belt' that stretched across the South defined its politics before the civil rights revolution, it is not a stretch to argue that the 'Bible belt' has defined the region's politics since then" (2012: 133).

Note that culturally oriented theories of partisan change focus on the attitudes of whites; even socially conservative African Americans tend to align with the Democratic Party.[12] Yet social conservatism has a long history among southerners; absent racial or class dynamics, how do we explain the dramatic late–20th century shift of *white* social conservatives from the Democratic Party to the Republican Party? This is a difficult question to answer, and it is the primary reason that cultural perspectives on southern partisan transformation rarely stand alone. Maxwell and Shields (2019) provide a masterful description of Republican efforts to curry favor among racially *and* socially conservative white southerners in *The Long Southern Strategy: How Chasing White Voters in the South Changed American Politics*. They argue that over the course of the latter part of the 20th century up through the present day, the "long" southern strategy included efforts to win social conservatives. These efforts were based on "family values" policy positions designed to attract Evangelicals, but they were also designed to build on and expand the bedrock of southern Republicanism which was opposition to the expansion and protection of civil rights, and racial conservatism more generally. White social conservatives, by themselves, were not (and still are not) a sufficiently large portion of the post-VRA southern electorate to generate widespread party success. Rozell and Smith rightly note that "[t]he [white] conservative evangelical vote is the solid core of the GOP in the region. . . . [but] As demographic trends point to an increasingly fast-growing minority population in the South, the GOP actually needs to both hold its evangelical core and broaden its appeal among other voters. Over time the evangelical vote cannot carry the GOP in the region" (2012: 149). An additional issue for cultural theories of partisan change in the South is the declining proportion of the white evangelical population—both due to the increasing minority population and the decreasing religious orientation of younger generations—during the time period in which the Republican Party was clearly growing in the South (the late 20th century).

If economic growth drives Republican support in the South, then my hometown and the county it sits in should not have been such a strong supporter of the president. As my hometown was also not a migrant magnet—experiencing a significant loss in population over the past 40 years—immigration dynamics touted by class theories of southern politics can't explain its partisan leanings. In a county in which 19 of every 20 persons are white, race-based theories of Republican growth also fail to provide any explanatory leverage. Cultural theories of partisan change offer a somewhat more promising perspective; evangelical churches are quite popular in the town and region where I grew up (see White 2014 and White 2019). But these churches were arguably more popular when I was a child. Religious attachment and religiosity in the United States is declining at a significant rate, even among Evangelicals (Cox et al. 2019 and Smith et al. 2019). If the foundation for Republican growth is white evangelicalism, why has this growth occurred at a time when white Evangelicals are declining?

Far from being an anomaly, my hometown is fully representative of many of the central features of 21st-century southern partisan politics. The core supporters of the Republican Party in the South—and across the United States—are white. They tend to be relatively older. They are less likely to have a four-year college degree. They are more likely to live in a rural area. A generation ago, these people would probably have been Democrats (just as our theories written for that time would have predicted). And a generation ago, they were. What happened? Or, more accurately, what is happening?

Old Theories Facing a New World

We are two decades into the 21st century, and in the context of southern politics, it is easy to view them as the fulfillment of the political arc that had already begun when Key was writing during those first few post-war years. Accelerated dramatically by the passage of the VRA in 1965, we might view President Trump's victory in 2016 as the apotheosis of the rise of the Republican Party in the South, a place where the GOP hardly existed a century ago. That interpretation would miss an important political transformation that has already begun—a change unlikely to disappear regardless of the winner of the 2020 election. In fact, President Trump's re-election is more likely to *accelerate* this transition than to end it.[13] I contend that the arc of southern partisanship has already shifted. The South is already becoming more Democratic. In fact, the southern electorate has been shifting subtly toward the Democratic Party for more than a decade, and only a sea change in who the parties are and what they stand for—an epochal national partisan transformation—will reverse that trend.

Why is the South shifting toward the Democratic Party? Because people *move*. Migration is arguably the central—possibly the defining—dynamic of American history. The earliest Americans arrived here from Asia thousands of years ago. For over half a millennium, people have come here from all parts of the globe. Having once arrived, they often set out to go new places. All of that still occurs; in many cases, it occurs in an especially caustic political environment.

Given the political parties' current demographics, international migration has been recognized for some time as a potential boon for Democratic fortunes in the South. But until recently, the literature on internal migration, particularly migration from other regions, held that new southern residents would be more likely to be Republicans than Democrats (see Hood, Kidd, and Morris 2012a and Scher 1992).[14] The ubiquity of the southern Democratic Party made it likely that in-migrants from the North would be more likely to be Republicans than Democrats. But the evidence increasingly suggests that in the 21st century, that partisan advantage has evaporated (Hillygus et al. 2017; McKee 2010; and McKee and Teigen 2016). Democrats are now advantaged by cross-regional migration.

What we have failed to account for is the political implications of *intra-regional* migration. Movers are different from non-movers. That's true whether they are moving across a regional boundary (e.g., from West Virginia to Virginia or Maryland to Virginia) or within a region (e.g., from Arkansas to Florida). I'll demonstrate that they are younger, better educated, and thus more progressive than their less-mobile neighbors. This is true both nationally (and so is true for migrants *entering* the South from other regions) and within the South (thus its importance for understanding intra-regional migration). Because of the demographic and *political* distinctiveness of the movers, the places that attract them become more progressive (and more Democratic). But this increased progressivism is only partly a function of the direct impact of new (and different) voters. These movers also influence *stayers*—the long-term residents of the communities in which they are arriving *and*, crucially, the long-term residents of the communities which they are exiting.

The key political implications of this migratory pattern do not, however, flow from conscious, politically motivated choices. Non-retirees make significant moves (to another county or to another city) for three primary reasons: (1) work, (2) family, and (3) housing.[15] These reasons are clearly related. A new professional opportunity in another area may provide the chance to choose a different type of dwelling or relocate closer to extended family members.

These rationales for moving are fundamentally at odds with Bishop's recent argument in *The Big Sort* (2009): migration is driven first and foremost by political preferences. In the context of *The Big Sort*, migrants are, first and foremost, seekers of ideologically compatible fellow partisans when they pick up and move to a new community. The migratory engine is politics, not jobs or family. But for the overwhelming majority of politically significant moves—those that cross important governmental boundaries like national borders, state borders, county borders, municipal borders—I agree with the demographers. Migration is primarily a function of work and family. However, more proximate, more subtle relocations—for example, moving from an apartment to a house while keeping the same job and keeping the kids in the same school district—might easily be partly driven by political considerations. Moves *within* major political boundaries may well be consistent with the "Big Sort" dynamic. Movers and stayers theory doesn't speak to this sort of migration; instead, it is intended to explain how politics change when people move across political boundaries.

If people move for jobs, then they are moving to where the jobs are. The vector of their migration is toward economically prosperous areas where the professional opportunities outstrip those available to them in their old hometowns.[16] These migrant "magnets" enjoy an influx of younger, more progressive adults. Movers and stayers theory argues that when long-term residents (stayers) interact with these new migrants, they tend to (1) become more accepting or (2) exit. Greater acceptance breeds the development of a more broadly progressive outlook (and, given the substantive politics of our time, a greater affinity for the Democratic Party). This is a manifestation of the traditional "contact hypothesis" (Allport 1954). "Exit" means just that: long-term residents leave the community in response to the influx of new neighbors. Note that it is occurring in communities with vibrant and vital economies—the primary rationale for the influx of migrants in the first place. With progressives moving into communities that then become more progressive due to increased interaction with the new migrants, movers and stayers theory predicts that population growth in a community will generate a more progressive orientation (and greater support for the Democratic Party) in that community.

And what of those communities that are left behind? If jobs are the primary reason for migrating, then these declining communities—those that are literally losing population or those growing so slowly that they are moving farther into the tail of the community population distribution in a growing region—are likely to face significant economic hardship. This is actually what we find in the data (see Chart 1.1). Chart 1.1 depicts a scatterplot of all southern counties on two dimensions: (1) the change in the adult population from 2006 to 2016 and (2) the change in the median income over the same time period. There is a strong positive relationship between population

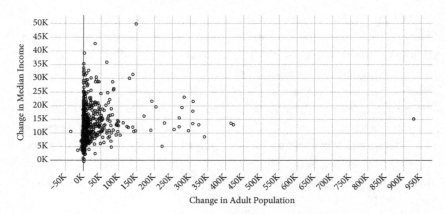

Chart 1.1. Change in Adult Population vs. Change in Median Income

change and income change, and that relationship is highly statistically significant. The places that people are moving to are also the places that are growing increasingly prosperous.

The chart also highlights the fact that this is not just a big city (or big county) story. Sure, metro areas centered in Austin, Atlanta, Charlotte, and Nashville have enjoyed population growth and financial success. But some of the fastest growth has occurred in smaller cities and counties—often in places that were quite small not that long ago. Take just two places in North Carolina: Asheville and Cary. Driving between college (Furman University) and my hometown took me through Asheville at a time when it had between 50,000 and 60,000 residents. Today, it has nearly double that number. When I arrived at UNC-Chapel Hill, Cary had fewer than 50,000 residents. Today, it has more than three times that number. Both Asheville and Cary are also considerably more prosperous than they were years ago. Asheville, the county seat for Buncombe County, is now the largest city and arguably the cultural center for fast-growing western North Carolina. Cary has become an increasingly popular location for tech-related businesses (e.g., SAS) and their employees, as well as the faculty and staff of the various colleges and universities in the area.

This chart also suggests that communities which are declining in population or growing at below-average rates tend to struggle economically as well. The causal relationship between income growth and population growth at the county level is not uncomplicated, but it is also difficult to deny. Long-term residents of these declining communities tend to feel *threatened*. This sense of threat was a key component of the Tea Party movement and, among whites, President Trump's base of support in 2016.[17]

In the context of movers and stayers theory, the response to threat is straightforward. In our highly polarized—and highly racialized—political environment, long-term residents respond to the threat they sense from the decline of their community by identifying more closely with the dominant political party of their social group. For whites, this will tend to be the Republican Party. Among African Americans, who already align with the Democratic Party at very high rates, the shift may be quite subtle, if we see it at all. Because Latinos partisan attachments vary across national identity groups, their response to threat, if it manifests at all, is also likely to be subtle, albeit in the Democratic direction. The key point is that neither blacks nor Latinos should respond to community decline by shifting towards the Republican Party—exactly what is expected of whites. At one time, a half-century ago or more, the racial divisions across parties were far more muted; those days are far behind us. Whites were far more evenly split among the Democratic and Republican parties. Blacks were somewhat more likely to identify as Republicans (see Farrington 2016), and Latinos and Asian Americans were a much smaller portion of the U.S. electorate.

Today our political parties are highly racialized. As Lee notes, "One of the most striking developments in the American party system since the 1990s has been the remarkable divergence in the racial and ethnic composition of the two parties in the mass electorate" (2020: 375). The primary reason for this divergence is the failure of the Republican Party to keep up with the increasing proportion of minorities in the electorate. Though the relative size of the white population has declined dramatically over the last 30 years, whites make up approximately the same proportion of the GOP as they did in 1990; Lee writes:

The GOP remains an overwhelmingly white party in a country that has become much more racially and ethnically diverse. . . . Over time, white voters' attitudes toward race emerged as a much stronger predictor of their partisan attachments, with white racial conservatives more likely to identify as Republicans. . . . The upshot of these long-term demographic and ideological changes is a party system increasingly cleaved along racial lines and thus primed to express racial and ethnic policy differences. (2020: 379)

In our racialized partisan environment, if whites threatened by community decline shift their allegiance to the Republican Party, and African Americans and Latinos threatened by community decline maintain or increase their allegiance to the Democratic Party, movers and stayers theory suggests that the conventional wisdom regarding Republican growth in rural areas is flawed. Rather than being constant, attachment to the Republican Party across rural (or previously rural) areas should vary—quite significantly—depending upon (1) the level of population growth or decline the community has experienced in recent years and (2) the relative size of the white population in those communities. Fast-growing rural (or previously rural) areas should have a larger proportion of Democrats than stagnating or declining rural areas. However, the impact of growth—or community size—on partisanship depends upon racial context. Declining majority minority communities might be *more* inclined toward the Democratic Party.

For white stayers, the relationship between population growth and alignment with the Democratic Party is positive and linear: long-term community residents become more conservative as population declines and more progressive as population increases.[18] For minorities, the relationship between population growth and attachment to the Democratic Party is more complicated. Given the relatively high baseline attachment to the Democratic Party, particularly among African Americans, the contact effects which move white partisanship in high-growth areas may not be sufficient to do the same among people of color. The effects of threat are more likely to influence the partisanship and political attitudes of people of color. Threatened by the social and economic repercussions of community decline, minorities—and African Americans in particular—will tend to become more attached to the party they view as representing their interests. Now more than ever, in our racialized political environment, that is the Democratic Party.

The responses of whites and minorities to the threat of community decline is fully consistent with recent work on *affective polarization* (Iyengar et al. 2019; see also Mason 2018). As the emotional dimension of partisan identity increases, both attachment to one's party and aversion to the opposition party are magnified. Community decline induces perceived threat; perceived threat intensifies existing partisan allegiance (and opposition). Even true independents (which are few and far between) are inclined to respond to communal threat by attaching to the party of fellow community members, and these attachments tend to break down along racial lines. In the case of population increase, the leftward shift is a function of increased contact with a more progressive population. Whether the threat effect or the contact effect is larger is an empirical question.

The primary implication of movers and stayers theory is that localized population growth boosts progressive attitudes and identification with the Democratic Party. What that looks like in the aggregate is presented in Chart 1.2. Chart 1.2 is a scatterplot of the southern counties on two dimensions: adult population growth from 2006 to 2016, and the difference in the two-party vote for Democratic presidential candidate Gore (in 2000) and Democratic presidential candidate Clinton (in 2016).[19] The regression line—strongly positive and highly significant—is bounded by a 95% confidence interval. Note that the slope is not an artifact of the relationship between population and Democratic voting in a small number of very large counties. The scatterplot is based on unweighted data, so each county is equally weighted. This data strongly suggests the presence of a relationship between population growth and voting that is not limited to the handful of large southern cities.

A second important implication of movers and stayers theory is that *geographic* polarization in the South is likely to grow. As migration fosters progressive politics in areas with vibrant, growing communities and economies, these areas will tend to become more Democratic. While the political responses to decline and stagnation will vary by the racial composition of the community, largely white communities—the overwhelming majority of

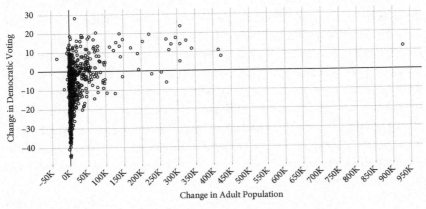

Chart 1.2. Change in Adult Population vs. Change in Democratic Presidential Voting

stagnating and declining communities—will continue their shift to the right, increasing their attachment to the Republican Party.

The political orientations of areas of growth and areas of stagnation and decline will become ever more disparate. Unlike the conventional wisdom in southern politics, the growth in geographic polarization will not cleave along the traditional Deep South and Rim South divide. Not all Deep South states are stagnating, and not all Rim South states are growing. Whether the Deep South and the Rim South are politically distinctive is increasingly a question for the past. The key to understanding the future political trajectories of each of the southern states—and cities, towns, and counties within the states—is not their place in the traditional sub-regional categorization scheme. The key is *growth*—or its absence. Movers and stayers theory implies that the Deep South/Rim South distinction will be overtaken by the Growing South/Stagnating South distinction (see Bullock 2020). If it does, students of southern politics will need to revisit the question of southern distinctiveness more broadly.

Outline of Chapters

The next chapter includes a more detailed introduction to the *movers and stayers* theory of southern partisan transformation. I elaborate on the ways in which existing theories, originally designed to explain the growth of southern Republicanism, fail to adequately account for the distinctive southern partisan shift occurring now. Whether focused on race, class, or culture, existing theories of southern partisan change are now poorly situated to explain the nascent shift toward the left. Chapter 2 includes a description of the various components of the movers and stayers theory and an explanation of the relationships between these components. In particular, I discuss my rationale for expecting 21st-century movers to be significantly more progressive than stayers and significantly more progressive than 20th-century migrants from other regions. Chapter 2 also includes a discussion of the *threat* dynamic and the *contact* dynamic on long-term community residents (stayers) and how and why the ideological and partisan implications of those dynamics vary across racial groups.

In Chapter 3, I examine the relationship between population growth and partisanship at the aggregate level. The central implication of movers and stayers theory is that population growth breeds increased attachment to the Democratic Party and greater support for its candidates. I provide empirical evidence broadly consistent with the hypothesized relationship between growth and partisanship. This chapter also includes an assessment of the recent trajectory of geographic polarization in the South. Are the Deep South and Rim South becoming more politically distinctive, or are they becoming more similar? And, more importantly, to what extent are the political leanings of residents of growing communities diverging from the politics of those living in locales that are stagnating or even declining? I provide answers to these questions in Chapter 3.

In the subsequent chapter, Chapter 4, I examine the empirical evidence for the distinctiveness of movers, a key aspect of the movers and stayers model. Movers are, in fact, different from stayers (and other non-movers). Using data from the Cooperative Congressional Election Studies from 2006 to 2018, I am able to access the demographic and political differences between recent movers and long-term residents of their current communities. The distinctions between the two are broadly consistent with the movers and stayers theory.

Chapter 5 is an examination of the demographic and political character of whites who are long-term residents of their communities (stayers) and whether or not we see differences between white stayers in growing communities and white stayers in declining communities. Movers and stayers theory has straightforward expectations for the relationship between community growth and the political attitudes and partisan attachments of white stayers—growth encourages progressivism. In growing communities, intergroup contact nurtures a more progressive orientation to social differences, and in our political environment that equates to increased identification with the Democratic Party. Conversely, the experience of threat associated with community decline incites a reactionary response and an increased attachment to the Republican Party. In this chapter, I evaluate these theoretical expectations.

Chapter 6 provides an examination of the extent to which the movers and stayers model accurately and adequately reflects the impact of movers on the ideological orientations and partisan attachments of stayers of color. Because movers and stayers theory predicts that people of color will respond to the threat posed by community decline differently than whites in the same circumstances—maintaining or increasing their identification with the Democratic—the relationship between population growth and the political attitudes of people of color is more complicated than the relationship for whites. I examine this relationship—and elaborate on the evidence—in Chapter 6.

I examine the special case of retiree migrants in Chapter 7. Do these movers—who by definition are not migrating in search of professional opportunities—counteract the effects of younger movers on existing community populations? Retirees are a distinctive lot, clearly different in many respects from the younger adults who dominate the "movers" category. Do the attitudes of mobile retirees mitigate or counteract the effects predicted by movers and stayers theory? I look at the evidence in Chapter 7.

In the concluding chapter, I provide a brief recap of the movers and stayers model, a description of the evidence for the various components of the model, and the key implication of the model: the direct relationship between population growth and Democratic Party support. The final chapter includes a discussion of the long-term implications of the movers and stayers theory for the future of southern partisanship, sub-regional distinctions within the South, and the distinctiveness of southern politics itself.

Though a full draft of the manuscript was submitted for review before the onset of the COVID-19 epidemic, I have taken the opportunity to discuss the potential impact of this international tragedy on the partisan trajectory of southern politics. Short of a transformation of the Democratic and Republican Party platforms, the fundamental relationship between growth and progressivism in the southern context will remain the same. However, the results of the 2020 elections may very well impact the baseline from which this dynamic reorganizes the region's politics.

If we are seeing the first stage of a Democratic resurgence in the South, movers and stayers theory can help us understand where and why it will happen (and where and why it won't). It will also give us a head start on the transformation of sub-regional politics in the South, and the changing relationship between "southern" politics and national politics. Southern politics—in state and nation—is not what it once was.

2

Migration and Partisan Change

Movers and Stayers

Democrats are gaining supporters and electing more public officials in the South. After two presidential elections in which Democrats failed to win a single southern state (2000 and 2004), Democratic candidates have won southern states in each of the last three elections (2008, 2012, and 2016). Democrats took a surprising number of Republican House seats in 2018, and three southern states (Louisiana, North Carolina, and Virginia) now have Democratic governors. In 2019, Democrats took control of the state legislature in Virginia for the first time since 1999. Virginia Democrats have not controlled both houses of the state legislature under a Democratic governor since 1994. Ironically, the places where Democratic growth is most prevalent tend to be the same places that saw the first significant inroads of Republicanism in the 1960s and 1970s, and the places where students of southern politics—particularly those focused on economic growth and migration as the engines of southern partisan change—expected to find the fullest flowering of Republican support: the Rim South.

Emerging Democratic strength in areas long thought to be Republican strongholds was unexpected, and a shift back to the right and a return of Republicanism remain real possibilities. But we may also be witnessing the early stage of a partisan transformation and a new southern politics. Think of this as *Southern Politics 4.0*. If we view Reconstruction—a time of Republican dominance and the widespread exclusion of southern whites from the electorate—as the first era of southern politics, then the end of Reconstruction in the late 1800s marks the beginning of the second era of southern politics. *Southern Politics 2.0* was a time of Democratic growth and then Democratic dominance. A concerted and successful effort to end African American suffrage resulted in the "Solid South," an unprecedented period of Democratic Party control, not seen in any other region of the country since the Civil War.

Cracks in the Solid South appeared well before the passage of the Voting Rights Act (VRA) in 1965. By the late 1940s, racially conservative southern Democrats bristled at the increasing support for civil rights by northern Democrats (such as Harry Truman). Strom Thurmond's Dixiecrat presidential campaign in 1948—an election in which he won four of the five Deep South states—illustrated the fault lines within the national Democratic Party in the middle of the 20th century. The Republican Party began a strategic shift to the right on civil rights issues in the 1960s, and the 1964 Goldwater campaign was only the most prominent early manifestation of this "Southern Strategy" (see Phillips 1969). When African Americans flooded into the electorate (and the Democratic Party) following the passage of the VRA, conservatives in the South fled the Democratic Party for the Republican Party (Hood, Kidd, and Morris 2012a). And so began *Southern Politics 3.0*, the era of Republican ascendance.

By the early years of the 21st century, Republicans enjoyed a level of political dominance not seen in any other region of the country by either party. But we are now seeing cracks in their control of southern politics, and Democrats are beginning to gain footholds in a growing number of southern states. In hindsight, the pre-Obama years appear to be the apotheosis of Republican dominance in southern politics, and the demographic foundations of the Obama victories and subsequent Democratic successes were developing at that time. We are now experiencing *Southern Politics 4.0*, an era with foundations stretching back to the earliest days of this century (if not farther).

Old Theories, New Politics

Unfortunately, our theories of southern politics were developed to understand previous eras, particularly the era of Republican ascendance. These explanations for partisan change fare poorly in the very different political context in which we now live. Our theories of partisan change in the South— designed for an older era of Republican growth—failed to predict this new attachment to the Democratic Party. They also prove to be of limited value in explaining this partisan shift. Theories of partisan change in the South tend to focus on class, race, or culture. How do each of these theories fare in the face of Southern Politics 4.0?

Class

Class-based theories (see, for example, Shafer and Johnston 2006; Levendusky 2009; Nadeau and Stanley 1993; Abramowitz 1994; Stonecash 2000; Stonecash and Brewer 2001; and Lublin 2004) of southern partisan change—the ebbing of support for the Democratic Party and the dramatic increase in support for the Republican Party—view economic growth as its engine. As certain parts of the South began to experience significant economic growth, they drew population both from across the South and from other regions. Those moving to these high-growth areas tended to be better educated and tended to earn higher incomes, at a time when those demographic characteristics were associated with greater attachment to the Republican Party. Additionally, the job-seeking migrants were more likely to be Republicans than the native southerners, who were overwhelmingly Democrats.

In the latter part of the 20th century, scholars focusing on the relationship between class and partisanship argued that economic growth would be an engine for Republican growth. Economic growth was expected to attract in-migrants from other regions, and these in-migrants were presumed to be more attached to the Republican Party than native southerners. Economic growth was also cited as the catalyst for a partisan realignment among native southerners. The greater the economic growth, the more attached to the Republican Party native southerners would become. Class-focused scholars hypothesized that economic expansion—driven, presumably, by Republican policy initiatives—would attract native southerners who had grown frustrated and disillusioned with the leftist leanings of the Democratic Party. In simplest terms: economic growth leads to population growth (from in-migration), and population growth leads to Republican growth (from Republican in-migrants and the rightward shift of native southerners).

Still, during the 20th century, class was not a strong dividing line in American politics—particularly partisan politics. This was especially true in the South. Class-based explanations for Republican growth in the South have largely faltered (to the extent they were ever accurate). While there is some evidence of a class-based dimension to the Reagan coalition, the ideological linchpin of that coalition (at least from a class standpoint) of fiscal conservatism and limited government was subsequently jettisoned by 21st-century Republicans. Trump apparently struck the death knell for Reaganites, both from an ideological perspective and a pragmatic political perspective. Arguably, the class component of the Reagan coalition either (1) played little or no role in the development of the southern Republican Party or (2) whatever role class played in the growth of southern Republicanism during the late 20th century was over by the 21st century. As Hood, Kidd, and Morris contend:

> . . . the attachment of small government conservatives to the Republican Party was relatively insignificant because of the limited role small government conservatives played in the development of the southern Republican Party in the first place. (2012b:345)

In accordance with this theory, we should expect to see the most significant and substantial Republican growth in the fastest growing urban, suburban, and exurban communities. As the preliminary evidence presented in Chapter 1 indicates, we do not see Republican growth in those locales with significant population growth. As counties grew over the past two decades, they actually became more Democratic (as indicated by support for Democratic presidential candidates). Republican support has waned in these counties over the course of the 21st century.[1] What is crucial from the standpoint of traditional class-based theories of southern politics is the strong relationship between economic growth, population growth, and Republican growth. As we saw in Chart 1.1, there is a strong relationship between economic growth and population growth. But as we saw in Chart 1.2, population growth is now associated with the expansion of Democratic support. Not only are communities in increasingly Democratic areas becoming larger; they are also becoming wealthier. The role of economics in the transformation of 21st-century southern politics surely isn't what it was decades ago.

Race

Race-based theories of southern partisan change tie Republican growth to local racial context. When it became clear by the mid-1960s that the Republican Party was to be the home for racial conservatives, Key's (1949) "black belt hypothesis" implied that the higher the proportion of African Americans in the local community, the more likely whites were to switch to the Republican Party. Hood, Kidd, and Morris (2012a) update and extend Key's logic to the post-VRA electoral environment in which whites reacted not to the relative size of the black population in their community but the relative size of the *politically mobilized* black population in their community. Theories of partisan change based on race relations struggle to explain the nascent growth of the Democratic Party and, even more important, the geographic locus of that growth. Since Key's introduction of the "black belt hypothesis," race-focused theories of southern partisan change have emphasized the relationship between white racial conservatism and *local* racial context. For Key (and sundry others), the relative size of the black population in a community drove white racial conservatism. As the "black belt"—an area where high concentrations of African Americans lived—cut a swath across the states of the Deep South, that was where racial conservatism developed most fully. There is considerable—though not unequivocal—evidence for this claim.

The shift to the Republican Party is a white story. Republicans in the South did not realize significant gains among African Americans, Latinos, or Asian Americans during this time period. Southern Republican growth during the second half of the 20th century was a white phenomenon. Racial dynamics played a "key" role in the growth of southern Republicanism; more specifically, racial dynamics played a role in the extent, the speed, and the geographic loci of Republican growth in the South.

Hood, Key, and Morris (2012a) outline the central mechanism driving the growth of southern Republicanism following the passage of the VRA in 1965—what they (we) refer to as the theory of "relative advantage." As African Americans moved into the electorate and, overwhelmingly, into the Democratic Party, the position of racial conservatives within the Democratic Party deteriorated. Once able to wield the power of the dominant party in state and local politics throughout the South, competition for control of the Democratic Party from liberal whites and newly mobilized African Americans intensified just as the national Democratic Party was veering away from the conservative positions of the southern wing of the party. These pressures were most intense where the size of the mobilized African American population was greatest. In predominantly African American communities, white conservatives struggled to maintain control of the Democratic Party.

Conservative Democrats who faced the most intense pressures from newly mobilized African Americans switched their allegiance to the Republican Party. Southern whites were faced with the choice between an unfamiliar Republican Party—though one that was newly conservative on issues of race—and a Democratic Party they could no longer control at the local level or support at the national level. The "relative advantage" of one party compared to the other was a function of the size of the African American electorate—the black proportion of the politically mobilized (Hood, Kidd, and Morris 2012a). As the size of the mobilized black population grew, conservative white control of the Democratic Party was compromised, and the GOP became an increasingly attractive option. Crucially, local (mobilized) black context drove party-switching.

As the Southern Strategy of national Republican leaders began to bear fruit among whites, racial context became more intimately tied to white support for the Republican Party. Following the passage of the VRA in 1965, the relative size of the mobilized black population drove both the increase in the size of the southern Republican Party and the geographic distribution of southern Republicans. Local racial context—specifically, the relative size of the local *mobilized* black population—drove the growth of southern Republicanism (Hood, Kidd, and Morris 2012a).

Today, the relationship between racial context—specifically, African American context—and attachment to the Republican Party among whites is quite different. According to the "black belt hypothesis," white racial conservatism was strongly and positively associated with local black context. As the relative size of the African American population in a community grew, so did the racial conservatism of the whites in the area. The theory of relative advantage (Hood, Kidd, and Morris 2012a) is based on a similar dynamic; here, however, the key independent variable is the relative size of the mobilized black population (post-1965), and the dependent variable is support for the Republican Party. At the time Key was writing, racially conservative southerners tended to be Democrats. In the post-VRA era, racially conservative southerners were increasingly likely to be Republicans. By the 21st century, racially conservative whites were overwhelmingly attached to the Republican Party.

In the absence of a relationship between local black context and Republican Party attachment (and white racial conservatism), the correlation between the relative size of the local black population and Democratic Party support is simply a function of the difference in the mean probability of Democratic support between African Americans and whites.[2] As African Americans are far more likely to identify with the Democratic Party and southern whites are far more likely to identify with the Republican Party, we would expect the correlation between black context and support for the Democratic Party (and their candidates) to be positive, quite large, and statistically significant.

If, on the other hand, white racial conservatism and support for the Republican Party are *directly* related to the relative size of the local black population, then the relationship between Democratic support and black context will be weaker. In the case in which no relationship exists between black context and white voting patterns, the replacement of a white voter by a black voter would have a positive impact on the expected aggregate Democratic support equal to the difference between the likelihood of a white voter supporting a Democratic candidate and a black voter supporting a Democratic candidate. However, if a positive relationship exists between an increase in the relative size of the black population and the likelihood that a white voter will identify as a Republican, then the Democratic advantage gained from the replacement of a white voter is mitigated by the extent that the additional black voter increases the likelihood that the *remaining* white voters will identify as Republicans. If conservative whites are very sensitive to black context, it is not difficult to imagine a scenario in which the replacement of a white voter by a black voter has *no* impact on the aggregate probability of support for the Democratic Party. It is even possible to construct an extreme "black belt" hypothesis scenario in which the replacement of a white voter by a black voter actually *decreases* the likelihood of aggregate support for the Democratic candidate.

The important takeaway here is that the strength of the relationship between black context and aggregate Democratic support is *inversely* related to the magnitude of the relationship between white racial conservatism/ Republican support and African American context. In an environment in which the mean probability of Democratic support among African Americans and the mean probability of Democratic support among whites is quite large—as it is, particularly in the South—then the *stronger* the aggregate relationship between relative black context and Democratic support, the *weaker* the relationship between relative black context and *white* Democratic support.

If the impact of local black context has diminished over time, we should expect the relationship between black context and Democratic support to have gained strength over time. We can assess the relationship between black context and Democratic support over time with demographic data from the Census and the aggregate county-level votes in presidential elections for each of the counties in the South.[3] In both 1996 and 2000, we see a relationship between black context and Democratic support, and the relationship is in the expected direction: as the size of the African American population increases, the level of Democratic support also increases. Significantly, the relationship is weaker (r = 0.48) in 1996 than in 2000 (r = 0.58). By 2016, the relationship has increased again (to r = 0.72). As African Americans were consistent supporters of the Democratic presidential candidates over this time period, this suggests a significantly stronger relationship between local black context and white conservatism or Republican support in 1996 and 2000 than in 2016.[4] This suggests that the localized relationship between black context and white voting is *much* weaker now than it was only 15–20 years ago.[5] In our era of nationalized politics, local racial context simply isn't as important as it once was. Local black context may no longer be a necessary or sufficient condition for the manifestation of racial conservatism. Today, diverse racial contexts may now foster progressivism (and Democratic Party attachment) among whites. By the same token, racial conservatism can grow in areas that have little if any racial diversity. In essence, we have learned to hate at a distance.

Culture

Alternatively, suppose culture is at the heart of partisan change. As the South has become more conservative and more Republican than the rest of the country, some scholars argue that it has become a magnet for both conservatives and Republicans. In *The Big Sort: Why the Clustering of Like-Minded America is Tearing Us Apart*, Bishop (2009) argues that American migrants sought communities that shared their cultural identities and chose their future neighbors accordingly. As native white southerners became more Republican, Bishop argues they were attracting ever-greater numbers of Republicans from *outside* the South. In fact, Bishop predicted significant growth in the number of Republican-dominated mega-counties during the early 21st century.

Migratory patterns—and the sorting they produce—also figure prominently in Richard Florida's work (see, for example, Florida 2008). Florida writes of the migration of the educated and wealthy "cultural creatives" to a handful of large cities and their surrounding suburbs. According to Florida:

[a] significant demographic realignment is currently at work: the mass relocation of highly skilled, highly educated, and highly paid people to a

relatively small number of metropolitan regions, and a corresponding exodus of lower and middle classes from those same place. (2008:93)

Florida's focus is on the movement to large metropolitan areas and, to a lesser extent, the forced relocation away from these areas by those with more limited resources. Significantly, the well-educated moving to these increasingly large urban areas are assumed to represent the range of the political spectrum, including both "the [progressive] cappuccino-drinking urban 'bourgeois-bohemian' ('bobo' for short) and suburbia's [conservative] 'patio man'" (2008:93).[6] Florida sees the manifestation of Campbell's "big sort" in this migration of the wealthy and educated to major urban areas—whether to the city centers or the suburbs or exurbs surrounding the city centers—but this in-migration is matched by the out-migration of those who can no longer afford these elite enclaves (Florida 2008).

Regardless of the variant of the "big sort" on which one focuses, a desire to live around those of similar *political* sensibilities drives political polarization. Progressives seek out politically compatible communities just as conservatives do. Progressive areas grow because progressives arrive; conservative locales flourish due to the influx of new conservatives. Communities decline because conservatives leave, and communities decline because liberals leave. Growth has no ideological or partisan vector. However, because of the distinctive conservatism of the South, the "big sort" dynamic should foster conservative (and Republican) growth within the region.

This culturally oriented tale of Republican ascendance is consistent with a recent work by Maxwell and Shields (2019) entitled *The Long Southern Strategy: How Chasing White Voters in the South Changed American Politics*. Maxwell and Shields describe how Republican elites strategically extended the core southern Republican constituency (based on racial conservatism) through the espousal of patriarchal values and the pro-life, anti-LGBTQ doctrines of the most conservative Christian Evangelicals. Where Maxwell and Shields (2019) seem to diverge from Bishop (2009) are in their expectations for the future. Though writing during a Republican presidency, Maxwell and Shields are somewhat less sanguine about the prospects of the Republican Party than Bishop.

According to Bishop (2009), these hypothetical migration and urbanization patterns should have produced Republican dominance in those areas that (1) grew most quickly and (2) attracted the largest numbers of migrants (often the same places). But that has not happened. Just as in the United

States as a whole, recent elections have shown that urbanized (and urban-izing) areas are increasingly Democratic while rural areas are increasingly Republican—even in the conservative South.[7] As we saw above, over the last two decades, where southern communities have grown significantly, the Democratic Party has benefited. If, ideologically speaking, like is simply drawn to like, this should not have happened. Why did it?

Movers and Stayers in the 21st-Century South

Existing theories of partisan change in the South were not designed to ex-plain the growing support for the Democratic Party. Our theories, and rightly so, were intended to help us understand why Republican supporters became so prevalent during the last half of the 20th century in an area where the political climate was (seemingly) so inhospitable. It should be no surprise that our theories of Republican growth failed to accurately predict the (ad-mittedly subtle) increase in support for Democratic candidates and attach-ment to the Democratic Party. Nor would it be fair to criticize these theories for failing to explain the geographic distribution of the southern Democratic vanguard in the first couple of decades of the 21st century. The fundamental problem is that extant theories of southern partisan change were predicated on political parties and partisans that are quickly fading into history. This is true in a philosophical sense and in a demographic sense.

Consider, again, the example of the county where I was raised. If eco-nomic growth drives Republican support in the South, then economically challenged Tazewell County should not have been such a strong supporter of the President. As Tazewell County has also not been a migrant magnet—experiencing a significant loss in population over the past 40 years—theories based on immigration dynamics can't explain its partisan leanings. And in an overwhelmingly white (>95%) county, race-based theories of Republican growth also fail to provide any explanatory leverage. From a theoretical standpoint, where I grew up is an outlier in every way.

But empirically, my hometown is fully representative of many of the cen-tral features of 21st-century southern partisan politics. The core supporters of the Republican Party are white. They tend to be relatively older. They are less likely to have a four-year college degree. They are more likely to live in a rural area. And while attachments to evangelical Christianity are prevalent in these rural areas (White 2014 and 2019), religiosity is not greater today than it was decades ago. In fact, it is broadly declining (Pew 2018a). If these religious attachments are waning, how do they provide the foundation cultural theories of Republican growth? Forty years ago, these people would probably have been Democrats (just as our theories written for that time would have predicted). And forty years ago, their parents and grandparents were Democrats. Why the striking disconnect between our theories and the facts on the ground? And what new theory can help us understand what the old theories failed to comprehend or no longer explain?

I have lived in a lot of southern places: as far west as Lubbock, TX, as far east as my current home in Cary, NC; as far South as Athens, GA (where I was born), and as far north as Cedar Bluff, VA. Over the course of the last half-century, the number of people in the South has grown dramatically—well in excess of national population growth. Texas is four times larger than it was in 1950, the year after V.O. Key published *Southern Politics in State and Nation*. Florida is almost eight times larger than it was in 1950. Today, there are more people in Texas and Florida than there were in all 11 southern states 70 years ago.

As is true for the South in general, population growth has been wildly uneven in the places I have lived. Some have grown dramatically. Cary has nearly quadrupled in size—from well less than 50,000 residents in 1990 to nearly 170,000 residents today—since I was in graduate school less than 25 miles away at UNC. Some have grown but at a much slower pace. Lubbock has doubled in size—from about 130,000 residents to around 260,000 residents—but it has taken 60 years to do so. Greenville (SC)— where I went to college—has a population that is only slightly larger than it had 60 years ago. And at least one place I have lived—my hometown, Cedar Bluff, VA—has not grown at all. In fact, its population has declined quite dramatically (from approximately 1,500 people to just over 1,000) over the past 40 years.

Students of southern politics have failed to appreciate the political implications of these differences—the variation in rates of population growth across the region. While we have been sensitive to the impact of regional in-migration on Republican growth during the last half of the 20th century, we have yet to grapple with the equally, if not more, significant role of migration more generally—not just inter-regional migration but also intra-regional migration—on Democratic growth in the 21st century. Significantly, these novel political implications are *not* the same as current theories of partisan change would lead us to expect.

What if the shifting sands of southern politics were a function of the character of migration both *to* the South and *within* the South? And what if we have misunderstood just who movers are? One explanation for the unexpected leftward shift in the trajectory of southern partisanship—particularly in those areas which grew most dramatically over the past two decades—is the changing character of in-migrants and their political attitudes and attachments. During the era of the Democrat-dominated Solid South, in-migrants from other regions tended to be more likely to be Republicans than native southerners, so as these in-migrants flowed into the South, they boosted the size of the Republican Party in the South (Hood and McKee 2010; see also Gimpel and Schuknecht 2001 on the impact of in-migration *in general* during this time period).

Political geographers have attributed this pre–21st century relationship between migration and Republican support to the demographic characteristics of *movers*. According to Jurjevich and Plane:

> Scholars have long inferred that because migrants are often younger, better educated, and have higher incomes, they are more likely to be Republicans compared to non-migrants. . . . Research has generally found that higher levels of mobility and migration are highly correlated with Republican Party identification. (2012:431)

Even though there is little question that in-migrants tended to be more Republican than native southerners during much of the second half of the 20th century, the impact of this flow of in-migrants on the overall trajectory of southern partisanship remains an open question. In fact, much of the most recent work suggests that the contribution of in-migrants to the growth of southern Republicanism—even if we limit ourselves to the pre-Clinton era—was more meagre than previously realized (see Hood, Kidd, and Morris 2012a and 2012b; Lang and Pearson-Merkowitz 2015; and Kuziemko and Washington 2018).

More significantly, all of the research referenced by Jurjevich and Plane (2012) focused exclusively on the last half of the 20th century. They provide no evidence—nor do they cite research that provides evidence—for the continuation of the relationship between migration and Republican growth into the 21st century. This is important because the demographics of partisanship have changed significantly over the past 20 years—with the exception of race, ethnicity, and gender, the characteristics that signaled "Republican" in 1990 and often signal "Democrat" today.

By the turn of the 21st century, the partisan attachments of in-migrants relative to native southerners had changed (see Hood and McKee 2010 and Jurjevich and Plane 2012). First, by 2000—obviously in the aftermath of the Republican Revolution in 1994—(white) native southerners were far more likely to be Republicans than they were during the Reagan era or earlier. Second, there was no similar shift in the partisanship of in-migrants from other regions; in fact, the most recent data indicate that in-migrants actually became *more* Democratic in their party attachments during the last twenty years (Hillygus, McKee, and Young 2017). As Hillygus, McKee, and Young write:

> ... white in-migrants contributed to the [Republican] partisan realignment of the South in the 1970s and 1980s. However, the relationship between in-migrants and natives subsequently flipped, with in-migrants diluting Republican presidential strength in the South by the 1990s. (2017:361)

Even if in-migrants were not more likely to identify as Democrats (which they are), they would still be less conservative than southern Republicans (particularly on social policy issues and issues related to race and ethnicity). Empirically, 21st century southern in-migrants are significantly more likely to identify as independents and to vote for Democratic candidates.[8]

So, where are the fast-growing southern Republican enclaves predicted by Bishop (2009), and why should we expect migrant Democrats to produce them? The contrast between the "big sort" narrative and the empirical record results from an underappreciation of the role of economics in relocation decisions. Migration patterns are far more sensitive to economics and economic circumstances than politically motivated theories of migration admit. In short, jobs matter as much as they ever have. And those who move for jobs are not a random cross-section of the American population. These movers tend to be relatively younger, more educated, and less likely to be white than the average American adult. Given those demographic distinctions, it comes as no surprise that they are also more likely to be Democrats.

Those locales that draw the largest numbers of migrants are then most likely to lean in the Democratic direction. And migrants moving into these fast-growing communities find themselves in more integrated neighborhoods than those in more economically stagnant communities. The Democratic leanings they bring with them are reinforced by the diversity of the communities in which they choose to live. Internal migration—whether between regions in the United States, states within the same region, or counties within the same states—is not *primarily* about politics. It is driven by economics. International migration—immigration from other nations—is also primarily about economics. To the extent there is a political component, the strong tendency for immigrants to identify as Democrats and support Democratic candidates mitigates against viewing this migratory stream as the foundation of new, fast-growing Republican-dominated cities, counties, and states in the South (or elsewhere in the United States).

These migration patterns—driven, fundamentally by a search for economic opportunity—also have important implications for the areas that migrants leave behind. Demographers distinguish between locations that *pull* or attract migrants and locations that *push* residents to emigrate. A vibrant job market is a strong pull; a stagnant or disintegrating job market—increasingly common in many rural areas in the South—can give a strong push to local residents. As economic opportunities evaporate, and the most able are pushed to emigrate (and pulled to other locations), residents who remain are threatened. There is the immediate economic threat, but with the loss of population comes a broader sense of social threat. How do stayers respond to this threat?

A central tenet of movers and stayers theory is that this perceived threat has important political implications: it fosters race-specific partisan growth. Under threat, citizens will be more likely to align with the dominant political party of their racial group. Whites will be more likely to align with the Republican Party. Note that this partisan reaction is not dependent upon the racial diversity of the local context. African Americans and Latinos will maintain or increase their alignment with the Democratic Party.

There are ideological reasons for this reaction, particularly among conservative whites. Increasing partisan polarization has been an important aspect of our politics for all of the 21st century. This polarization has led to a more *nationalized* politics (Hopkins 2018), but the ideological and policy distinctiveness of the two parties is still more complicated than much of the literature suggests (see, for example, Grossman and Hopkins 2016).

In *Reactionary Republicans: How the Tea Party in the House Paved the Way for Trump's Victory* (2018), Bryan Gervais and I argued that Donald Trump capitalized on a distinctive (and growing) strain of Republicanism in 2016, the same strain of Republicanism upon which the Tea Party movement was built following the Great Recession and the election of Barack Obama in 2008. What set this strain of Republicanism apart from those which had gone before it was (1) the preoccupation with issues related to social policy and civil rights and (2) the complete disregard for both fiscal conservatism and free trade, central facets of post–New Deal Republicanism. Cultural issues did not divide the parties to a significant extent until substantial constituencies within the national Republican Party sought to attract conservative southern whites disillusioned with the increasingly progressive stance of the national Democratic Party on issues related to race (see, for example, Maxwell and Shields 2019). These cultural issues included abortion, LGBTQ rights, gun control, and religious liberty. While the national Republican Party's increasing emphasis on conservative positions on issues of race, class, and culture may well have grown the southern Republican Party during the last third of the 20th century, changing circumstances and changing Republican strategies have eroded this growth potential in the 21st century (particularly in the last decade). There are three main reasons for this.

First, the Great Recession eliminated whatever electoral advantage Republicans enjoyed on the management of the economy. Policy responses to the Great Recession—massive new government spending, ballooning deficits, and historically expansionary monetary policy—manifested a full-scale repudiation of Reaganism. Arguments drawing a causal relationship between income or class and partisan voting in the South, in which Republicans are the party of wealth and economic growth and Democrats are the party of the working class, are no longer apt. Shafer and Johnston, writing in the early 2000s (but prior to the Great Recession) argue:

> From the 1960s and ever onward, *at least as this is being written* [emphasis added], the wealthy became most likely to vote Republican, in the South and not just the North. In our terms, the top tercile became most likely to vote Republican, the bottom tercile least so. (2006:27)

This is a statement that simply has not accurately characterized class dynamics within southern partisan politics for at least a decade. To the extent that economic development was ever a significant "Republican accelerator" (Shaffer and Johnston 2006:92), it is clearly not that today. Another proponent of the centrality of class-based explanations for southern partisan change writes:

> Economic growth has been rapid in the South since the Civil Rights Movement, allowing the region to narrow considerably the gap in prosperity between the South and the rest of the nation. Growing Republicanism might unsurprisingly accompany this rise in prosperity. (Lublin 2004:210)

Today, this dramatic rise in prosperity is accompanied by growing numbers of Democrats. Whatever we once considered the role of class in the transformation of southern partisanship, it does not play that role (or it plays that role in an entirely different way) today.

The genesis of the organizational Tea Party movement—though not the foundation of mass public support for the movement—flowed from this ideological transformation within the Republican Party. Any class-based advantages enjoyed by the southern wing of the Republican Party—advantages that tied greater wealth and income to support for the Republican Party and its candidates—experienced a precipitous erosion. Today, wealth and income among southern whites is nearly unrelated to partisanship. Education, a building block for future income and wealth, on the other hand, is related to support for Democratic Party candidates.

Second, demographic dynamics have eroded the relative size of the southern white population over the course of the 21st century. If Republican candidates were equally adept at attracting minority supporters as white supporters, this demographic trend would not have compromised their dominant position in southern politics, but Republican candidates have struggled to appeal to non-white voters (in the South and more broadly).

Finally, generational change has eroded Republican support in the South—even among whites. Younger generations are far less likely to identify with a religious denomination or to attend church than Baby Boomers and members of the Silent Generation. According to data collected by the Pew Research Center (2018b), Millennials and Generation Z adults are significantly less likely to be affiliated with a religious community than older Americans. Of particular importance for the Republican Party is the fact that this generational difference is *greatest* for Protestants—the backbone of social conservatism in the Republican Party (Pew Research Center 2018a).

Reactionary Republicans, a manifestation of an overwhelmingly *white* political movement, see no progress—economic, political, social, or otherwise—in the first decades of the 21st century. It would be inaccurate and unfair to suggest that all Republicans are of a reactionary bent, but it is an extremely common attitude within the party, and the party itself is over-whelmingly white—more so than at any time in modern history. The two major political parties are more demographically distinct than at any time in American history. Of particular significance is the racial and ethnic dis-tinctiveness of the two major parties. The racial and ethnic composition of the Democratic Party is comparable to—though admittedly somewhat more diverse than—the adult U.S. population as a whole. However, there is a large gap between the racial/ethnic makeup of the Republican Party and the ra-cial/ethnic makeup of the U.S. population. The percentage of Republicans who are minorities is approximately the same today as it was 40 years ago (Lee 2020). Obviously, during that time the relative size of the minority pop-ulation has grown dramatically. This minority growth has been captured by the Democratic Party.

Reactionary Republicans are rooted in the Tea Party movement (see Gervais and Morris 2018). And like Tea Partiers, reactionary Republicans see only regression and decline over the last two decades and especially over the last decade, in the years since the election of Barack Obama. They see the slow disintegration of their local communities and the rise of a host of "others"—people of color, members of the LGBTQ community, immigrants, the unchurched—and they blame the struggles of their local communities on the rise of the others, following in lockstep the narrative of leaders of this movement (e.g., Donald Trump).

The early literature on polarization focused on the role policy distinctions played in the widening gap between the major political parties (Levendusky 2009, McCarty, Poole, and Rosenthal 2006).[9] Within the southern con-text, policies related to civil rights issues were crucial in this regard, and the shift of racially conservative southern Democrats to the Republican Party in response to the increasing conservatism of the Republican elites and the increasing liberalism of (national) Democratic elites is arguably the linchpin of polarization in late 20th century politics (see Hood, Kidd, and Morris 2012b).

The most recent research, however, suggests that polarization is increas-ingly driven by non-policy dynamics. As Americans become more attached to political parties, and as partisanship becomes an increasingly impor-tant aspect of our identities, we develop an affinity for fellow partisans and, more significantly, an antipathy toward opposing partisans that cannot be explained solely in terms of policy differences. *Affective* forces play an ever-larger role in the polarization of our politics (Iyengar et al. 2019 and Mason 2018). *Affective polarization* refers to this emotional affinity for fellow partisans and the (often) passionate animosity toward opposing partisans. Iyengar et al. describe the manifestation of affective polarization as follows:

> Ordinary Americans increasingly dislike and distrust those from the other party. Democrats and Republicans both say that the other party's members are hypocritical, selfish, and close-minded, and they are unwilling to socialize across party lines, or even to partner with opponents in a variety of other activities. (2019:130)

Affective polarization is a relatively recent phenomenon, so we are just beginning to understand the political and non-political factors that drive it. Ideological polarization appears to foster affective polarization. As societal groups become more ideologically homogenous and increasingly share the same partisan identity—think of the shift in partisan consistency among white Evangelicals in the South over the last three decades of the 20th century—the number of cross-cutting identities *within* the group declines. If members of a congregation, for example, are split relatively evenly between Democrats and Republicans, it is more difficult for parishioners to develop an animosity toward opposing partisans than if all (or nearly all) parishioners identify with the same party. In the absence of these cross-cutting identities, affective polarization grows (Huddy et al. 2015 and Mason 2018). Affective polarization also influences non-political aspects of social life. There is evidence that partisanship plays an increasingly important role in our personal relationships, our economic behavior, and, in some cases, even professional decisions (Iyengar et al. 2019:136).

In this extremely polarized context, responses to threat will also be partisan. Threat will increase the partisan attachment of existing partisans (and independent leaners). Among true independents—quite a small share of the electorate—movers and stayers theory leads us to expect an increase in partisan attachment in the direction of the partisan alignment of an independent's primary social group (race, class, religion) where *no* significant cross-pressuring exists. As race is an increasingly important social identity—often trumping class and religion when cross-pressures occur— white independents will tend to gravitate toward the Republican Party when under duress, and independents of color will tend to gravitate toward the

Democratic Party.[10] Where cross-pressuring is significant—a vanishingly rare situation in our current political environment—movers and stayers theory has no partisan prediction.

Declining or stagnating locales—unless they are overwhelmingly populated by minorities—will tend to become increasingly Republican. Minority communities facing the threat of stagnation and decline, on the other hand, will tend to become, if possible, even more leftward leaning. In the 21st century, there is still a "big sort" occurring—and that sort has political implications. But the areas of growth in the South are not becoming more Republican; they are becoming more Democratic. It is the areas of waning population that are tending to become more Republican. Sorting is occurring, but it is not the sorting described by Bishop—at least not since the Great Recession. And as long as party differences are driven by racial, ethnic, and cultural differences, this dynamic will continue.

Movers and stayers theory is not logically inconsistent with the proposition that movers seek out neighborhoods where their political preferences are reflected. A Republican moving from rural West Virginia to Raleigh, NC, might seek out a relatively more Republican neighborhood in Raleigh. A Democrat moving from suburban Maryland to Raleigh might, likewise, seek out a Democratic neighborhood in Raleigh. Those neighborhoods might be in different state legislative districts—or even distinct congressional districts—but not necessarily.

Movers and stayers theory can accommodate short, local moves driven by neighborhood concerns—moves focused on changing schools, upsizing or downsizing housing, or (even) political outlooks. Short moves within the same political boundaries have, by themselves, no net effect on the partisan makeup of a broader legislative or congressional district. Even so, as the size of the in-migrant population increases relative to the size of the existing community, the *enclave* strategy becomes more and more difficult to implement. In fact, areas that have grown dramatically over the past few decades tend to be significantly *less* segregated than areas which have declined in population.[11]

According to movers and stayers theory, those who relocate—the movers—and those who remain in place—the stayers—are demographically and politically distinct. In fact, they are politically distinct in large part because they are demographically distinct. In Chapter 4, I present recent data showing that southern in-migrants (and those moving *within* the South) are younger, more educated, and more diverse than native southerners—and for all of these demographic reasons, they are more likely to be Democrats.[12] Southerners making politically meaningful moves within the South—to other states, other congressional districts, and other counties—are also demographically disposed to the Democratic Party. And when they arrive in their new communities, the increasingly diverse (and integrated) places they call home foster the progressivism to which they are demographically disposed.

Among whites, the mirror image of this dynamic occurs in the areas which southerners are leaving. Those who remain behind when movers leave tend to be older, less educated, and less progressive than movers, and so those communities drift in a conservative direction. This drift is augmented by the threat associated with community decline and the Republican shift in partisan attachment in response to that threat. In majority-white rural communities in the South, the movers and stayers theory explains their increased conservatism (and increased support for the Republican Party and its candidates). The conjunction of the movers dynamic and the stayers dynamic implies a progressive shift *in the aggregate*: growing areas becoming more Democratic and declining (white) areas becoming more Republican. The joint effects of the movers and stayers dynamics provide an explanation for the particular version of geographic polarization—growing areas becoming more progressive, stagnating areas becoming more conservative— that is becoming increasingly common in the South.

This *national* political narrative resonates within largely white communities experiencing a decline and stagnation. Residents of declining communities—those growing at the very slowest rates or those actually declining in population—have come to connect the waning of their local communities with the historic political decline they have also experienced. The attribution of *local*-level ills and disappointments to *national*-level causes is important (and novel). Rather than attributing local problems to local context—the central theoretical thrust of group conflict theory—long-term community members (stayers) attribute local problems to national causes, a pattern reinforced by the growth of affective polarization. In our political environment, partisan attachments drive the perception of these national causes (Hopkins 2018). Threat (at the local level) then engenders a partisan response informed by national-level politics. I expect this effect is uniquely strong in the South. Maybe for the first time, we are finding a significant disjuncture between local problems and local solutions in southern politics.

Today, local problems prompt reactions that are conditioned on national-level political narratives. Fifty, sixty, or seventy years ago, local issues elicited responses framed by local conditions, particularly in the realm of race. Key's (1949) "black belt" hypothesis is predicated on this local-level dynamic. According to Key—and much subsequent research (Giles 1977; Giles and Hertz 1994; Giles and Buckner 1993; Glaser 1994 and 1996)—racial context drove racial conservatism among whites. As the relative size of the African American population grew within a community, the racial conservatism of whites grew accordingly. In the 1940s and 1950s this does not produce a concomitant rise in the support for the Republican Party in the South, largely because whites still controlled the ballot box and the southern branch of the Democratic Party more generally.

However, as I note above, following the passage of the VRA, conservative southern whites' influence within the national Democratic Party waned at the same time that the political mobilization of African Americans made it difficult (for racially conservative whites) to maintain control of their local Democratic Party apparatus (Hood, Kidd, and Morris 2012a). The shift to Republicanism among southern whites during the late 20th century was function of *local* racial context, though not the same local racial context that Key focused on. When federal law required the effective extension of the suffrage to African Americans, the prevalence of mobilized African Americans—rather than the simple proportion of African Americans in the community—became the key determinant of the partisan activities of conservative white southerners. Both Key's (1949) and Hood, Kidd, and Morris' (2012a) theories are consistent with variants of *group conflict theory*.

But the impact of local racial context on white political behavior is no longer what our race-based theories of southern politics predict. This inconsistency is a function of the nationalization of our partisan system. Proponents of group conflict theory assert that proximity to and contact with "others" engenders perceptions of threat. As the relative size of the other group increases within one's community, perceptions of threat increase. So, in the southern context, group conflict theory would predict that as the relative size of the African American population (or mobilized African American population) increases, whites' proximity to and contact with African Americans increases, and the threat perceived by conservative whites increases. Conservative white responses (i.e., greater attachment to the Republican Party) shift in response to variation in perceived threat.

The perception of threat is based on the prevalence of the "out" group within one's local community, and partisan responses flow from local demographic dynamics. Within our nationalized partisan environment, local demographic contexts may no longer drive levels of partisan attachment. Today, social and economic experiences may influence one's relative attachment to one political party or the other—and that party's positions on social or racial/ethnic issues—without any mediation from the local demographic context.

Imagine a white voter living in a depressed economic area. Maybe coal mining was the main industry for many years, and the decline of coal—or at least the decline of the workforce associated with coal extraction and the income it provided for many communities in the Appalachian Mountains—has brought difficult economic circumstances to the community where this white voter lives. Nostalgia for a past of greater economic prosperity is easy to understand. Let's also assume that this white voter is demographically average in this community, so job prospects are limited, and age and family ties make moving for work personally unattractive. Is it then a surprise that recent Republican appeals—particularly Trump's promise to bring back coal—find a welcoming audience here? Likewise, is it any surprise that blame for the community's current conditions is successfully laid at the feet of an array of "others"—minorities, the unchurched, immigrants, elites, urban professionals, etc.?

At one time, political identity was subject to an array of cross-cutting pressures. For example, one's economic status might encourage attachment to one political party at the same time that one's religious identity might encourage attachment to the other major political party. Consider how a working-class evangelical Christian would have been cross-pressured in the 1970s. Now assume that our cross-pressured voter is white. Does that change our calculation? What if our voter lives in Michigan? Do we need to update our predictions regarding the voter's party identification? In the 21st century, this sort of cross-pressuring is far more limited. As white conservatives left the Democratic Party in the late 20th century, identities tended to coalesce. Note that racial and ethnic identities hold a privileged position in the mutually reinforcing character of 21st century political identities (see Mason 2018).

The key, of course, is that these successful efforts to demonize "others"—those who don't look like our white voter or share the same faith (or culture) as our white voter—do not depend on the local presence of the population targeted for blame. In a nationalized political environment in which affective forces drive partisan attachments, the perception of "group threat" in this scenario—an increasingly common scenario—is fully divorced from the prevalence of the "threatening" group (or groups) in the local community. Our white voters' willingness to accept the blame narrative is unrelated to their personal experience (if any) with the targets of blame. This is a very different group threat dynamic. The absence of "others" also precludes the manifestation of the *contact hypothesis* dynamic.[13] If personal experience of living in a community with those who might be considered "others" is unavailable, then the opportunity for contact and interaction to ameliorate (or at least mitigate) feelings of threat is also unavailable.

This dynamic is unlikely to manifest in the cases of other demographic groups. We would not necessarily expect African Americans, for example, to have the same political response to economic deprivation and community decline as whites (particularly conservative whites in the South). The reactionary dimension to Trump's version of Republicanism is simply unlikely to resonate with people of color to the same extent it does conservative whites. Why would people of color seek to return to a time when they could not vote, or to a time where their basic civil rights were largely unprotected? In short, they wouldn't. This does not mean that people of color would not be threatened by the deterioration of their local economy or the decline of the community, but we should not expect their response to be the same. The threat associated with population decline and economic decline may not draw people of color to the Republican Party in the way that it does whites (conservative whites, in particular). Both population and economic decline are threatening regardless of race or ethnicity. However, people of color are more likely to respond to this threat by increasing their attachment to the *Democratic Party* rather than the *Republican Party*. The distinctiveness of the response flows from (1) traditional group attachments to the Democratic Party (a la "shared fate," Dawson 1994) and (2) the increased racialization of the two major political parties.

Party-switching in our current polarized political environment is, however, much less common. Affective polarization makes it nearly unthinkable. As conservative white southerners flooded out of the Democratic Party in the latter half of the 20th century, supporters of the two major political parties have become more demographically and ideologically distinctive.[14] For our purposes, the central feature of this partisan realignment is the increasingly racialized nature of the partisan division; as southern whites were shifting out of the Republican Party, the people of color were increasing their attachment to the Democratic Party.

Though African Americans have primarily been Democrats since the New Deal coalition, the flow of blacks out of the Republican Party picked up momentum in the 1960s and 1970s (Farrington 2016). Though the shift for Latinos occurred much later (in the 21st century) and engendered subtler results, we still see evidence of an increased attachment to the Democratic Party. With pundits struggling to explain why Trump received just over a quarter of the Latino vote in 2016, it is easy to forget that George W. Bush received over a third of the Latino vote in 2000 and 40% of the Latino vote in 2004 (a 20% increase) (Suro, Fry, and Passel 2005). While policy differences between the parties played an important role in the racialization of the party system, the growing racial disparity between the two parties has taken on a life of its own. As Mason writes:

> . . . party identity is strongly predicted by racial identity, not racial policy positions (Mangum 2013). The parties have grown so divided by race that simple racial identity, without policy content, is enough to predict party identity. The policy division that began the process of racial sorting is no longer necessary for Democrats and Republicans to be divided by race. Their partisan identities have become firmly aligned with their racial identities, and decoupled from their racial policy positions. (2018:33)

In our racialized partisan era, people of color facing the threat of community decline will align more closely with the Democratic Party.

In the case of population growth (and the attendant economic growth), people of color will develop more progressive political attitudes and an increased attachment to the Democratic Party. This is the same response movers and stayers theory predicts for whites in fast-growing communities, and the causal mechanism is the same: increased intergroup contact (see Allport 1954 and Pettigrew et al. 2011). Allport (1954) asserted that an increase in social interactions between two or more societal groups can mitigate intergroup prejudice. In the earliest expositions of the "contact hypothesis," the criteria for prejudice-reducing contact were extensive. Groups were to be of equal status, and their interactions were to be non-competitive, focused toward a common goal, and sanctioned by the appropriate authorities (see Mason 2018). Over time, the thrust of the literature suggests that activities and interactions may facilitate the development of more cooperative and appreciative intergroup attitudes even when one or more of these criteria are not met (Pettigrew et al. 2011). My own research on the impact of racial context on attitudes toward immigration (Hood and Morris 1997 and 2000) is consistent with contact effects in the absence of intergroup interactions that would satisfy the stringent criteria set by the earliest work in this literature.

My work in this area also highlights the difficulty of realizing contact effects in those environments in which there is competition, or in which the groups are clearly unequal, or in which there is no shared goal (or at least no *perception* of a shared goal) (Hood and Morris 1998). That is why movers and stayers theory posits the presence of contact effects in those environments in which the effects of competition, and the perceptions of inequality, and the absence of common goals are most muted: fast-growing, economically vibrant communities.

Note that contact effects are unlikely to be constant across racial groups. In the case of whites, increased interracial contact is relatively more important to the transformation of political attitudes than I expect it to be for minorities. For African Americans and Latinos, both groups that tend to be relatively conservative on social policy issues (such as abortion rights and LGBTQ rights) (see Philpot 2017), increased contact with the more socially progressive movers (of all races and ethnicities) is the engine for increased progressivism and greater attachment to the Democratic Party. However, as in the case of responses to threat from population decline and community decay, the ideological and partisan shifts among minorities should be subtler than the ideological and partisan shifts among whites because of the high level of minorities' existing attachment to the Democratic Party.

Given both of these dynamics, what we should see is a non-linear relationship between threat and attachment to the Democratic Party among people of color. If a partisan shift occurs among people of color, the hypothesized relationship between perceived threat (induced by population decline) and attachment to the Democratic Party is non-linear—support for the Democratic Party is high at the extremes (fastest decline and fastest growth) and more moderate in the middle (average population growth). There is no *a priori* reason to expect population decline to have a greater partisan effect on African Americans or Latinos than population growth. Given the existing levels of attachment to the Democratic Party among African Americans and the partisan variability among national identity groups within the Latino community, aggregate-level shifts in the Democratic direction are likely to be very subtle (at best). Given the relative ideological conservatism of African Americans—and the strong ideological conservatism of

Latinos—community decline could elicit a rightward shift in ideology (particularly among Latinos). According to movers and stayers theory, the threat associated with community decline should result in a shift toward the dominant partisan or ideological position of one's racial group. Note that for people of color, that could be "Democrat" and "conservative" in a manner we don't see among whites.[15]

For whites, on the other hand, I expect to find a linear relationship between population growth and identification with the Democratic Party: as population grows, whites are increasingly likely to support the candidates of the Democratic Party. As these partisan shifts manifest among long-time community residents (stayers) responding to the influx (or the exit) of a demographically and politically distinct set of migrants (movers), we should see a shift in the partisan tide in southern politics. But this regional tide will be stronger in some places and weaker (or non-existent) in others. Movers and stayers theory provides a new conceptual technology for understanding the economic, social, and political foundations of this political sea change as well as the geographical variation in its prevalence. Movers and stayers theory is simply a new tool for a new time. Let's see if it works.

3

Population Growth and Partisan Change in the South

We are witnessing a growing attachment to the Democratic Party and increasing support for its candidates in the South: nothing short of a sea change in southern politics. At the point when Key was writing *Southern Politics*, the transformation of the Democratic Solid South into a region dominated by Republicans was nearly impossible to imagine. But the seeds of change had been planted, and for those studying the region with the greatest care, hints of a partisan shift were evident. Now, signs of a new partisan transformation are beginning to emerge.

Just as the Republican era which followed the Solid South never reached the level of partisan dominance and exclusivity manifest in the earlier era, we should not expect the growing southern progressivism to usher in an era of Democratic dominance that matches either of the earlier partisan eras. Even so, there is considerable room for Democratic growth. Movers and stayers theory is an effort to understand the engine of this current and (potentially) future growth. Movers and stayers theory provides an explanation for the subtle shift to the left we are experiencing, and it can help us understand where the progressive lean is strongest (and where there is likely to be a conservative reaction).

Movers and stayers theory begins with the premise that migration drives the growth in Democratic attachment and support we see in various locales throughout the South. But this is not the traditional in-migration story. Rather than focusing solely on in-migrants from the North, movers and stayers theory incorporates migration within the South. Instead of the conservatively oriented, Republican migrants of the 1970s and 1980s, migrants in the 21st-century movers and stayers story are young and progressive. And unlike existing treatments of the impact of in-migrants on southern politics, movers and stayers theory focuses on, as its name implies, both movers and stayers.

Migratory effects on a community are both direct and indirect. Community growth fostered by an influx of progressive migrants produces a more progressive political climate because (1) the proportion of progressives in the community is relatively (and immediately) larger because of this influx of migrants (direct effect) and (2) the average attitudes of long-term residents (stayers) become more progressive due to the increased contact with the new community members (indirect effect). Emigration, or population loss, also has direct and indirect effects on a community. The direct effect of the exit of movers (who are assumed to be progressive) will be a decline in progressive attitudes (and Democratic Party support) and an increased sense of community threat. Movers and stayers theory predicts that whites will respond to perceived threat by increasing their attachment to the Republican Party— the dominant party in their racial group (in the South). On the other hand, people of color are expected to respond to this perceived threat by increasing their attachment to the Democratic Party—the dominant party of their racial groups. Thus, the impact of population decline on partisanship and ideology should be conditioned by the relative size of the minority population in a community.

In this chapter, I examine the empirical support for the central claim of movers and stayers theory: population growth yields greater attachment to the Democratic Party and support for its candidates. I also examine the effects of minority context (a conditioning component of the movers and stayers model) and population size (an alternative explanation for Democratic growth) based on the shift in political attitudes and partisan attachments.

In the next section I describe the data that I analyze and the methods used to conduct the analysis.

Data and Methods

To begin to evaluate the movers and stayers theory, I examine the relationship between population growth and partisan voting in the South, focusing specifically on the relationship as it manifests at the county level from the late 1990s to 2016 (the latest presidential election year). I focus on the last two decades of electoral history because students of southern politics view the late 1990s as a transitional period in partisan politics in the region. The processes and dynamics that produced the widespread and extensive growth of Republican support in the region were largely played out. As Myers writes about the literature on party transformation in the South:

> The analyses in much of the aforementioned work tend to stop in the late 1990s, by which time it is more or less presumed that the long-term process affecting the South that began in the 1960s had largely run its course . . . an implicit theme in much of the literature is that the period between the 1960s and the 1990s constituted a tumultuous transitional period, and that by the 1990s a set of political arrangements had taken hold that are likely to endure for some time. (2013:49)

I agree that the late 1990s (and early 21st century) were an important time in the history of southern politics. However, this point in time was not so much an endpoint as a point of inflection. Dramatic political change continued after the turn of the 21st century, but the character (and partisan vector) of that change shifted to the left. If in-migrants were a source for Republican growth during much of the last half of the 20th century, they are now—and have been for at least a couple of decades—a key component of Democratic growth in the South. Additionally, internal migration—whether from one southern state to another southern state or one southern county to another southern county (even if the counties are in the same state) played an important role in the growth of Democratic support in a variety of locales throughout the South during the last 20 years.

Some will argue that the leftward shift in southern politics—to the extent they admit its existence—is a much more recent phenomenon, one that dates from the first Obama election in 2008. I argue that the dynamics upon which President Obama's southern successes were founded obviously pre-existed his campaign and election. No doubt President Obama's 2008 election was a milestone in southern politics, but the partisan tides were shifting well before that.

I focus on counties because partisan balance aggregated to the state level obscures very important, localized variation in the relative strength of the two major parties. Congressional districts are also too large—on average—to fully manifest the trajectory of relative partisan support. And congressional districts are also subject to change—a change often driven by partisan factors. Finally, metropolitan areas are also subject to boundary alterations that make it difficult (if not impossible) to effectively gauge the underlying partisan change in the broader geographic areas. Voting precincts are, obviously, far too small.

Partisanship

I am trying to understand the impact of population growth on partisan change. Conceptually, my dependent variable is partisanship or, more specifically, the aggregate-level change in partisan attachments and related voting behaviors. I operationalize aggregate partisan attachment as the percentage of the two-party vote for the Democratic presidential candidate. Presidential vote is an imperfect measure of partisanship. Partisans don't always vote for the presidential candidate from their party (though the relationship between individual-level partisan identity and vote choice—particularly at the presidential level—has grown stronger over the past several decades). Likewise, self-described independents may often vote for a particular party's presidential candidate without behaving (at least in other ways) like self-avowed partisans. But vote choice is such an important part of partisan attachment—it is by far the most significant behavioral aspect of partisan attachment—that there are strong theoretical rationales for using presidential vote choice to gauge partisan attachment, particularly at the aggregate level.

The alternative most commonly offered in the literature is partisan self-identification taken from voting rolls (see Abrams and Fiorina 2012). The primary criticism of presidential votes as a measure of partisanship is that they are inherently unstable—that is, voters choose candidates for a variety of reasons unrelated to partisanship—and so idiosyncratic qualities of any election (such as the personalities of the candidates) obscure the extent to which vote choices reflect underlying partisanship. I mitigate this problem by evaluating the robustness of the substantive results by repeating the analyses with different base years (and, necessarily, different Democratic and Republican candidates). Though I focus solely on the results associated with 1996 as the base year, the results from analyses in which 2000 is the base year are fully comparable. Another advantage of the presidential vote measure is that Bishop (2009) employs presidential election returns as the primary measure of partisanship for his book *The Big Sort*. As I am offering an alternative to Bishop's characterization of the partisan implications of migration, I use his measure of partisanship to preempt claims that the inconsistency of my results with his theory are an artifact of a different measure of partisanship.

Finally, the proposed alternative to presidential votes—self-identification on voting rolls—is clearly inferior for my purposes. Voter registration data (by party) for a sufficiently large (and representative) number of southern states simply is not available, even for 21st-century elections. For the entire United States this limitation is far less important. As Abrams and Fiorina explain:

> The drawback of voter registration is that not all states have partisan registration—29 states plus the District of Columbia have it today and somewhat fewer—23 had it in the mid-1970s. . . . [but] scholars who have worked closely with such data have concluded after a number of validity tests that "The 21 states for which we were able to collect party registration data are surprisingly representative of the country as a whole" (McGhee and Krimm 2009, 351). (2012:204)

Unfortunately, states which collect partisan attachments through their registration process are far more common outside than South than within it. Thirty-one states now allow voter registration by party, but only three of those states are in the South (Florida, Louisiana, and North Carolina). So, while well greater than a majority of states have party ID voter registration, less than 30% of southern states have it. Whatever claims to representativeness are reasonable in the context of the entire United States, those same claims are clearly unjustified for the South. Generating county-level estimates of partisanship for the entire South based on the information for Florida, Louisiana, and North Carolina alone simply is not workable. Thus, this is not a viable option to an election-based measure of aggregate partisanship.

As I am interested in the change in partisanship, the dependent variable is the difference between the percentage of the two-party Democratic vote in the base year (1996) and the most recent presidential election year (2016). There is a reasonable theoretical case to be made for using either 1996 or 2000 as the base year—that point in time when the traditional 20th-century migration dynamic—more migration, more Republican support—had ended, and the new demographic dynamic—more population growth, more Democratic support—had begun. As indicated above, I focus solely on the results from analyses using 1996 as the base year. Results from analyses using 2000 as the base year are fully comparable.

Population Estimates

Ideally, we would have no need for population estimates. But much of the behavior that I want to understand occurred between decennial censuses—either after 2010 or before 2000. Thankfully, I will not need to generate my own county-level interpolations of census population figures.

The population data are taken from the National Cancer Institute's (NCI) Surveillance, Epidemiology, and End Results Program (SEER). In order to determine the relative prevalence of (and mortality associated with) cancer across the United States, the NCI has generated annual, intercensal estimates from 1969 to 2017 based on the U.S. Census Bureau's Population Estimates Programs. Because this data also includes information on the size of various age cohorts, we can focus specifically on the population of adults rather than the overall population. Given my interest in partisan attachment (and partisan voting), I focus the analysis on those individuals who are at least old enough to vote rather than the entire population.[1] These authoritative estimates cover nearly all of the relevant time period of this analysis (minus 2018). (For more information on these population estimates, see https://seer.cancer.gov/popdata/.[2])

The primary independent variable is the log of county-level population change. Counties vary dramatically in size, both in geography and population. In the South, the average county population has ranged between 20,000 and 25,000 since the mid-1990s. However, the range in adult population goes from just over 50 (Loving County, TX, the least populous county in the continental United States) to over 3 million (Harris County, TX—a major portion of the Houston metropolitan area and the third most populous county in the continental United States).[3] The range in county-level population change over this time period is also extraordinary—from population loss in the tens of thousands to growth well in excess of 1 million people in Harris County. The distribution of population change has a very high peak and, not surprisingly, a very long positive tail.

Given the nature of our dependent variable—change in percentage of two-party vote cast for the Democratic presidential candidate—we should not expect a linear relationship between population growth and partisan voting. A linear relationship between the percentage change in population and the percentage change in the Democratic proportion of the two-party vote is more likely (and more consistent with the movers and stayers theory). While we could use the percentage change in population as an independent variable, the prevalence of very small counties (from a population stand-point)—the types of counties where the shift of a few hundred (or few thousand) people might dramatically affect the percentage of population growth in a way that is not true for larger counties—implies that the errors in the simple percentage change in population variable are heteroskedastic. Using the natural log of population growth allows me to avoid each of these methodological problems. However, as a number of counties had negative population growth from 1996 to 2016 and/or 2000 to 2016—Orleans County, Louisiana for example—prior to taking the log of the difference in population, the 1 + the minimum population growth figure was added to each county's growth rate (to avoid logging negative numbers). Note that this does not alter the relative position—in terms of growth—of any of the counties, regardless of the size of population growth in that county for the time period of the analysis.

Alternative Explanatory Variables

In evaluating the relationship between population growth and partisan change, we must evaluate the possibility that if a relationship does appear to exist, it is a causal relationship rather than a spurious relationship. To evaluate the potential spuriousness of the relationship between population growth and partisan change, I examine a set of alternative explanations for partisan growth in the South. These explanations include (1) change in racial and ethnic context, (2) population size, and (3) change in economic context.

Nearly two decades into the 21st century, there appears to be an increasingly strong relationship between population size and Democratic voting throughout the United States *as a whole*. In fact, one of the most widely discussed phenomena of the 2016 presidential elections was the stark difference between Democratic support (or, conversely, Republican support) between urban areas and rural areas. I include a measure of current population to account for the potential effect of this dynamic on Democratic support.

A significant strand of research with the literature on southern politics argues that economic growth and general economic well-being are associated with increased support for the Republican Party and its candidates. This is the central theme of Lublin's (2004) argument in *The Republican*

South: Democratization and Partisan Change and Shafer and Johnston's (2006) *The End of Southern Exceptionalism: Class, Race, and Partisan Change in the Postwar South*. In this vein of research, economic prosperity in the South is the driving force—for migrants and native southerners—behind the increasing attractiveness of the Republican Party. If this dynamic manifests during the time period of my analysis—as it should, if this argument is correct—we should see a negative relationship between improvements in economic context (e.g., higher median incomes, lower unemployment) and relative change in Democratic support. I include measures of median income and unemployment to tap the effects of this theorized partisan dynamic.

Racial context has always played a role in southern politics, albeit a role that has never been uncomplicated. Seventy years ago, Key (1949) noted that white conservatism was directly related to black context—as the relative size of the African American population grew in a locale, the more conservative the white voters became. Similarly, following the broad mobilization of African American voters following the VRA, Hood, Kidd, and Morris (2012a) find that support for the Republican Party among whites was directly related to the size of the mobilized black population in a community. However, now well into the 21st century, the racial disparities in the demography of the political parties is so striking—whites make up a far, far larger portion of the Republican Party than they do the general adult population—that we may now be at the point where the percentage of whites in a community is strongly (and positively) related to support for the Republican Party. To assess the impact of racial demographics on partisan support, I include a measure of the percentage of whites in a county. I have also included a dummy variable for Orleans County to account for the unique effects of Hurricane Katrina on this locale.[4] The reported results are robust to the exclusion of this variable.

Unemployment rate data is taken from the Bureau of Labor Statistics. Income data is taken from the U.S. Census Bureau. When and where necessary, missing values were imputed using multiple imputation in the "Amelia" package in R (Honaker, King, and Blackwell 2011).[5] County-level presidential voting data are taken from various editions of the *CQ Voting and Elections* collection. Multivariate results are standard ordinary least squares (OLS) coefficients with robust standard errors.

Results

The South has grown dramatically since the days of V.O. Key, and some states (and counties) have grown much faster than others. Table 3.1 provides the ranked order of southern states based on their growth rate between the two most recent censuses, 2000 and 2010.[6] The range of growth is striking. The growth rate in Texas (the fastest growing southern state) is nearly *fifteen* times the growth rate in Louisiana (the southern state with the slowest growth rate). The size of this differential is at least partially attributable to the population exodus following Hurricane Katrina, but that only explains the paucity of Louisiana's growth, not the dramatic robustness of Texas's growth. (See Table 3.1.)

For students of southern politics, it will only take a quick glance at the order of states to realize that the population of the Rim South (Arkansas, Florida, North Carolina, Tennessee, Texas, and Virginia) has grown much faster than the population of the Deep South (Alabama, Georgia, Louisiana, Mississippi, and South Carolina). The two highest growth states (Texas and North Carolina)—and three of the top four (Texas, North Carolina, and Florida)—are Rim South states. At the other end of the distribution, the three states with the lowest levels of growth—Louisiana, Mississippi, and Alabama—are all in the Deep South. In fact, the Rim South states have grown

Table 3.1. Population Growth in the Southern States

State	Percent Growth (from 2000 to 2010)
Texas	20.6
North Carolina	18.5
Georgia	18.3
Florida	17.6
South Carolina	15.3
Virginia	13
Tennessee	11.5
Arkansas	9.1
Alabama	7.5
Mississippi	4.3
Louisiana	1.4

Source: U.S. Census at https://www.census.gov/prod/cen2010/briefs/c2010br-01.pdf

at an average rate that is more than 60% greater than the growth rate of the Deep South states.

The relationship between population growth and Democratic support at the state level is likely to be more muted than at the county level. First, the movers and stayers dynamic presumes contextual effects associated with community-level integration. This process occurs at the neighborhood or local community level, not the state level. Second, states are economically and demographically diverse, so they include areas that manifest population growth as well as decline. The aggregation of these disparate areas is likely to dampen the effects we expect to find at the local level.

Still, I expect the hypothesized relationship between population growth and Democratic support to manifest at the state level (albeit a subtler version than we should find at the county level). If we regress the state-level change in the Democratic candidates' percentage of the two-party vote between 2000 and 2016 on the percentage change in population over the same time period, we find a strong positive relationship between population growth and change in Democratic support. The population growth coefficient is 0.41 (indicating just less than a half point increase in Democratic support for each full percentage point increase in population). The coefficient is significant at the .05 level (two-tailed), no mean feat in a sample of 11 observations, and population growth explains over a third of the variance in the change in Democratic support. If we look at the difference in the change in Democratic support between the five fastest growing southern states and the five southern states with the slowest growth rates, we see that Democratic support grew by more than 4% in the high-growth states, and Democratic support fell by over 7% in the low-growth states. So even though our theorized dynamic was not designed for the state level, the aggregation of localized processes still generates significant evidence of state-level impacts.

Now let's look at the counties that are leading the way in population growth and the counties that are lagging the furthest behind. Table 3.2 provides a list of the 15 fastest growing counties in the South.[7] (See Table 3.2.) Note how many of the counties are in the fastest growing states. More than half of the fastest growing counties are in Texas (the fastest growing state), a third of the fastest growing counties are in Florida, and the three remaining counties are in North Carolina (the second fastest growing state) and Georgia (the third fastest growing state).[8]

In Table 3.3, we have a list of the counties that experienced the most significant population decline (or lowest level of growth) from 1996 to 2016. Notice

Table 3.2. Fastest Growing Counties in the South

County	State	Population (2016)	Population Growth (1996–2016)
Harris	TX	3256287	1096082
Tarrant	TX	1427941	512157
Bexar	TX	1370459	471985
Orange	FL	987720	412303
Collin	TX	668840	409156
Dallas	TX	1832715	391266
Travis	TX	903106	385637
Hillsborough	FL	1029610	365037
Wake	NC	763902	364474
Broward	FL	1466330	353844
Palm Beach	FL	1140723	338266
Denton	TX	580540	335373
Mecklenburg	NC	776242	326751
Fort Bend	TX	517210	323566
Gwinnett	GA	634741	292877
Lee	FL	577034	263136

how few of these counties are in the faster-growing states. With the exception of two counties from Virginia—the state with the median growth rate for the southern states—all of the remaining "high" decline counties are from three of the four states with the lowest overall growth rates: Louisiana, Mississippi, and Arkansas. Hurricane Katrina clearly played some role in the population decline in certain counties in Louisiana and Mississippi, but the same can't be said for population loss in locales like Buchanan County, Virginia.[9]

As we did at the state level, we find evidence of a relationship between adult population growth and a positive change in Democratic support in presidential elections at the county level. In Figure 3.1, the box plot depicts the distribution of change in Democratic support by quartile of adult population growth.[10] The largest difference is clearly between the highest growth counties and all of the others. Democratic support is only slightly higher than in the first two quartiles, and Democratic support is actually lower—albeit very slightly—in the second quartile than in the first quartile.[11]

Table 3.3. Fastest Declining Counties in the South

County	State	Population (2016)	Population Growth (1996–2016)
Orleans	LA	304325	–35191
St. Bernard	LA	32447	–16038
Washington	MS	33654	–8290
Danville City	VA	31407	–6837
Jefferson	AR	52255	–6150
Sunflower	MS	19539	–5059
Leflore	MS	20527	–4384
Buchanan	VA	17804	–3784
Mississippi	AR	30444	–3762
Phillips	AR	13593	–3734
Coahoma	MS	16542	–3187
Bolivar	MS	23468	–3152
Union	AR	29369	–3097
Henry	VA	40499	–2813
Ouachita	AR	18117	–2474

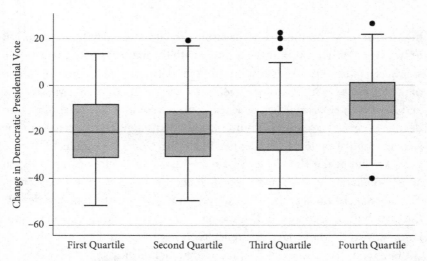

Figure 3.1. Democratic Presidential Vote and Population: Population Growth and Change in Democratic Support

One factor that may obscure the relationship between population growth and Democratic support is racial context. Because minority voters—particularly African American voters—consistently support Democratic candidates at far higher rates than white voters, we do not expect population change to generate the same effect in majority-minority communities. For example, if a largely African American community (e.g., New Orleans or Orleans County) suddenly lost a substantial portion of its population, we would not expect it to become significantly more Republican in its political orientation. However, high-growth majority-minority communities may well see an increase in Democratic support.

Where we would expect to see the greatest effect of population growth is in predominantly white communities. In Figure 3.2, we see that the effect of population growth on Democratic support is stronger if we limit ourselves to majority-white communities. There is clear—though initially subtle—monotonic increase in Democratic support as we range across the quartiles of population growth.[12] As in the full sample, the most dramatic difference is between the change in Democratic support in the fastest growing communities and all of the remaining communities.

Limiting our analysis to majority-minority communities tells a somewhat different story. The highest growth areas are still likely to see the greatest increase in Democratic support, but the difference between the highest growth

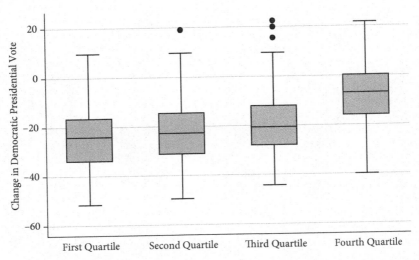

Figure 3.2. Democratic Presidential Vote and Population: Population Growth and Change in Democratic Support—Majority White

counties and the remaining counties is somewhat smaller than for the majority-white counties. We also see that there is no relationship between population growth and Democratic support when limiting ourselves to the counties outside the top growth quartile. As expected, the hypothesized relationship between population growth and Democratic support is far subtler, to the extent it exists at all, in majority-minority communities—communities that were overwhelmingly supportive of Democratic candidates in the first place.[13] (See Figure 3.3.)

Evidence of a first-order relationship between population growth and change in Democratic support is a key aspect of the assessment of the movers and stayers theory. But we would also like to know whether or not this relationship is driven by other factors that we might reasonably expect to influence partisan support.

The relationship between population and Democratic support is of special importance. Following the 2016 election, scholars and pundits highlighted the relationship between urbanization and the Trump vote; in far less populated rural areas, Trump was far more popular than he was in highly populated urban areas. Clinton, on the other hand, received significantly more support in the most densely populated urban areas than in rural areas.[14] In an important respect, the urban/rural partisan divide is consistent with movers and stayers theory. And over the past 20 years, shifting

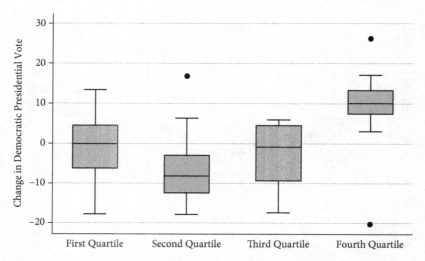

Figure 3.3. Democratic Presidential Vote and Population: Population Growth and Change in Democratic Support—Majority-Minority

populations—migrants—have dramatically influenced county-level population size; in fact, population size and population growth (over the past two decades) are highly correlated.

The traditional explanation for this "big city" versus "backwoods" distinction is that these areas are populated by completely different people. Coastal urban areas are populated by a wealthy, educated elite, and poor and working-class whites fill the small towns and rural areas of the rest of America. Movers and stayers theory offers a more nuanced explanation for these partisan differences. First, it provides an explanation for partisan *change* which the simpler urban/rural divide does not. Second, it helps us understand key partisan *differences* obscured by the urban/rural distinction. For example, Trump did not run well in all rural areas in the South; he did particularly poorly in rural counties with a majority-minority population. Not all rural areas are alike. Finally, movers and stayers theory helps us understand the 21st-century political trajectories of many places that are too small to be big cities and too big to be tiny rural areas; in short, much of the South.

What about the evidence for the more traditional explanations for relative partisan support in the South: changes in racial or ethnic context and changes in economic context? The influence of race and ethnicity on aggregate partisan leanings in the South is complicated. At the individual level, whites are clearly far more likely to be Republicans and to support the Republican candidate than minority voters.[15] But in the aggregate, minority context has tended to have a conservative impact on whites in the South. So, as the size of the minority (or more specifically, the African American population) grew, the more conservative (read: Republican) whites became. Traditional theories of race and southern partisanship thus suggest a relatively weak relationship between percent white and aggregate partisanship.

On the other hand, a key aspect of movers and stayers theory is the premise that intergroup conflict does not require *localized* contact. Because of the nationalization of our politics and the increasing prevalence of affective polarization, whites may develop very conservative racial attitudes even in the absence of a significant local black population. Movers and stayers theory also predicts that intergroup contact—increasingly common in the highest growth areas—will be associated with more progressive white opinions on issues of race. In contrast to traditional race-focused theories of southern partisanship, movers and stayers theory suggests a strong *direct* relationship between the percentage of whites in a county and Republican attachment and support for Republican candidates.

In a similar way, the relationship between economic context and aggregate-level partisanship is complex. Traditionally, income (and employment) tended to be positively related to Republican support. In contrast, a foundation of movers and stayers theory is that population growth and economic growth coincide. At the state level, this relationship is clearly manifest. "Growing" states are getting bigger and wealthier just as "stagnating" states are languishing—in terms of population and economics (Bullock 2020 and Bullock et al. 2019). We should see the same dynamic at the county level. To the extent we find an economic effect on partisanship (while accounting for population growth), movers and stayers theory predicts a positive relationship between income and Democratic support and an inverse relationship between unemployment and Democratic support.

The results of the multivariate model explaining the change in Democratic support (again, from 1996–2016) are clearly consistent with the hypothesis that population growth is directly related to growth in Democratic support over the same time period—even when controlling for the most prominent alternative explanations.[16] *Ceteris paribus*, places that have seen robust population growth have seen greater growth in Democratic support (or a lesser decline) than in areas that have seen a decline in population (or more meager population growth). What is also clear is that the relationship between population growth and Democratic support is not an artifact of a mutual relationship with community size. There is simply no evidence of a relationship between population size and *change* in Democratic support. We have no evidence that large (small) communities have grown more Democratic (Republican) because they are large (small). Communities have become more Democratic (Republican) because they have grown larger (smaller).

Racial and ethnic context also plays a significant role in partisan change over the last two decades and in a manner fully consistent with movers and stayers theory. As the relative size of the white population in a county declines, the relative support for Republican candidates also declines. Evidence regarding the impact of economic factors on partisan support is mixed. Change in median family income is directly related to increased Democratic support. Interestingly, this result turns the class-based explanation for Republican growth in the 1980s and 1990s (Lublin 2004 and Shafer and Johnston 2006) on its head. In the 21st century, income growth is no longer associated with Republican growth. That said, I see no evidence of an unemployment effect on partisan loyalty.[17] Given the increasing levels of support for the Republican Party provided by working-class whites—a group highly likely to be affected by even subtle shifts in unemployment—this result is not especially surprising. Finally, we see that Orleans County's experience—post-Katrina—really was distinctive.

Obviously, a host of factors influence presidential election results in the aggregate: economic context, public approval of the current president, party of the current president, length of partisan regime, etc. I argue that population growth (in the South) is one of the election "fundamentals" (like economic context). Campaigns and candidates influence electoral outcomes, but their influence comes within a context driven by fundamentals. In the southern context, we can no longer ignore the role of population growth in influencing presidential election outcomes.

Note that this is a very conservative test. Even in a context in which factors clearly correlated with the dynamics of movers and stayers theory are incorporated in the model, population growth matters. The changing character of southern politics is not just an urban/rural story. It's also a story of race and a story of class, but the role of race and class are not what they once were. The story of southern partisan change is following a new narrative—a migrant story.

Population Growth and Geographic Polarization

The evidence strongly supports the presence of a significant direct relationship between population growth and progressivism. As I note above, not all types of population growth lead to more progressive politics. Subtle growth in relatively small areas—even when that growth represents a significant portion of the population—may not be large enough to alter the underlying demographic *and* political profile of the locale. Population growth driven by economic forces *unlikely* to attract more-educated migrants (e.g., tourism or mineral extraction) or migrants of conventional age (e.g., retirement hubs) should not be expected to drive ideological or partisan change (or *economic* growth) to the extent seen in areas with population growth driven by a more diverse array of economic forces (manufacturing, education, health care, IT, etc.).

But even accounting for these limited exceptions, we see a broad relationship between population growth and increasingly progressive politics, particularly as that progressivism is manifest in partisan shifts. An important implication of the role of population growth in increased progressivism is that population growth also exacerbates geographic polarization in the South. One of the more interesting facets of this growing geographic polarization is the extent to which it blurs traditional sub-regional political distinctions. Historically, the geography of political divisions in the South centered on the distinction between the Rim South and the Deep South. But growth and stagnation have not manifest in equal parts in these two sub-regions. Although growth has been relatively greater in the Rim South, there are some states within this sub-region that suffer from stagnation. Twenty-first century population growth in Arkansas and Tennessee has lagged well behind population growth in Florida, North Carolina, and Texas. Likewise, while the Deep South has not experienced the overall growth of the Rim South, some of the states in this sub-region are clearly outpacing their fellows in the Deep South. Recent population growth in Georgia (and to a lesser extent, South Carolina) has kept pace with all but the very fastest growing states in the Rim South.

Spatial political distinctions—*geographic* polarization—is an important characteristic of any country or region. Traditional political distinctions between the Rim South and the Deep South flowed from variance in the relative size of the African American population between the two. Key's (1949) "black belt" was securely centered in the Deep South—the sub-region with a far larger proportion of African Americans. As the politics of the South centered on the position of the African American, so the politics of the two sub-regions varied—though for decades, only in subtle ways.

As we saw in Chapter 1, the sub-regional distinctions in partisan presidential voting have been eroded over the course of the early 21st century. New sub-regional distinctions—those intimately related to population growth or its absence—are rising in their places. Presidential votes mirror patterns of growth and stagnation more closely than they do the traditional distinction between the Rim South and the Deep South. And it's not just presidential voting that follows this pattern. The same pattern exists in legislative elections, at the federal level and at the state level.

From 2000 to 2018, party differences between the legislative arenas in the Rim South and the Deep South have declined at a much faster rate than the party differences between the fast-growth states and the slow-growth states. In some cases, the partisan gap between the slow-growth states and the fast-growth states has grown, and in every case the current legislative partisan gap between the fast-growth states and the slow-growth states easily exceeds the legislative partisan differences between the states of the Rim South and those in the Deep South.

At the federal level, the percentage of Republicans in House delegations from both the Deep South and the Rim South has grown since 2000, but the gap between the Republican presence in the two sub-regions' legislative delegations has declined dramatically, from more than 11% to just over 5% (see Figure 3.4). On the other hand, in 2000, the percentage of Republicans in House delegations from the fast-growth states was only slightly larger (1.3 percent) than the percentage of Republicans in House delegations from

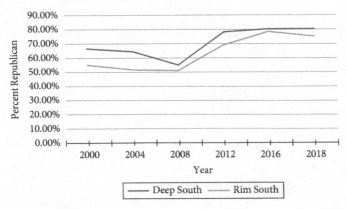

Figure 3.4. Republican Percentage of U.S. Representatives by Geographic Region, 2000–2018

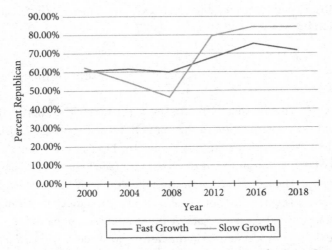

Figure 3.5. Republican Percentage of U.S. Representatives by State Growth Rate, 2000–2018

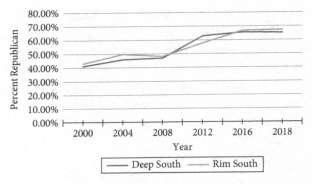

Figure 3.6. Republican Percentage of States' Upper Chambers by Geographic Region, 2000–2018

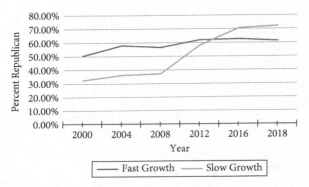

Figure 3.7. Republican Percentage of States' Upper Chambers by State Population Growth, 2000–2018

the slow-growth states. In 2018, that gap was nearly 10 times larger (see Figure 3.5).

The same dynamic manifests in state legislatures. The 2000–2018 trend in Republican representation in the upper houses of southern legislatures is nearly identical in the Rim South states and the Deep South states: an upward trajectory tapering off in the most recent past (see Figure 3.6). The partisan trajectories for the fast-growth states and the slow-growth states are dramatically different. The trajectory of Republican growth is much flatter in the fast-growth states, and there is a slight downturn in the recent past that we do not see in the slow-growth states. As in the case of House delegations, the partisan gap between the fast-growth states and the slow-growth states in the most recent past is significantly greater than the partisan gap between the Deep

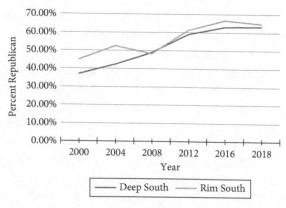

Figure 3.8. Republican Percentage of States' Lower Chambers by Geographic Region, 2000–2018

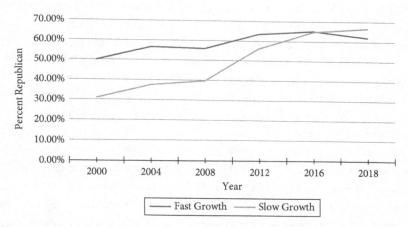

Figure 3.9. Republican Percentage of States' Upper Chambers by State Population Growth Rate, 2000–2018

South states and the Rim South states. We also see a higher percentage of Republicans in slow-growth states than in fast-growth states (see Figure 3.7).

The distinction between fast-growth states and slow-growth states also signals a much more significant partisan difference than the difference between Deep South states and Rim South states in the lower houses of the southern state legislatures. What was a nearly 10 percentage point partisan gap between the prevalence of Republicans in lower houses of the Deep South states and in the lower houses of Rim South states has all but disappeared (see Figure 3.8). But we still see a partisan gap between the lower houses of the fast-growth states and the lower houses of the slow-growth states. And, unlike in 2000, the Republicans hold the advantage in the slow-growth states rather than the fast-growth states (see Figure 3.9).

From a legislative standpoint, Republican representation has grown—in some states, dramatically—over the course of the 21st century. More recently, however, this partisan advantage has begun to dissipate. In Virginia, as of 2019, it disappeared altogether. Does this mean that the leftward shift of the 21st century is only a couple of years old? No, Obama's election in 2008 provided a clear outward sign of a progressive shift in several fast-growing states. Just as southern Republicans' successes in legislative elections lagged their successes in presidential elections in the second half of the 20th century,[18] Democrats' legislative successes have lagged their successes in presidential elections in the 21st century. But the foundations of this progressive shift predate the electoral results which are the evidence of its significance—just as the foundation of the growth in Republican identification predated their successes in federal and state legislative races at the end of the 20th century. As these data show, the foundation of the leftward shift in southern politics was not—and is not—equally distributed across the region. The foundation—*migration*—is more prevalent in fast-growth states and locales than in slow-growth states and locales. This migratory gap has important implications for geographic polarization.

The growing geographic polarization of the southern states—and the locales within the southern states—has considerable substantive significance. If the old sub-regional distinctiveness flowed from the locus of the black population in the early- to mid-20th century South—Key's (1949) "black belt"—then the fulcrum of southern politics was the position of the African American, and their geographic location drove political differences. Today, migrants are the geographic fulcrum of southern politics.

African Americans still play a crucial role in southern politics, and issues related to civil rights remain of paramount importance in the region and nationally. For Key, the centrality of African Americans for the trajectory of southern politics revolved around the impact of their geographic dispersion on *white* political attitudes, not their own independent political roles (which were very limited in the late 1940s when Key was writing). The relationship between black context and white political attitudes today is weaker (and more complicated) than it was 70 years ago.

Group threat may still play an important role in the formation of whites' political orientations and attachments, but there are also areas in the

South where few minorities live *and* where whites have very conservative attitudes on issues related to race. In other parts of the South, whites living in communities with significant minority populations have much more progressive views on issues related to race. The overwhelmingly white areas where racial conservatism is prevalent tend also to have experienced stagnation or very slow growth. More diverse communities where whites have more progressive orientations toward issues related to race and ethnicity tend to be growing at a much faster pace. As movers and stayers theory explains, migration—both its *direct* effects and its *indirect* effects—is the key to these political distinctions, and migrants are the political fulcrum. They alter their new homes just as their departures change the places they used to live.

Discussion and Conclusion

The South is undergoing a new, 21st-century partisan transformation. The shift to the right (and the Republican Party) of white southerners that began during the middle of the 20th century and picked up appreciable speed following the passage of the VRA (see Hood, Kidd, and Morris 2012a) is giving way to a subtler—but still important—shift to the left (and the Democratic Party).

Ironically, southern migration patterns in the latter half of the 20th century and the first two decades of the 21st century had progressive vectors—in both cases. But importantly, the migratory progressivism was not founded in economic attitudes and beliefs. In the latter half of the 20th century, Republicans moving to the South tended to have more progressive attitudes on issues related to civil rights than the racially conservative southern Democrats that dominated regional politics. Today, Democrats moving to the South tend to have similarly progressive attitudes—not only on issues related to race but also on issues associated with social policy (such as gay marriage)—than conservative southern Republicans. Though the parties have flipped identities, the migratory vector is still in the progressive direction.

The progressive pressure of in-migration—and migration within the South—need not always foster progressivism. Suppose, for example, that partisan competition revolved around economic policies—the traditional party differences model from the literature on macroeconomic

Table 3.4 Explaining Change in Partisan Vote, 1996–2016

Δ Democratic Presidential Vote	b	Robust SE	T	P > t
Ln (Δ Adult population)	18.83	5.79	3.25	0.001
Adult population	5.1e–06	7.05e–06	0.72	0.473
Δ White population (percentage)	–91.74	9.26	–9.90	0.000
Δ Median income	0.00016	0.000062	2.67	0.008
Δ Unemployment rate	0.11	0.17	0.67	0.503
Orleans County	32.72	3.20	10.22	0.000
_cons	–252.17	70.21	–3.59	0.000

politics—rather than social policy and civil rights policy. Then migration would likely not have the progressive effect on the South which it has had for more than a half century. Those seeking locations with economic opportunities may well choose a political party for the same reason. Recent developments in both parties—but particularly the Republican Party—provide little reason to expect that party divisions will be based on economic policy any time soon.[19]

But why is this progressive shift occurring in these burgeoning locales? Is it solely a function of movers? Do stayers also play a role in this shift? And if they do play a role, what is that role? Is the growth in progressivism in growing communities married to a similar increase in conservatism decrease in declining communities? Movers and stayers theory provides hypothetical answers to these questions. I now examine the evidence for each of these hypotheses.

4

Players in the Migration Game

Understanding the Distinctiveness of Movers

"A man [or woman] goes on a journey . . ." (John Gardner)[1]

There is a substantial literature on migration's role in the creation of political change. Migratory patterns play a central part in explanations of the transformation of the solid Democratic South to a region in which Republicans are ascendant.[2] Research in this vein focuses on the demographic and political differences between the areas or regions from which migrants emigrate and the regions to which they immigrate. So, for example, migratory patterns drove the rise of the Republican Party in the South because northern migrants were leaving for more Republican areas—and thus were far more likely to be Republicans—than residents of the Democratically dominated southern states to which they were moving (Bass and DeVries 1995, Lublin 2004; Scher 1992). However, more recent research on the impact of migratory trends in the South makes a similar argument in the other direction: now that the South is much more Republican than the Democratic northern areas from which migrants move, the partisan vector favors Democrats (Hillygus, McKee, and Young 2017; Hood and McKee 2010; McKee and Teigen 2009). In both cases, the key differences are regional. Partisan change occurs because the region of emigration and the region of immigration have distinctive partisan cants.

The logic of this regional focus depends upon two key assumptions: (1) movers are not demographically or politically distinctive from non-movers in their home region, and (2) movers do not target demographically or politically distinctive areas (i.e., movers from liberal regions only move to liberal regions). Attributing the political impact of migration to the partisan distinctiveness of migrants' home region and target region presumes that migrants' political orientations fully reflect those of the home region.

Migration from a primarily Republican region to a primarily Democratic region only provides an explanation for a rightward shift in the target region if migrants' attitudes reflect those of the home region in the first place. If migrants from the home region happen to be significantly more Democratic than the home region more generally, then their migration to a Democratic region may actually reinforce the status quo rather than foster partisan change.

Even if migrants are *perfectly* representative of their home region—that is, movers and stayers are demographically and politically indistinguishable— significant demographic and political differences between home and target regions may not manifest in demographic or political change in the target region if immigration patterns are non-random. Consider the case of the late 20th-century South again. Even if northern emigrants are significantly more Republican than the primarily Democratic target region (the South), if only the northern Democrats move to the South (while the northern Republicans move to the West, for example), then migration has no partisan vector—the South remains primarily Democratic. This is the crux of Bishop's (2009) "Big Sort" argument. Migration is non-random; people move to places where current residents share their political orientations. Regardless of existing regional disparities, if Republicans move to places dominated by Republicans, and Democrats move to places dominated by Democrats, we should not expect to see regional shifts in partisan attachment. What we should see is parties strengthening their existing regional advantages. This is the increased partisan polarization predicted by Bishop (2009). Blue regions should become bluer, and red regions should become redder. Blue states should become bluer, and red states should become redder.

But that is not what we see. In the South, while some red states are becoming even more red (Arkansas, Tennessee), some red states have stabilized. And other red states—and remember, at the turn of the 21st century, *all* of the southern states were red states (see 2000 and 2004 presidential election results)—are becoming purple (Florida, Georgia, North Carolina, and Texas) or blue (Virginia). Nascent Democratic growth could be attributed to the changing character of extra-regional migration to the South. At one time, the South was the most Democratic region on the country. An influx of migrants from other regions provides at least a partial explanation for the shift to right and the Republican Party. Now that the South is the most Republican region of the country,[3] migration from areas that tend to be more Democratic might explain some portion of the increasingly widespread shift to the left.

This still leaves the even more dramatic aspect of the partisan transformation which the South is currently undergoing—the partisan polarization of southern geography—without an explanation in the existing literature. The subtle but increasingly significant leftward shift of the region is not uniform. During the 21st century, some parts of the South have clearly become more Democratic. Republican George W. Bush won more than 61% of the vote in Texas in 2004; Republican Donald Trump's proportion of the Texas vote in 2016 was almost 10 points less. Republicans easily won Virginia in 2000 and 2004, and Democrat Hillary Clinton won Virginia by more than five percentage points in 2016. In both Texas and Virginia, high-growth areas have tended to lean more toward the Democratic Party in recent years. In Texas, we see this especially in the Austin, Houston, and San Antonio urban areas. In Virginia, growth in Democratic Party support has coincided with population growth in the Washington, D.C. suburbs in northern Virginia (Alexandria, Arlington, etc.).

Other parts of the South have become somewhat more Republican. More rural states such as Tennessee and Arkansas have become significantly more Republican since the turn of the 21st century. And rural areas in general, such as the Appalachian Mountain areas of Tennessee and Virginia, have become significantly more Republican over the past two decades. If the migration of Democrats from the North, the Midwest, and West explains the leftward shift of the region as a whole, how does it explain the rightward shift—and sometimes a sizable rightward shift—of significant sub-regions in the South? Simply put, it can't.

Again, there are two central facets of southern partisan change during the 21st century:

1. Region-wide, a net shift to the Democratic Party.
2. A dramatic increase in geographic partisan polarization, both between states and within states. Some locales have become significantly more Republican while other communities have become significantly more Democratic.

A migratory explanation for both facets of southern partisan change must take a far broader view of migration, in both its direct and indirect effects, than the existing literature affords. Migratory theories of political change in the South have focused exclusively on the character of in-migrants from other regions (and countries), their political distinctiveness, and the direct effects of these new residents on party fortunes in imminent elections.[4] This ignores the broader, and admittedly more subtle, potential impact of in-migrants on existing residents—both of the communities they are joining and those they are leaving. And because existing theory has ignored these indirect effects, it has failed to fully account for the political impact of *intra*-regional migration. If in-migrants from other regions can influence the residents of existing southern communities, the same is true for migrants from other parts of the South.

Migratory theories of southern partisan change that focus solely on arrivals from other regions (and other countries) are hopelessly incomplete. A migration-based theory of southern partisan change must incorporate the migration of current southerners to other parts of the South. It must manifest an understanding of just who is moving (not a random sample of the southern population), what happens when they get to where they are going (politically speaking), and—at least as significantly—what happens to the places they leave behind. There are movers *and* stayers, and both play roles in this 21st-century southern political drama.

One of the central premises of my argument is that movers and stayers are different and, crucially, different in ways that have important political implications. Specifically, movers have demographic characteristics that consistently incline them toward the Democratic Party in ways that are not manifest among more stationary adults. Two key aspects of this demographic distinctiveness are *age* and *level of education*. I present data below illustrating that movers are younger and more highly educated, and these distinctions are broadly true for southern migrants whether they come from another region or not.

Historically—at least since the middle of the 20th century—migrants were demographically distinct in ways that tended to make them more likely to identify as Republicans and support Republican candidates. As Jurjevich and Plane claim:

> Scholars have long inferred that because migrants are often younger, better educated, and have higher incomes, they are more likely to be Republicans compared to non-migrants. (2012:431)

Campbell et al. (1960) also noted that "movers" were distinctive 60 years ago. They wrote:

> Who are the *movers* (emphasis added)? As a single gross category they are men who tend to be somewhat better educated and who have considerably

better jobs and higher incomes . . . professional and business men on the make and on the move, leaving home territory for greener pastures. (Campbell et al. 1960:445)

Campbell et al. (1960) find evidence that movers entering the South were also better educated and wealthier than native southerners, and, not surprisingly, the movers were far more likely to be Republicans than native southerners. They also found no evidence that these movers, once established in southern communities, shifted their allegiances to the Democratic Party more than did migrants to other, considerably less Democratic regions.[5]

More recent data suggests that the relative preponderance of Republicans among movers (compared to stayers or natives) was not a phenomenon limited to the Eisenhower era. Writing about a much more recent time period, Gimpel (1999) argues that the relationship between Republican identification and migration activity is based on an economic calculus, one very similar to that posited by Campbell et al. (1960). Gimpel writes:

. . . population growth from domestic sources [our *movers*] is a sign of expanding economic opportunity likely to attract the best educated, most upwardly mobile populations and therefore likely to benefit the GOP at the expense of Democrats and third parties. (1999:335)

Brown (1988) also presents evidence that migrants were significantly more likely to identify with the Republican Party than were stayers. This is true regardless of the timing of migration, though more recent migrants tended to be more Republican than earlier migrants (Brown 1988). In the case of the North-to-South migration, the partisan distinctiveness was particularly stark:

The north-south migrants were Republican. They identified with the Republican party and voted Republican for presidential candidates . . . . When Republicans began to compete for seats in the South in the early 1960s, these migrants voted for them. Over time, the partisan hue of this group has not changed. (Brown 1988:62–63)

Gimpel simply concludes that movers "are more likely to have a Republican than a Democratic profile" (1999:1350).

The overall Republican bent of (white) migrants in the mid-to-late 20th century fits well with the migratory explanation for southern partisan change during this same time period. As migration to the South increased with an influx of new residents who were not only more likely to be Republicans than to be Democrats, but were *far* more likely to be Republicans than long-term residents because of the overwhelming preponderance of native southern Democrats, the overall partisan leaning of the southern states shifted to the right (or the Republican side).

In-migration from the North also plays an important role in theories of 20th-century southern partisan transformation which revolve around economic growth and development (see Lublin 2004 or Shafer and Johnston 2006). As economic opportunities increased in the South, the region became an increasingly attractive destination for the young, well-educated professionals that leaned heavily in the Republican direction (see Black and Black 2002 on the urban magnets of northern Republicans). Even for those who espouse a more ecumenical view of the causes of the late 20th-century shift to the Republican Party in the South (i.e., Bass and DeVries 1995 and Scher 1992), inter-regional migration plays a key role in Republican growth. As Scher concludes, "one of the most important factors contributing to the Republican success in the South has been in-migration" (1992:143).

But times change. Research focused on the mid- to late 20th century did not capture this change because it had not yet occurred, and the demographic composition of the Republican Party is not what it once was. The same is true for the Democratic Party, particularly the white contingent of the Democratic Party. The shifting compositions of the two political parties suggests that northern in-migrants may have a somewhat different effect on the partisan orientation of the South in the 21st century than they did in the 20th century. The most recent research—that which captures the early portion of the 21st century—is fully consistent with an altered partisan vector for in-migrants. Where northern in-migrants might once have driven southern Republican growth, it now appears that they may be driving a resurgence of the Democratic Party in the south (see Hood and McKee 2010; McKee and Teigen 2016; and Hillygus, McKee, and Young 2017). Likewise, internal migrants—people moving from one town or city or county in the South to another town, city, or county in the South (possibly even in the same state)—are also fostering Democratic growth—and sub-regional polarization—across the region.

The traditionally distinctive characteristics of migrants[6]—that they are younger, better educated, and wealthier—no longer suggest such a strong attraction to the Republican Party.[7] Republicans are now significantly older than Democrats. Twenty-five years ago, members of the Silent Generation—some of whom are now in their 90s—were more likely to be Democrats than Republicans. The subtle generational differences in partisan attachment of the late 1990s have given way to dramatic ideological differences between young and old in the 21st century. Now, the Silent Generation—or more accurately, whites in the Silent Generation—are overwhelmingly Republican. White Baby Boomers also skew to the right, but Generation Xers lean more toward the left, and Millennials skew strongly to the left.[8] When migrants were more likely to align with the Republican Party in the mid- to late 20th century, this generational partisan gap simply did not exist. Generational differences in partisan attachment were more subtle, and the youngest generation wasn't the most Democratic (Fisher 2020). This growing generational gap has influenced the partisan leanings of movers.

In the 1990s, educational attainment was strongly associated with identification with the Republican Party. According to a recent Pew study (2018a), those with some college experience in the mid-1990s were more likely to be Republicans than Democrats, and those with a college degree were significantly more likely to be Republicans than Democrats. Those with some postgraduate education who expressed a partisan identification were relatively evenly divided between Democrats and Republicans. Only among those who never went to college were Democratic identifiers more common than Republican identifiers.

The current relationship between partisanship and educational attainment is a mirror image of the earlier pattern. Today, respondents with some postgraduate experience are more than twice as likely to identify as Democrats. Likewise, a college education is associated with a strong preference for the Democratic Party. For those with less than a college education, the Republican Party holds a slight advantage. For whites with no more than a high school education, the attachment to the Republican Party is especially strong.

The defining characteristics of movers—at least movers within the United States—during the latter part of the 20th century—the characteristics which clearly tied them to the Republican Party at that time—may no longer be true (in the case of income and wealth) or may no longer tie them to the

Republican Party (in the case of age and education). In the next section of this chapter, I investigate the demographics of 21st-century migrants with a particular focus on migrants in the South.

Age and Migration

Migration occurs at all stages of life. I moved when I was 4, 6, 18, 22, 27, 31, 40, and 52. Every time I moved to a different county and a different state—every politically significant move—I was moving for professional reasons, either for a job or an education. When I was four, my family moved for my dad's job. Then I moved for college and for graduate school, and there were moves for three different jobs. When I was six, we moved from an apartment to a house in the same small town.[9] At 40, my family and I moved between houses in adjacent towns in the same Maryland county. Politically significant moves for jobs (and family). Local moves for housing. Completely conventional. And the number of moves, by American standards, is about average.[10] You'll note that the frequency of moves has slowed down now that I have reached (late?) middle age—also common in the American context—and it is likely that I will move at least once more (around retirement age).

During the late 20th century, movers tended to be younger (as we discussed above). If my experience is any indication, the same should be true today. And, in fact, the same is true today: movers tend to be younger than stayers. Consider the data from the Cooperative Congressional Election Studies (CCES) (Kuriwaki 2018). If we look at responses to the CCES question "*How many years/months have you lived in this city?*"[11], we find that younger people have lived shorter amounts of time in their current cities of residence than older people. One explanation for this difference is the generational variance in mobility. Younger people have lived a shorter period of time in their current city of residence than older people because they move more frequently and so are more recent arrivals to their current city than older residents. But even if no one ever moved, older people would have lived more time in their current city of residence than younger people; so *time in residence*, by itself, provides us with limited leverage on the question of the relationship between age and migration patterns.

To rigorously assess the relationship between age and mobility, we must distinguish migrants from non-migrants and then examine the generational character of both groups. Migration has two key dimensions: space and time. What is the geographic relationship between the community the migrant left behind and the community to which the migrant moved? And when did the migrant move?

Demographers, geographers, sociologists, and political scientists employ a wide range of geographic distinctions to delineate internal migratory patterns.[12] While some scholars focus on the subtlest category of migration— from neighborhood to neighborhood—others have focused on the most dramatic category of residential changes—from one region of the country to another.[13] I focus on county-level migration because it is (1) a common unit of analysis in the migration literature and (2) the smallest unit of analysis that is both *temporally consistent* and *politically distinct*. Except for a very small number of boundary adjustments, county boundaries are consistent across time. The same is obviously not true for municipal boundaries. And when migrants move across a county border, they are moving to a new political jurisdiction. Migration within a county—even when crossing between census tracts—may not result in a transition to a new political environment. On the other end of the analytical spectrum, states are simply too large to provide the sole basis for a comprehensive assessment of the political impact of migration. According to movers and stayers theory, intrastate migration has significant political implications. Operationalizing migration at the state level completely ignores those effects and precludes a meaningful empirical assessment of the theory.

To investigate the temporal dimensions of migration—and the age-distinctiveness of migrants—I created two *migrant* variables. Having moved within the past year certainly qualifies one as a migrant, but as years in the new city accumulate, the "migrant" appellation becomes less apt. *One-year migrant* is coded "1" for all respondents who have spent less than a full calendar year in their current city. It is coded "0" otherwise. To avoid a single, somewhat arbitrary, temporal distinction between migrants and non-migrants, I also created a migrant variable with a slightly longer (four years) time frame. *Four-year migrant* is coded "1" for all respondents who have spent less than four calendar years in their current city. It is coded "0" otherwise. One-year migrants make up 6.3% of the weighted sample; 23.7% of the weighted sample are four-year migrants.[14]

In the full U.S. sample (all regions), migrants are clearly significantly younger than natives. This is true for both the one-year migrants and the four-year migrants; relatively recent arrivals are younger—on average—than

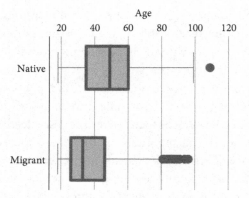

Figure 4.1. Age and Migratory Status: One-year Migrants vs. All Others

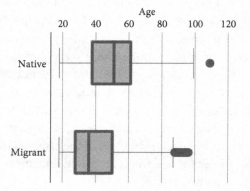

Figure 4.2. Age and Migratory Status: Four-year Migrants vs. All Others

the people who have been living in the area for years (see Figures 4.1 and 4.2). Figure 4.1 depicts the age distribution of that set of individuals who have moved in the past year and the age distribution for those individuals who have not moved in the past year (natives).[15] Those who have made a significant move in the past year are quite a bit younger than respondents who have not. The mean age of one-year migrants is more than a decade younger, and while the bulk—the middle quartiles—of natives are in their late 30s to 60, the bulk of one-year migrants are in their late 20s to mid-40s. The dramatic age gap between migrants and natives also manifests in the graphic depicting the age distribution of four-year migrants and natives (see Figure 4.2). Not surprisingly, four-year migrants are slightly older than one-year migrants because we have added some longer-term residents to the migrant groups.

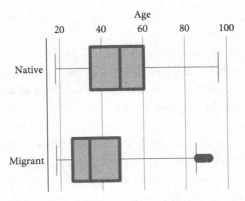

Figure 4.3. Age and Migratory Status: One-year Migrants vs. All Others in the South

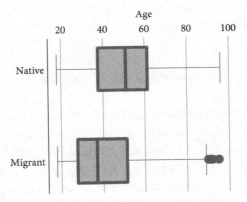

Figure 4.4. Age and Migratory Status: Four-year Migrants vs. All Others in the South

But the age differential is still quite clear; migrants are still much younger than natives[16].

Migrants are younger than natives in the South, too (see Figures 4.3 and 4.4). Figure 4.3 graphically represents the age distribution of one-year migrants and natives in the South,[17] and Figure 4.4 graphically represents the age distribution of four-year migrants and natives in the South. The migrant–native age differential we find in the United States as a whole is fully reflected in the South. One-year migrants in the South are well over a decade younger than natives, and the same is true for four-year migrants in the South. Migrants are much younger than natives, and this is true whether we define migrants as those who have moved in the last year or those who have moved in the last four years.

Just as was true in the latter part of the 20th century, movers are much younger than stayers in the 21st century—in the South and the United States as a whole.[18] The key difference is that age was inversely related to Democratic Party identification. In the mid- to late 20th century, older voters tended to be more likely to support Democrats, and younger voters tended to be more likely to support Republicans or to identify as independents.[19] This was especially true in the South (see, for example, Black and Black 1987). More recently, the trend has shifted. Today, younger voters are more likely to align with the Democratic Party, and older voters are more likely to align with the Republican Party.[20] In the most recent past, this partisan age gap has grown considerably. Just as before, younger Americans are more likely to move than older Americans. Years ago, that meant movers were more likely to be Republicans; today, it means that movers are more likely to be Democrats.

Education and Migration

Another widely accepted facet of the migrant population in the latter part of the 20th century was its relatively high level of education. Are 21st-century migrants still more highly educated than the native population? As in the case of the relationship between age and migration status, the answer is yes: migrants are more highly educated than natives, though the schooling differentials are subtler than the age differentials.

The CCES educational attainment question I use to assess educational differences between migrants and natives is, "What is the highest level of education you have completed?" The coding categories are as follows:

1. No HS
2. High School Graduate
3. Some College
4. 2-year
5. 4-year
6. Post-Grad

Based on responses to this question, I created a *High School Only* variable which is coded "1" if the respondent had "No HS" or if the respondent was a "High School Graduate." All other non-missing responses—from "Some College" to "Post-Grad"—were coded "0."

While the differences are subtle, migrants are more educated than long-term residents, and these differences are statistically significant in every case: for the United States as a whole, for the South specifically, and for both one-year and four-year migrants. Chart 4.1 depicts the relative differences in educational attainment for migrants and natives throughout the United States and in the South. The height of each bar is based on the percentage difference in the prevalence of any educational attainment beyond high school[21] between a certain category of migrants and natives and for a certain geographic area. So, for example, the 3.93% atop the first bar in Chart 4.1 indicates that the percentage of individuals in the United States with at least some college-level educational experience is nearly four points higher for one-year migrants than for the remaining population.[22] The figure is significantly higher for four-year migrants as compared to the remaining population (natives).

In the South, these differences are smaller. One-year migrants are only slightly more highly educated than natives.[23] But in the case of four-year migrants, the educational gap is nearly as large as it is for the United States as a whole. In general, in the United States and in the South specifically, migrants tend to be more highly educated than longer-term residents.

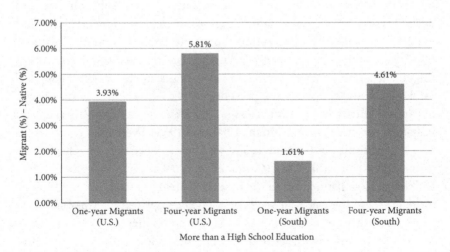

Chart 4.1. Migrant Population vs. Native Population

The educational gap between natives and migrants which existed in the latter half of the 20th century remains in the 21st century. However, as noted above, the partisan implications of this educational gap have reversed polarity since the 20th century. An educational gap that favored Republicans (migrants more educated than natives) in the 1970s and 1980s now plainly favors Democrats.

Migration and Income

At one time, in the late 20th century, wealth enabled migration. As Brown notes, "those who moved more recently are likely to be drawn from relatively higher status groups" (1988:25). Migrants during this time period were more likely to be professionals or have white-collar jobs, have a high income, and consider themselves upwardly mobile than natives (Brown 1988). This is fully consistent with the Campbell et al. observation from the 1950s that movers:

> ... have considerably better jobs and higher incomes than the natives of the regions they leave ... [they are] professional and business men on the make and on the move, leaving home territory for greener pastures. (1960:445)

Socioeconomic distinctions between migrants and natives in the latter part of the 20th century had political implications. The Republican Party had been the party of moneyed interests, the wealthy, and the upper class (at least outside the South) since the 19th century (and arguably since its creation). During the 20th century, wealth and social class played a significant role in the constellation of partisan attachments. Franklin Roosevelt's New Deal (and the Great Depression that preceded it) played a key role in the growth of support among the working class for the Democratic Party. This support remained extremely strong into the 1950s and 1960s. Even in the overwhelmingly Democratic South of the 1950s, we find evidence of an upper-class tilt toward the Republican Party (Campbell et al. 1960). In every other region, the class-based distinctions in the base of the two political parties was even more evident. The role that socioeconomic class played in American politics does not rival the role of class in European politics, but "class is clearly one of the underlying dimensions of party affiliation in the United States" (Campbell et al. 1960:159).

Signs of the gradual disintegration of the class-based substructure of the American party system have become increasingly common in the past two decades. Recent evidence suggests that the very wealthiest voters are now more likely to be Democrats than Republicans (Drutman 2016). In the aggregate, the income and wealth of political constituencies that have tended to support Democratic candidates has grown in the recent past. Conversely, the income and wealth of the most staunchly Republican constituencies has declined somewhat over the same time period (Edsall 2019).

But among the members of the mass public, vestiges of the socioeconomic architecture of the party system remain. In particular, members of the working class are still more likely to identify with the Democratic Party than the Republican Party, and wealthier Americans are more likely to identify with the Republican Party (Pew Research Center 2016). Voters with family income above $50,000 identify more frequently with the Republican Party than the Democratic Party. The opposite—more likely to identify with the Democratic Party than the Republican Party—is true among voters with family incomes below $50,000. We see a similar dynamic among whites, African Americans, and Latinos, though the baseline support for the Republican and Democratic parties in each group varies considerably, and the particular character of the relationship between income and party support varies as well. For example, among whites, support for the Republican Party may be higher among middle class voters than upper-class voters. But among the poorest voters—those making less than $30,000—support for the Democratic Party is slightly greater than support for the Republican Party, the only income group for whom this is true among whites. Though African Americans are overwhelmingly supportive of the Democratic Party, working class blacks are still more supportive than higher income blacks. Among Latinos, the class distinctions in the support levels for the two parties are even greater. Still, the strength of the relationship between class and party identification has apparently ebbed over time.

If the relationship between income and partisanship has weakened over time, has the relationship between migration and class weakened as well, or has this 20th-century characteristic of migrants carried over to today? Are migrants still wealthier than natives; do movers come from higher socioeconomic classes than stayers today? I find that this relationship has weakened considerably. To the extent that there is any current class-based distinction between migrants and natives/movers and stayers, the stayers tend to be slightly better off than the movers.

Looking at the data from the CCES, we see years of continuous residence in the same city are largely unrelated to income. Taking the average years of continuous residence by income level, we see that across the income levels from $20,000 to more than $150,000, the average times of residency for each of the income classes are statistically indistinguishable. Within this income range, if I knew a person's income (or their family's income), I could not improve upon a random draw when guessing their time in continuous residence at their current home. However, those at the lowest income levels—$10,000–$20,000 and below $10,000—had significantly shorter periods of continuous residence than those in the other income categories. Those in the lowest income category—below $10,000—had, by far, the shortest average period of continuous residence. This pattern holds true in the South and the United States more broadly. Significantly, the average time of continuous residence in the South is lower than for the United States as a whole in *every single income category*. In the 21st century, migration is more and more a southern thing, and that's true regardless of one's income or class.

Looking at recent migrants—either one-year migrants or four-year migrants—migrants have lower incomes than natives. For the United States as a whole, the median (family) income category for natives is $50,000 to $60,000; for both one-year migrants and four-year migrants, the median income category is $40,000–$50,000. Income data manifest the same migrant–native differences in the South.[24] Natives in the South have a median family income of $40,000–$50,000. One-year migrants have a median family income of $30,000–$40,000. In the South, four-year migrants have the same median income as natives. However, if we take the mean of the income codes for both four-year migrants and natives, the statistic for four-year migrants is smaller, suggesting a lower average family income. In both the South and the United States as a whole, when compared to natives, 21st-century migrants are relatively less well off than 20th-century migrants.

This income gap suggests that migrants might be somewhat more likely to align with the Democratic Party than their 20th-century forebears. But as we noted above, the strong and consistent relationship between income and partisanship that manifested in the 20th century has been weakened since the turn of the 21st century. Upper-class attachments to the Republican Party and working class attachments to the Democratic Party (particularly among whites) are not what they once were. While this evidence of a migration income gap implies that migrants are more likely to support the Democratic

Party, we might reasonably expect no more than a subtle partisan support differential.

Race, Ethnicity, and Migration

Research on the racial/ethnic composition of the flow of immigrants to the United States is voluminous. This detailed research includes extensive annual data and detailed information on region of origin (Latin America, Europe, Africa, etc.) of documented migrants. There are also significant efforts to assess the racial and ethnic composition (or the country of origin) of *undocumented* immigrants. The same cannot be said for our efforts to understand the racial/ethnic composition of the various flows of internal migration, especially if we are interested in the composition of these flows into or among the southern states.

Immigrants from Asia and Latin America make up by far the largest portion of the external migrant population in any given year, and that has been true for years (Center for Immigration Studies 2017). For many years, more immigrants came from Latin America than any other region of the world, but most recently the size of the immigrant population from Asia has nosed ahead (Center for Immigration Studies 2017). International migrants are also more likely to favor the Democratic Party than the Republican Party (Mayda, Peri, and Stengress 2016), but only those who become naturalized citizens can vote, so the arrival of international immigrants alone does not directly affect the voting rolls.[25] Except in relatively unusual circumstances, international migrants must satisfy a number of quite stringent criteria— including a five-year residence requirement and a 30-month continuous residence requirement—to even *apply* for naturalization (which is required to vote). Because of the stringent requirements to become a naturalized citizen, not all international migrants—even if they are legally resident in the United States—choose to become citizens. Recently, the United States has taken over a million immigrants on an annual basis (Radford 2019). During the same time period, the number of newly naturalized citizens has hovered around 800,000 (Radford 2019).

Residency requirements complicate the counting of international migrants for the purposes of assessing the impact of recent migrants—national and international—on localized population and partisanship. The modal *recent* international migrant simply isn't eligible to vote. The formal requirements insure newly naturalized citizens have been legal residents of the United States for at least five years, but the average citizen—at naturalization—has been in the United States far longer. Median residency time for naturalized citizens is eight years; median residency for immigrants from some regions is significantly longer (Blizzard and Batalova 2019). The median period of residency for immigrants from North America (i.e., including Mexico, the country that regularly sends the largest number of immigrants to the United States) is over a decade (Blizzard and Batalova 2019).

There is a gap—often of many years—between the arrival of an immigrant and the first time he or she casts a ballot. Population growth due to the arrival of international immigrants only has a direct effect on shifting partisan tides with a lag. But that effect is no less real, even with the lag, and there is every reason to think that in the 21st century, that effect favors the Democratic Party.

Still, assessing the short-term partisan implications of immigrant flows remains difficult. The same is true for assessing the political implications of the racial and ethnic dynamics of internal migrant flows, particularly as they manifest in the South. When the focus turns to citizens (at least, primarily)—and the movement of citizens across a significant political boundary (rather than a move within the same immediate area or neighborhood)—the complications associated with the assessment of the political implications of migrant streams only grow. We simply do not know a great deal about the relative propensity of citizens of different racial/ethnic groups to make significant moves to and within the South.

The racial/ethnic composition of internal migration streams has important political implications because of the variation in partisan attachment across racial/ethnic groups. African Americans have overwhelmingly identified with the Democratic Party since the New Deal (and especially since the mid-1960s), and this is true regardless of their migrant status (White and Laird 2020). Latinos and Asian Americans have historically had a more heterogeneous orientation to the major political parties. Cuban Americans have long been strong supporters of the Republican Party, and Asian Americans have also supported Republican candidates at significant levels. However, during the last two decades, Latinos and Asian Americans have shifted toward the Democratic Party (see Thee-Brenan 2014). Whites are now far more supportive of the Republican Party than other racial/ethnic groups, and this is true regardless of region (Lee 2020). According to Lee (2020) the Republican Party has become an overwhelmingly "white" party since the turn of the 21st century. If the presence of people of color is higher among migrants than among natives—if people of color are more likely to be movers than stayers—this will influence the political implications of migration.

Among the CCES survey respondents, residency patterns vary widely across racial/ethnic groups. Whites are largely distinctive from other racial groups, but there are important differences among people of color as well (see Table 4.1). On average, whites have lived in their current cities longer than members of any other specific racial or ethnic group.[26] The average white respondent has lived in the same city 18 months longer than the average African American, over two years longer than the average Hispanic respondent, and more than five years longer than the average Asian American. Native Americans, those of Middle Eastern descent, and those of mixed race also have much shorter residences than whites.

Among southern respondents, we see subtle differences in these patterns. First, northerners—in general—have lived in their current cities significantly longer than southerners. With the exception of Hispanics and those of Middle Eastern descent, the average residency figures are lower for every racial/ethnic group in the South than they are for the United States as a whole. Obviously, if we looked at a North-only sample, we would see an even starker difference. This is fully consistent with the broad demographic trends indicating significant regional in-migration to and in the southern states. Second, the residential gaps between people of color and whites in the South tend to be smaller than the same gaps for the United States as a whole (and, implicitly, the non-southern states). The key exception is among Native Americans,

Table 4.1. Mean Residency (in Years) by Racial/Ethnic Group (U.S.)

Racial/Ethnic Group	Mean Years in Current City
White	16.2
Black	14.7
Hispanic	14.1
Asian	10.7
Native American	15.6
Mixed	12.1
Other	16.6
Middle Eastern	11.8

Table 4.2. Mean Residency (in Years)
by Racial/Ethnic Group (South)

Racial/Ethnic Group	Mean Years in Current City
White	14.8
Black	14.0
Hispanic	14.3
Asian	8.9
Native American	15.4
Mixed	10.7
Other	15.2
Middle Eastern	11.8

who have longer residences than whites (in the South). Again, respondents indicating "Other" have remained in place longer than southern whites. In sum, the residency data suggest that people of color make up a larger portion of the migrant population—or have made a larger portion of the migrant population over the course of the 21st century—than whites (in both the North and South). (See Table 4.2).

A similar pattern emerges when we examine the distinctions between one-year migrants, four-year migrants, and natives. For the United States as a whole, migrant populations are more diverse—include significantly more people of color—than native populations. As in the previous charts, the size of the bars is based on the percentage difference between a specific migrant population and a corresponding native population. Chart 4.2 depicts the differences in the relative size of various racial and ethnic groups between one-year migrants and natives in the United States as a whole. The relative size of the white population in the group of one-year migrants in the United States is 3.32% smaller than it is among the native population. This is the largest gap between the one-year migrant and native groups, and it is in the expected direction; migrants are less likely to be white than natives. The next three largest gaps—among blacks, Asian Americans, and those of mixed descent—all indicate a greater preponderance of people of color among migrants than among natives. We see even starker results when comparing the racial/ethnic composition of four-year migrants and natives. The gap between the white composition of four-year migrants and natives is even larger than the gap between one-year migrants

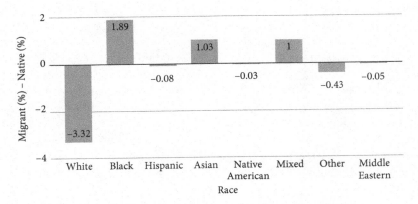

Chart 4.2. Native/Migrant Proportions by Race (One-year Migrants, U.S.)

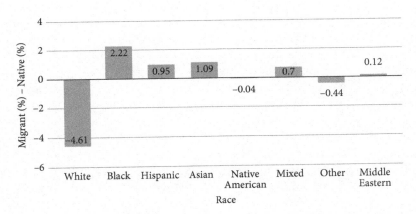

Chart 4.3. Native/Migrant Proportions by Race (Four-year Migrants, U.S.)

and natives, and in this case blacks, Hispanics, and Asian Americans make up a larger proportion of the migrant population than the native population (see Charts 4.2 and 4.3).

In the South, we find larger racial and ethnic disparities between the groups of migrants and the native populations (see Charts 4.4 and 4.5). Whites make up a significantly smaller proportion of the migrant population—both one-year migrants and four-year migrants—than in either of the native populations. African Americans make up a significantly larger proportion of both migrant populations, and Asian Americans and Hispanics also make up larger proportions of both migrant populations

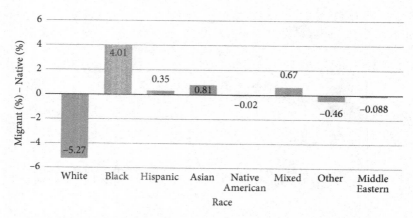

Chart 4.4. Native/Migrant Proportions by Race (One-year Migrants, South)

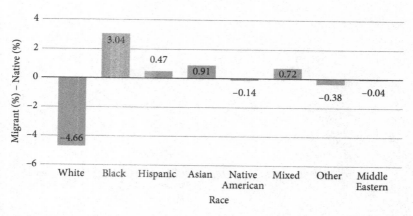

Chart 4.5. Native/Migrant Proportions by Race (Four-year Migrants, South)

than the native populations. Migrants are simply more likely to be people of color than white.

It is important to note that these figures may underestimate the Hispanic proportion of the migrant population. And, in fact, they do. A small percentage of individuals of Hispanic descent do not self-identify as Hispanic on the race question but do identify as Hispanic on the subsequent direct question regarding Spanish or Hispanic descent. A higher percentage of those of Spanish or Hispanic descent—even if they did not identify as a member of the Hispanic race—are migrants than natives. This is true regardless of the operationalization of migrant (one-year migrant or four-year migrant), and it is true in the South as well as the United States more broadly. Regardless of the operationalization of the migrant (and native) populations, the evidence suggests migrants are a more racially and ethnically diverse population than non-migrants.

Demographics and Migration: A Summary

In the analysis above, I focus on the first-order relationships between various demographic factors long thought to be related to migration—age, income, education, race/ethnicity—and 21st century migratory behavior. Obviously, these demographic factors are not orthogonal. Age and income tend to be positively related. Income varies systematically across racial/ethnic groups. Education and income are correlated. Even age and race/ethnicity are related: whites tend to be older than African Americans, who tend to be older than Latinos. Those tendencies are borne out in the CCES data and the differences are stark. So, for example, the mean age of whites in our sample is 48. The mean age of African Americans in the sample is 43. For Latinos, it is 40. The mean age of Asian Americans is 36.

Given the relationships between these various demographic factors, we must consider the possibility that only a subset of these factors drives migratory habits. Perhaps the first-order relationships between certain demographic factors and migratory activities do not reflect a causal relationship. To examine this possibility, I estimate a set of multivariate models including the full range of demographic factors examined above: age, education, income, and race/ethnicity. The dependent variables in these multivariate models were the same indicators of migration employed in the bivariate analyses above:

1. Length of residence in current city
2. One-year migrant dummy variable (less than one year in the current city of residence coded "1," all others coded "0")
3. Four-year migrant dummy variable (less than four years in the current city of residence coded "1," all others coded "0")

Length of residence models are estimated with OLS regression. Models with a one-year migrant dummy variable or a four-year migrant dummy variable are estimated with logistic regression. Standard coefficient errors are robust

Table 4.3. Explaining Time in Current City (U.S.)

Years in Current City	b	Robust SE	t	p > t
Age	0.35	0.02	20.06	0.00
Family Income	0.14	0.03	4.95	0.00
No High School	−1.21	0.34	−3.54	0.00
Some College	−1.57	0.19	−8.12	0.00
2-year Degree	−1.81	0.30	−6.03	0.00
4-year Degree	−2.54	0.22	−11.71	0.00
Post-Grad	−3.43	0.29	−11.99	0.00
Black	0.65	0.34	1.93	0.06
Hispanic	0.69	0.66	1.03	0.31
Asian	−0.77	0.38	−2.02	0.05
Native American	−0.01	0.67	−0.02	0.99
Middle Eastern	0.31	0.91	0.35	0.73
Mixed	−0.47	0.28	−1.66	0.10
Other	0.27	0.49	0.55	0.59
Constant	−0.71	0.42	−1.68	0.10

$R^2 = 0.16$

and clustered by state. Results for each of the multivariate models are generated from weighted samples[27] (see Tables 4.3 through 4.8).

Two results consistently appear across the full set of multivariate models. First, migrants are younger—substantially younger—than natives. It is only a slight exaggeration to suggest that movers and non-movers are *generationally* distinctive. And this generational gap appears without any accounting or controlling for retiree migration; these results are based on samples that include the full age range. Migrants were younger in the latter part of the 20th century; they are still younger in the 21st century. But while youth signaled identification with the Republican Party in the 20th century, today it implies just the opposite: attachment to the Democratic Party. And the generational gaps in party support—younger voters increasingly favoring the Democrats, and older voters increasingly favoring the Republicans—are growing wider.

The second consistent result is the role of a college degree in migratory habits. College graduates have spent significantly less time in their current locations, and college grads are much more likely to be movers than respondents without a college education. We see some evidence that any

Table 4.4. Explaining Time in Current City (South)

Years in Current City	B	Robust SE	t	p > t
Age	0.31	0.03	9.94	0.00
Family Income	0.07	0.04	1.57	0.15
No High School	−0.27	0.54	−0.51	0.62
Some College	−0.89	0.25	−3.55	0.01
2-year Degree	−0.99	0.54	−1.84	0.10
4-year Degree	−1.94	0.39	−5.03	0.00
Post-Grad	−2.75	0.51	−5.40	0.00
Black	1.30	0.51	2.54	0.03
Hispanic	1.76	1.59	1.11	0.29
Asian	−1.35	0.34	−3.95	0.00
Native American	0.65	1.18	0.55	0.60
Middle Eastern	2.23	0.85	2.61	0.03
Mixed	−0.90	0.73	−1.23	0.25
Other	0.07	0.54	0.12	0.91
Constant	−0.12	0.74	−0.16	0.87

$R^2 = 0.13$

college experience fosters mobility, but the evidence for this aspect of the education effect is mixed, particularly in the South. Again, we find both similarity and contrast between migratory patterns and their political implications across time. Just as migrants were more educated than non-migrants in the 20th century, movers are more educated than stayers in the 21st century. But while education was positively related to support for the Republican Party in the 20th century, it is now associated with identification with the Democrats. And, as discussed above, this educational gap in partisan support is only growing. Not only have the partisan allegiances flipped between the 20th and 21st centuries, but over the last 15 years, the gap in partisan support between those with a four-year college degree and those with no more than a high school degree has grown substantially.

The evidence for a relationship between income and migrant status is mixed. In the national sample, natives tend to have more resources than migrants. In the southern sample, I find no evidence of a relationship between income and migrancy. In the 20th century, income was positively associated with the likelihood of identifying with the Republican Party, but

Table 4.5. Movers vs. Stayers: One-year Migrants and Natives in the United States

One-year Migrant	b	Robust SE	t	p > t
Age	−0.04	0.00	−23.14	0.00
Family Income	−0.08	0.01	−12.81	0.00
No High School	**0.19**	0.08	2.23	0.03
Some College	**0.20**	0.05	3.86	0.00
2-year Degree	**0.20**	0.05	3.77	0.00
4-year Degree	**0.31**	0.05	6.05	0.00
Post-Grad	**0.37**	0.07	5.60	0.00
Black	−0.06	0.07	−0.94	0.35
Hispanic	−0.29	0.10	−2.80	0.01
Asian	−0.01	0.18	−0.04	0.97
Native American	−0.12	0.17	−0.67	0.50
Middle Eastern	−1.27	0.34	−3.74	0.00
Mixed	0.13	0.07	1.79	0.07
Other	−0.27	0.10	−2.68	0.01
Constant	−0.59	0.05	−11.23	0.00

Table 4.6. Movers vs. Stayers: One-year Migrants and Natives in the South

One-year Migrant	b	Robust SE	t	p > t
Age	−0.04	0.00	−9.18	0.00
Family Income	−0.07	0.01	−6.52	0.00
No High School	0.06	0.13	0.49	0.62
Some College	0.06	0.10	0.56	0.57
2-year Degree	0.16	0.10	1.54	0.12
4-year Degree	**0.29**	0.13	2.17	0.03
Post-Grad	0.22	0.12	1.90	0.06
Black	0.00	0.08	−0.02	0.99
Hispanic	−0.16	0.16	−1.05	0.29
Asian	0.08	0.16	0.47	0.64
Native American	0.00	0.26	0.01	1.00
Middle Eastern	−1.18	0.32	−3.71	0.00
Mixed	0.03	0.13	0.23	0.82
Other	−0.20	0.11	−1.74	0.08
Constant	−0.68	0.08	−8.82	0.00

Table 4.7. Movers vs. Stayers: Four-year Migrants and Natives in the United States

Four-year Migrant	b	Robust SE	t	p > t
Age	−0.04	0.00	−28.63	0.00
Family Income	−0.08	0.01	−13.88	0.00
No High School	0.15	0.05	2.79	0.01
Some College	0.25	0.03	8.65	0.00
2-year Degree	0.23	0.04	6.30	0.00
4-year Degree	0.35	0.04	9.85	0.00
Post-Grad	0.49	0.04	11.37	0.00
Black	−0.03	0.04	−0.70	0.49
Hispanic	−0.14	0.06	−2.16	0.03
Asian	0.02	0.09	0.28	0.78
Native American	−0.09	0.11	−0.74	0.46
Middle Eastern	0.11	0.22	0.50	0.62
Mixed	0.00	0.05	0.00	1.00
Other	−0.22	0.07	−3.12	0.00
Constant	0.90	0.05	17.25	0.00

Table 4.8. Movers vs. Stayers: Four-year Migrants and Natives in the South

Four-year Migrant	b	Robust SE	t	p > t
Age	−0.04	0.00	−13.65	0.00
Family Income	−0.06	0.01	−7.94	0.00
No High School	0.06	0.09	0.60	0.55
Some College	0.17	0.06	2.99	0.00
2-year Degree	0.20	0.07	3.06	0.00
4-year Degree	0.29	0.07	3.92	0.00
Post-Grad	0.40	0.08	4.95	0.00
Black	−0.06	0.06	−0.99	0.32
Hispanic	−0.15	0.12	−1.27	0.20
Asian	0.12	0.12	1.01	0.31
Native American	−0.16	0.18	−0.90	0.37
Middle Eastern	−0.45	0.26	−1.75	0.08
Mixed	0.07	0.14	0.47	0.64
Other	−0.13	0.14	−0.92	0.36
Constant	0.79	0.08	9.42	0.00

that relationship has weakened considerably over time (particularly among whites). Some might argue that there is little evidence of a lingering relationship between income and partisanship (after controlling for education), and to the extent a relationship still exists, it favors the Democrats. There is a growing body of aggregate-level evidence (i.e., at the county or congressional district level) that suggests wealthier constituencies now tend to lean to the Democratic side. Regardless of the actual relationship between partisanship and income over the time period of this analysis, there is no evidence of a relationship between income and migrant status (at least in the South).

Finally, we find relatively little evidence of racial or ethnic differences in migratory habits. Even limiting our focus to the results based on the southern sample, we fail to find significant, consistent differences between the migratory patterns of racial/ethnic groups across the various analyses. This should probably not be too surprising, First, while CCES samples (when weighted appropriately) are designed to represent all U.S. adults, the actual percentage of non-citizen immigrants in average samples is quite low (on the order of 1%) (see Richman, Chatta, and Earnest 2014). Second, we are controlling for age, education, and income, and we know there are significant differences across racial/ethnic groups on these demographic dimensions. When the focus is the internal migration of voters, the theoretical foundations for the impact of age, education, and income are simply much stronger than the rationales for the impact of racial and ethnic identity.

So, demographically speaking, migrants should be politically distinctive from natives. I expect movers to be more attached to the Democratic Party than stayers. The question is simple: are they? I answer that question next.

Migration and Partisanship

The old story regarding migrants was that they had a certain demographic profile—relatively young and relatively well educated, in particular—fully consonant with support for the Republican Party, at least the Republican Party of the 1970s and 1980s. As the analysis presented above demonstrates, that profile is still largely accurate. But the consistency of the migrant profile belies the stark transformation in the partisanship attachments associated with it. Today, those young, well-educated Republicans are Democrats. The demography of the migrant profile, largely consistent across the latter half of the 20th century and the first decades of the 21st century, is now far more consistent with attachment to the Democratic Party than the Republican Party. As I note above, recent research in southern politics has begun to pick up on this migratory transformation among *regional* migrants, movers coming to the South from another part of the United States, and immigrants (or international migrants) (see, for example, Hillygus, McKee, and Young 2017).

Although consistent with the "new" southern in-migration literature, my argument is also broader. Southern migrants are more likely to be Democrats than they were generations ago. And they are more likely (overall) to identify with the Democratic Party than those staying put—the natives. Not only are in-migrants—the conventional term for migrants from other regions—more likely to be Democrats than they were in the latter part of the 20th century, migrants—people moving within a region (i.e., from one part of the South to another part of the South)—are more likely to be Democrats than they were a generation ago. As I note above, there is a good bit of research on in-migrants to the South; there is much less work on migrants within the South.

The analysis presented above highlights key demographic differences between movers and stayers, across the United States and those residing in the South. And those demographic differences, once suggestive of attachment to the Republican Party, now indicate identification with the Democratic Party. But where is the direct evidence that movers are really more closely attached to the Democratic Party than the Republican Party than stayers? I turn to that analysis now.

Apart from the demographic profile of migrants, is there any other reason to think that migrants are more likely to align with the Democratic Party than the Republican Party? Yes, there is. On average, Republicans tend to live in the same city longer than Democrats. The CCES data suggests this residential pattern is manifest in the South and the United States as a whole. In the United States, the mean residency for a Republican is more than a year and a half longer than the mean residency for a Democrat. The median residency for a Republican in the South is more than two years longer than the mean residency for a Democrat in the South. In the South, the partisan gap between median residencies is the same; the partisan gap between average mean residencies is (slightly) larger. Democrats don't live in the same place as long as Republicans do. The reason for that is that they migrate more frequently. Democrats are more likely to be migrants than Republicans. It is true if we look at short-term migration (migration during the past year) or longer-term migration (migration within the past four years).

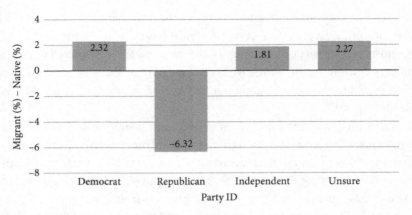

Chart 4.6. Native/Migrant Partisanship (One-year Migrants, U.S.)

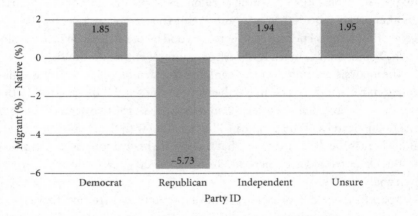

Chart 4.7. Native/Migrant Partisanship (Four-year Migrants, U.S.)

In the United States, recent movers (one-year migrants) are signifi-cantly more likely to be Democrats than Republicans. Natives are also more likely to be Democrats than Republicans, but the gap is much smaller[28] (see Chart 4.6). As in the previous charts, the bars in the following charts de-pict the difference in the prevalence of migrants relative to natives in each of the categories on the x-axis. In Chart 4.6, we see that the percentage of Democrats in the sample of one-year migrants in the United States as a whole is 2.32% higher than the percentage of Democrats among natives. Likewise independents and those who indicate that they are unsure of their parti-sanship are relatively more common among migrants than among natives.

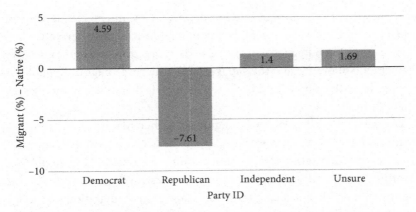

Chart 4.8. Native/Migrant Partisanship (One-year Migrants, South)

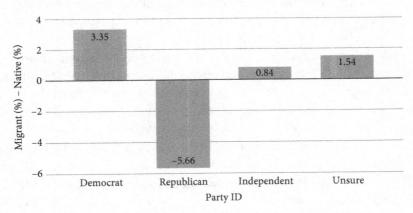

Chart 4.9. Native/Migrant Partisanship (Four-year Migrants, South)

Conversely, the percentage of Republicans in the sample of natives is significantly higher than the percentage of Republicans in the migrant population. We see a nearly identical pattern when we focus on four-year migrants in the United States as a whole. These movers tend to be overrepresented in groups of Democrats, independents, and those who are unsure about their partisanship. The opposite is true for Republicans; stayers are overrepresented in this group (see Chart 4.7).

In the South, we see an even starker gap between the partisan attachments of movers and stayers (see Chart 4.8 and Chart 4.9). Among one-year migrants, the percentage who identify as Democrats is nearly 5% higher than the percentage of natives who identify as Democrats. Independents also make up a larger portion of the migrant population than the native population. Only Republican identification is more common among natives than among migrants, and the gap is sizable. The percentage of Republicans among the native population is nearly 8% higher than it is among one-year migrants in the South.

We see a similar partisan configuration when we focus on four-year migrants. Democrats, independents, and those who are unsure of their party attachment manifest in larger percentages among migrants. Only Republican identification is more common among natives. While the patterns are slightly subtler when basing our operationalization of migration on a longer time period—four-year migrants vs. one-year migrants—the contours of the pattern are identical. The partisan composition of the migrant population is more Democratic and more independent than the composition of the native population (see Chart 4.8 and Chart 4.9).

To put these partisan figures into an explicit political context, consider the states which most closely represent the partisan allegiances of the various migrant and native populations based on the results of the 2016 election. Among one-year migrants in the South, 59% aligned with the Democratic Party; in 2016, 59% of New Yorkers voted for Democrat Hillary Clinton. Among four-year migrants in the South, 56% associated with the Democratic Party. That figure is comparable to the support for Hillary Clinton in Illinois—President Obama's home state. And the 50.5% of natives aligning themselves with the Republican Party is comparable to the level of support for Republican Donald Trump in Georgia in 2016. Those are the partisan gaps between migrants and natives in the South, the partisan gaps between states such as New York and Illinois on the migrant side and states like Georgia on the native side. It is no mean distinction. And the partisan differences between movers and stayers have broad political implications for southern politics in the 21st century.

Migration and Ideology

During the 20th century, even much of the second half of the 20th century, the ideological distinctions between Republicans and Democrats were far more muted than they are today. On some issues, primarily those related to economic policy, Republicans were more conservative than Democrats. In other areas, such as civil rights policy, Republicans tended to be more conservative than one component of the Democratic Party (northern Democrats) and more liberal than the other primary component of the Democratic Party (southern Democrats). To what extent do the partisan distinctions between movers and stayers (migrants and natives), particularly movers and stayers in the South, reflect these historic (i.e., 20th century) patterns and, conversely, to what extent do the party differences between movers and stayers reflect the much more distinctive ideological cants of 21st-century partisan politics? Does the stark partisan divide between movers and stayers reflect an equally stark ideological divide?

Based on the available evidence, the partisan divide between movers and stayers is fully reflected in a comparable ideological schism. Movers are far more liberal than stayers. In the full U.S. sample, one-year migrants are significantly more likely to identify as liberal or very liberal and significantly less likely (than natives) to identify as conservative or very conservative (see Chart 4.10). An even starker pattern emerges when we operationalize movers as four-year migrants; movers are more likely than stayers to identify as liberal, very liberal, or moderate (and as "not sure"). The only categories where stayers are in the majority—and it is a sizable majority—are the conservative and very conservative categories (see Chart 4.11).

While southerners are generally more conservative than respondents from other regions, the ideological distinctions between movers and stayers throughout the United States are fully reflected in the southern sample. Movers in the South are significantly more likely to identify as liberal or very liberal than southern stayers. Conversely, southern stayers are more likely to identify as conservative or very conservative than southern movers. This is true regardless of the temporal operationalization of "mover." It is true if we focus on one-year migrants (depicted in Chart 4.12) or four-year migrants (depicted in Chart 4.13).[29]

Conclusion: Movers, Non-movers, and their Differences

Movers are different. This is nothing new. Movers were different a half-century (and longer) ago. In some ways, the long-ago differences are the same today. Just as the authors of the *American Voter* (Campbell et al.

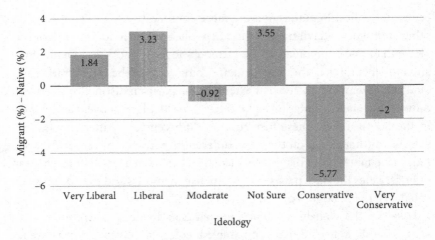

Chart 4.10. Native/Migrant Ideology (One-year Migrants, U.S.)

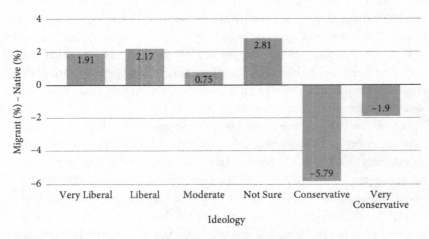

Chart 4.11. Native/Migrant Ideology (Four-year Migrants, U.S.)

1960) described movers as younger, better educated, and wealthier than stayers in the mid-1950s, we could say the same is true for movers today. They are (much) younger. They are (somewhat) better educated. And, at least some evidence suggests, they are wealthier.

Where the time-period differences between movers diverge is in their ideological orientations and political allegiances. Movers during the mid- to late 20th century were more likely to be Republicans. Younger people were more likely to be Republican. More educated people were more likely

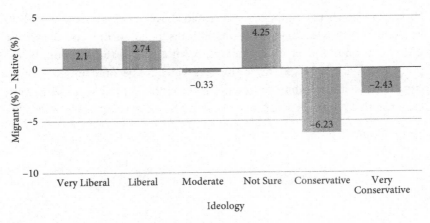

Chart 4.12. Native/Migrant Ideology (One-year Migrants, South)

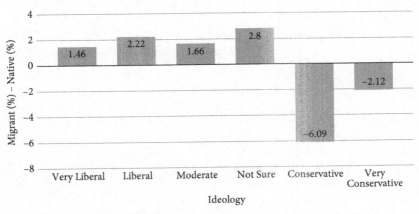

Chart 4.13. Native/Migrant Ideology (Four-year Migrants, South)

to be Republican. Wealth and income were also positively associated with Republican identification.

But movers weren't necessarily more conservative than non-movers. In the mid-to late 20th century, neither major party was ideologically cohesive to nearly the extent we see today. Movers might well have been more conservative on issues related to economic policy, but they probably did not have more conservative positions on civil rights issues than more stationary adults.

Today, the demographic profile of movers—younger, better educated, more racially and (to a lesser extent) more ethnically diverse—is more consistent with identification with the Democratic Party than the Republican

Party. And we see that in the data presented above: movers are more likely to be Democrats and less likely to be Republicans than non-movers. This is true if we focus on the most recent movers, but it also true (to, as would be expected, a slightly lesser extent) for movers who have become settled in a new city. It is true if our frame of reference is the entire United States. And most importantly for our purposes, it is true if our frame of reference is the South.

5

Migrant Magnets

How Movers Change the Politics of Their New Homes *and* the Places They Leave: The Case of Whites

The small town where I grew up had nearly 1,300 residents when I graduated from high school in 1989.[1] Far fewer people live there today. A beautiful place deep in the Appalachian Mountains, Cedar Bluff's population history reflects that of the county in which it resides, Tazewell County, Virginia. Historically, the primary business was coal mining. As mechanized mining took over, the numbers of good union jobs dwindled. While the area has seen other economic engines take root—the local community college, for one, and the hospital in neighboring Richlands—the area still struggles to recover from the slow and seemingly inexorable exit of the coal industry.

In 1980, Tazewell County had over 50,000 residents.[2] A decade later the population had dropped by nearly 10%. The latest estimates suggest that the current population is nearly 20% less than it was at its 1980 height. As population has declined, support for Republican candidates has increased dramatically. Tazewell County went big for Bill Clinton in 1992 and 1996, but after that, the fortunes of Democratic candidates cratered. Nearly 82% of *all* ballots cast in the 2016 presidential election—not just the ballots cast for Trump or Secretary Clinton, but those cast for third-party candidates as well—went to Trump. In Tazewell County, Trump received five times more votes than did Secretary Clinton.

Conventional wisdom suggests that the explanation for Tazewell County's political transformation is size. A standard explanation focuses on the conservatism of rural areas relative to urban areas and the increasing conservatism—and concomitant support for the Republican Party and its candidates—in rural areas. In *Why Cities Lose: The Deep Roots of the Urban-Rural Political Divide*, Jonathan Rodden explains the growth of rural conservatism as follows:

> We are currently in the midst of what is being called the third industrial revolution. The rise of the knowledge economy has led to the concentration of jobs and prosperity in global cities . . . . The knowledge-economy revolution may have ushered in something else as well: a nationalist backlash of the rural periphery against globalization, immigration, cosmopolitan values, and free trade. (2019:253–254)

According to this perspective, jobs and opportunities migrated to burgeoning megacities, leaving residents in the vast majority of far more rural counties frustrated with change beyond their control and disappointed with the current prospects for themselves and the future prospects for their children.

But is size destiny? A little less than five hours up Interstate 81 from my hometown, there sits a small city named Winchester. Also in Virginia—a state in which independent cities such as Winchester (technically, Winchester City) are governmentally comparable to counties like Tazewell County—it is very near the West Virginia border. Situated in the Shenandoah Valley, Winchester is, like Tazewell County, within the broader Appalachian Mountain range. As a city, Winchester is obviously not a "rural" area (as defined by the U.S. Census), but it is surrounded by rural area. It is also much smaller, at least in population, than Tazewell County. The most recent estimates indicate that Tazewell County is approximately a third larger than Winchester.

Winchester's commercial base was never predicated on coal, and so the decline of the coal industry's workforce—particularly the unionized workforce—did not destabilize Winchester's economy as it did Tazewell County's. The more diverse commercial environment (health care, light manufacturing, and education) has provided for economic growth in Winchester, and with that economic growth has come population growth. Though Winchester is smaller than Tazewell County, it has experienced consistent population growth over the same time period that Tazewell County has witnessed a considerable decline. Winchester has twice as many residents today than it did in 1970, and since 1980, the population has grown by nearly 40%.

With population growth—even in such a small place—has come partisan change. Rather than the dramatic upswing in support for Republican presidential candidates, voters in Winchester have leaned in the progressive direction. President George W. Bush beat Senator John Kerry by nearly 15 percentage points in 2004; in 2016, Secretary Clinton beat President

Trump. Even in small places—places where relatively few people live—population growth has political implications. Contrasting implications are equally real for many places that have lost and are losing population.

The differences between Tazewell County, Virginia, and Winchester, Virginia, are not reducible to the rural–urban divide that conventional wisdom claims dominates our politics.[3] This is not to say that size is politically irrelevant. But the preoccupation with the number of people in a community obscures the crucial role that the *growth* or *decline* in the number of people in a community, and the demographic and political characteristics of that migrant growing edge, have on a locale's politics.

In Chapter 3 I provided the aggregate-level empirical case for the broad claim that population growth—adult population growth—is directly related to support for Democratic presidential candidates. Even when accounting for population size, population growth has an independent and significant impact on residents' voting decisions, and the impact is in the progressive direction. Chapter 4 provided an initial explanation for the progressive effect of population growth: the demographic and political characteristics of *movers*—the engine of political change. Movers are clearly different from long-term natives; in fact, movers are different from non-movers more generally, even if the non-movers haven't spent decades in their current residences. The recently mobile are younger, more educated, more attached to the Democratic Party, and more progressive (in general) than their more geographically stable neighbors.

Previous research on the political implications of migration focused nearly exclusively on the changes in aggregate partisanship resulting from the demographic characteristics and political orientations of the new community members (see Rice and Pepper 1997 and Frendreis 1989; Carlson and Gimpel 2019 are an exemplary exception). For example, southern in-migrants during the 1970s and 1980s were thought to boost support for Republicans in the communities where they settled because of their own relatively conservative orientation (when compared to the existing population in the South). The in-migration argument did not extend to a subsequent transformation of native southerners' political attitudes driven by the influx of migrants from other regions. More commonly, research focused on the possibility that the political orientations of natives would transform the ideology and partisanship of the newcomers (Brown 1988).

This may have been the full migration story during the latter part of the 20th century in the South, but this continued preoccupation with the movers themselves has resulted in an incomplete and overly simplistic understanding of the political transformation in the 21st-century South. From the perspective of movers and stayers theory, it is no surprise that efforts to assess the direct effect of migration on partisan polarization—ignoring any indirect effects on stayers—reveal that the direct effects are far too small to explain the level of polarization that we see (Martin and Webster 2018). We must seriously consider the possibility that movers shape stayers, and realize that movers can shape the political orientations of the stayers in the communities to which they are moving, and, equally important, that they may shape the political orientations of the communities they are leaving. With very few exceptions, the literature completely ignores this latter dynamic.

Still, a central facet of the movers and stayers explanation of the relationship between community-level (county-level) population growth and increased support for Democratic candidates is the political character of movers, the people driving adult population growth. Younger and more educated than stayers, movers are more liberal than stayers and more likely than stayers to identify with the Democratic Party. This is true outside the South but is especially true for movers in the southern states. This finding does not depend upon a specific or particular definition of movers. It is true for those who have moved very recently (in the last year) and for those who moved a few years ago. Movers simply are different from stayers, and they are different in ways that tend to lead them to identify more closely with the Democratic Party than the Republican Party (and, in some cases, identify as independents).

On average, movers are demographically and politically distinct from stayers. Obviously not all movers are more liberal (or more likely to identify as Democrats) than stayers. It is possible for a local community to grow in a demographically unusual way that would not foster greater progressivism. Localized growth might be overwhelmingly driven by retirees, movers who are significantly older and somewhat more conservative than average.[4] Likewise, the economic foundation (i.e., tourism) of a local area may foster population growth without attracting significant numbers of highly educated job seekers. Finally, certain areas may experience growth without an increase in racial and ethnic diversity. In some comparatively rare cases, this growth may come at the expense of racial and ethnic diversity.

Consider the case of Brunswick County, North Carolina.[5] The fastest growing county in the state, it is a coastal area that includes an array of family beaches including Sunset, Ocean Isle, Holden, and Oak Island.[6] Its economy is largely based on tourism—likely one of the reasons it is now included in the Myrtle Beach-Conway-North Myrtle Beach metropolitan area centered in neighboring South Carolina rather than the metropolitan area of the nearest major city in North Carolina, Wilmington. It is one of the largest counties in the state without a single four-year college or university.

Though Brunswick County has experienced dramatic population growth over the past 50 years—over 40% in each of the last four decades—it has remained a relatively Republican area. In the 2004 presidential election, just over 40% of the vote went to Republican incumbent George W. Bush. In 2016, Trump received over 62% of the popular vote, and Clinton received less than 35% of the popular vote. The last Democratic presidential candidate to receive such a small portion of the popular vote in Brunswick County was Hubert Humphrey in 1968—the year American Independent Party candidate George Wallace won this county.

The demographic character of Brunswick County's growth is distinctive. Over the course of the past two decades, it has become significantly older and significantly whiter without becoming significantly wealthier. The percentage of the population that is white has grown from 82% in 2000 to 86% in 2018.[7] During this same time period, the relative size of the African American population declined by 25%. In 2000, 17% of the population was 65 or over; in 2018, nearly a third of the population was 65 or over. While income in this county has grown, it has not kept pace with population growth, nor is it dramatically higher than the average for North Carolina counties as whole. Average income in Brunswick County is significantly lower than the average income in the second-fastest growing county in North Carolina, Wake County. So it is certainly possible for a county to grow—and grow at a quick pace—and maintain its conservative Republican leanings. It simply isn't easy (or common).

And apart from these relatively rare exceptions, the political character of the citizens driving population growth—the movers—is still a powerful force driving increased attachment to the Democratic Party and its candidates in the South. But it is only one facet of the relationship between population growth and increased progressivism. What if population growth also influenced the political attitudes and partisan preferences of stayers? What if stayers in areas experiencing significant population growth—above-average population growth—became more liberal and more closely aligned with the Democratic Party as the population in their communities increased? And what if exactly the opposite happened in those communities experiencing below-average population growth or even population decline? What if stayers in those areas became more conservative or attached to the Republican Party? This "stayers" dynamic would reinforce the migration effect. We would then expect the political implications of population change to be even more precipitous than if migrants monopolized the political vector for the local community. In the next section, I outline a theoretical rationale for just this demographic and political dynamic.

Contact Hypothesis, Group Conflict Theory, or What?

A central feature of movers and stayers theory is that movers *influence* stayers. Movers have a direct effect on partisan dynamics, but their mobility also has indirect effects on the political orientations of their neighbors—both their new neighbors and their old neighbors. As I noted in Chapter 2, movers and stayers theory predicts that the character of these indirect effects are contextually dependent: the impact of movers on the political orientations of stayers varies according to stayers' racial and ethnic identities. For white stayers, we should see a direct relationship between population growth—in some communities, movers coming in; in other communities, movers leaving—and attachment to the Democratic Party and support for Democratic Party candidates. As population grows, progressivism grows. Conversely, as population declines, conservativism and identification with the Republican Party and its candidates grows.

For black stayers and Latino stayers, the effects of population change are both more subtle and more complex. Significant growth *and* significant decline should boost support for the Democratic Party and its candidates. But because the Democratic Party is already the party of choice for Latinos and African Americans, overwhelmingly so in the case of African Americans, substantively significant shifts in partisan attachment may result in no more than a gain of a few percentage points. This suggests that substantively important shifts in partisanship among people of color are *less* likely to be statistically significant than substantive shifts in white partisanship.

Among people of color, partisan effects may not be consistent with ideological effects. While the ideological effects of population growth should be consistent with partisan effects—if ideological changes manifest in people of color in high-growth settings, those changes should be in the progressive direction—the same is not necessarily true for people of color facing the threat of declining communities. As blacks and Latinos tend to be relatively conservative—particularly Latinos—movers and stayers theory predicts a shift in the conservative direction, the dominant ideological position for the racial group. Again, the effect should be more pronounced among Latinos (because of their greater conservatism).

In growing communities, we should see evidence of a *contact hypothesis* dynamic. First, as population growth implies economic growth, community natives (stayers) are less likely to be economically threatened by newcomers. Second, newcomers (movers) are likely to increase the relative size of the Democratic contingent in the community and may well increase the racial diversity in the community. Increased stayers' contact with these more progressive groups through interactions with new movers should tend to mitigate resistance to increased support for Democrats among community natives. Third, natives who find the new members of the community most objectionable—whether because of their age, their political orientations, or their race or ethnicity—are likely to exit (and become movers themselves).[8]

Declining communities (or those simply growing at a much slower rate than average) are more likely to feel threatened for a host of reasons. Communities experiencing population declines often experience economic declines as well. These economic downturns may last for years or, in some cases, decades. Knowing that movers tend to be younger and better educated, it is easy to infer that the adults leaving these declining areas are the same ones on which any new economic growth would need to be built. Those in the best position to staunch the loss of jobs and income are the same ones who are most likely to leave. As the areas decline, these communities are unable to replace the energy and talent lost to native emigration with a sufficient number of immigrants.

The loss experienced by these declining communities goes far beyond the degradation of the workforce. Families split. Community organizations struggle to survive. Schools close. Married to whatever economic loss is incurred when movers exit is often a deep personal loss. A recent article in the *New York Times* (Porter 2019) chronicled the effects of population decline in Grundy, Virginia, a small town near where I grew up. Grundy was once a thriving coal town:

> At the peak of coal's fortunes in the 1970s, more than 35,000 people lived in Buchanan [County]. Over 5,000 worked in the mines. Mr. Rife [a local resident] remembers downtown sidewalks in Grundy, the county seat,

packed with thousands of people on weekend shopping expeditions. Karen Brown, the principal of Grundy High School, recalls Porsches and Mercedes-Benzes parked in the high school lot when she went to school there. (Porter 2019)

Those days are long gone. County population has declined by more than a third. Fifteen percent of the county's residents are receiving disability benefits (Porter 2019). Grundy High School once had 1,000 students; today, the number is close to 400. It's not that the coal industry has completely disappeared. It still employs about 1,000 workers, but that's a significant decline from the height of the industry, and these jobs pay far less than earlier mining jobs.

Not surprisingly, people have left and are leaving, and it is primarily young adults leaving for jobs—often in other parts of the South. According to Porter:

> Migration, as economists would have predicted, has become an increasingly compelling option: Those lucky enough to find work somewhere else leave. They include Ms. Brown's two daughters—Peyton, 23, and Bailee, 25—who last summer followed their husbands from the coal industry to more stable jobs at the Toyota plant in Georgetown, KY. (2019)

A long-term resident (stayer) simply said, "We lost one generation to Detroit, another to the Carolinas . . . . These days, workers will go anywhere" (2019). Grundy and Buchanan County more generally have tried desperately to keep these workers. Millions of dollars have been spent on industrial facilities, the Cumberland School of Law, and the Appalachian School of Pharmacy. For many years, Grundy—a town built on a river—struggled to deal with perennial flooding problems. Finally, state and federal funding (and the expertise of the Army Corps of Engineers) literally moved the town to higher ground. Cost estimates for this municipal migration exceed $170,000 for every single town resident (Porter 2019). And all to seemingly little avail. These losses are substantial, and they can manifest in extremely troubling ways. Life expectancy is often below average in declining communities. Suicide rates are higher in declining areas, and disability rates are significantly higher than the national average in rural areas.[9]

This is as staunch a Republican stronghold as there is in the state of Virginia. In a county that is more than 95% white, Trump won more than 80% of the vote in the last election. According to the *Times* article, "Overwhelmingly, they support President Trump, who promised to bring coal back. But it doesn't look as if they have much faith in the promise. As Hoot Dellinger said, leaning over the edge of his booth, 'This community will never prosper again'" (Porter 2019). In Key's South, the "black belt"—that crescent of land in the Deep South where African Americans were most prevalent, in some communities outnumbering whites—was home to the most conservative whites. Though very Republican (and thus, very conservative), Grundy's political trajectory is clearly not a "black belt" story.

Still, communities in decline tend to target "others" for blame. In these white, often rural, communities, "others" are people of color, city people, the unchurched, and the government that they perceive to be dominated by "others": in short, Democrats. The attribution of blame follows a script authored by our nationalized politics: the "others" are a threat; only renewed support for our own (Republicans) can ward off the great dangers the "others" pose.

Our *national* political narrative has dramatically affected these dwindling communities. White residents of declining communities—those growing at the very slowest rates or those actually declining in population—have come to connect the waning of their local communities with the historic political decline they have also experienced. The attribution of *local*-level disappointments to *national*-level causes is important (and novel). Rather than attributing local problems to local context—the central theoretical thrust of group conflict theory—long-term community members (stayers) attribute local problems to national causes.[10] In our polarized environment, partisan attachments drive the perception of these national causes (e.g., elites, immigrants, "the Deep State," etc.). Threat (at the local level) then engenders a partisan response informed by national-level politics. I expect this effect is uniquely (and surprisingly) strong in the South.

Today, local problems prompt reactions that are conditioned on national-level political narratives. There is a disconnect between local context (i.e., racial and ethnic context) and the political reactions that local conditions engender—such as lost jobs, lost incomes, and, for a growing number, lost futures—and this disconnect is a function of the nationalization of our partisan political system. Proponents of group conflict theory assert that proximity to and contact with "others" engenders perceptions of threat. As the relative size of the other group increases within one's community, perceptions of threat increase. So, in the traditionally racialized politics of the South, group conflict theory predicts that as the relative size of the African American population (or mobilized African American population) increases, whites' proximity to and contact with African Americans increases, ultimately heightening the threat perceived by conservative whites. Conservative white responses (i.e., change in attachment to the Republican Party) shift in response to variation in perceived threat.

According to group conflict theory, perceptions of threat are based on the prevalence of the "out" group within one's local community, and partisan responses flow from local demographic dynamics. Within our nationalized partisan environment, local demographic contexts no longer drive levels of partisan attachment. Today, social and economic experiences may influence one's relative attachment to one political party or the other—and that party's positions on social issues or issues related to race—without mediation from the local demographic context.

Imagine a white voter living in a depressed economic area. Maybe coal mining was the main industry for many years, and the decline of coal—or at least the decline of the workforce associated with coal extraction and the income it provided—has brought difficult economic circumstances to the community where this white voter lives. Nostalgia for a past of greater economic prosperity is easy to understand. Let's also assume that this white voter is demographically average in this community, so job prospects are limited, and age and family ties make moving for work personally unattractive. Is it any a surprise that recent Republican appeals—particularly Trump's promise to bring back coal—find a welcoming audience here? Likewise, is it any surprise that blame for the community's current conditions is successfully laid at the feet of an array of "others"—minorities, the unchurched, immigrants, elites, urban professionals, and the like? The key, of course, is that these successful efforts to demonize "others"—those who don't look like our white voter or share the same faith (or culture) as our white voter—focus blame on groups that are largely (or completely) absent from the local community in which our white voter lives. The perception of "group threat" in this scenario—and increasingly common scenario—is fully divorced from the prevalence of the "threatening" group (or groups) in the local community. Our white voter's acceptance of the blame narrative is unrelated to their personal experience (if any) with the targets of blame. This is a very different group threat dynamic from the one Key (1949) described 70 years ago.

The absence of "others" also precludes the manifestation of the *contact hypothesis* dynamic—just what we expect to see in growing, thriving communities. If personal experience of or living in a community with those who might be considered "others" is unavailable, then the opportunity for contact and interaction to ameliorate (or at least mitigate) feelings of threat is also unavailable. So, the theoretical expectation is as follows: county-level adult population decline is inversely related to Democratic support among white stayers. In the next section, I describe the data and methods used to assess the empirical content of this hypothesis.

Data and Methods

To assess the impact of population change on stayers (long-term residents), I again leverage the individual-level data available from the cumulative 2006–2018 file from the Cooperative Congressional Election Study (CCES). As in the previous chapter, because of the absence of a question indicating period of residence in current city in the cumulative file, I drew that information from individual-year surveys in which relevant questions were asked and appended this data to the cumulative file. As a reminder, the survey questions tapping time of residence in current locale are the following:[11]

1. How long have you lived in your current city of residence? (Response in years)
2. How long have you lived in your current city of residence? (Response in months).

The responses to these two questions were cleaned[12] and merged into a single variable that indicated a respondent's period of residence in their current city (in years with percentages for partial years). *Stayers* were defined as individuals whose period of residence in their present city met or exceeded the 75th percentile on the distribution of time indicated by responses to the current city of residence questions.

I operationalize population growth as the logged value of the 10-year increase in the adult population. The 10-year time frame is particularly apt in this case because the distribution of respondents' time spent in the current city of residence was such that those at or above the 75th percentile of that distribution was well more than 10 years. Using a significantly longer time frame would, however, require the assumption that movers and stayers theory can be extended backward, well into the 20th century.[13] If population

Table 5.1. Mean Time in Residence in Current City in the South, by Race

	Mean	Standard Error
All	14.49	.08
White	14.85	.09
Non-white	13.77	.14

change were calculated over a 20-year time frame, for example, that would require the presumption that movers and stayers dynamics were driving partisan attachment and ideological orientation in the 1980s (at least for respondents to CCES surveys fielded in the early 2000s). There simply isn't a sufficient empirical or theoretical foundation to justify this backward-focused temporal expansion that using a significantly longer time frame for measuring population change would require.

While *movers* and *stayers* are mutually exclusive categories by construction, they are not exhaustive. A significant number of respondents satisfy the criteria for *neither* category. They have lived in their current city of residence for too long to be considered movers but not long enough to satisfy the criteria for the stayer category. Practically speaking, I would expect respondents who fit in neither the stayer or the mover category to behave as if they were some amalgam of movers and stayers.

The summary statistics for the time in residence variable is presented in Table 5.1.[14] Table 5.1 provides the mean and standard error of the mean for the number of years southerners have spent in their current city of residence. The average time in current city of residence is just less than 14.5 years for the full southern sample. Not surprisingly, the mean time in current city of residence is somewhat longer for white southerners (just under 15 years) than it is for non-white southerners (just under 14 years). This is both a substantively and statistically significant difference.[15] As would be expected given the findings in the previous chapter, this data is consistent with a more active migratory pattern among non-whites than whites (see Table 5.1).

Not surprisingly, stayers have lived in their current cities of residence *far* longer than the average person. Table 5.2 provides the mean time in residence in their current cities for stayers (as whole), white stayers, and stayers of color. The average stayer has spent over 34 years in their current city of residence. Only eight months separates the average time in residence for white stayers and non-white stayers—in this case, non-white stayers have slightly

Table 5.2. Stayers' Mean Time in Residence in Current City in the South, by Race

	Mean	Standard Error
All	34.57	.13
White	34.49	.14
Non-white	34.76	.26

more longevity in their current homes—but this small difference is not statistically significant. As I am focusing on the impact of population dynamics on white respondents in this chapter, subsequent analyses presented in this chapter will include only white respondents.

Beyond the large gap in time in their current cities of residence, how are stayers different from everyone else? In particular, given the focus of this chapter, how are *white* stayers different from *white* non-stayers? First, while stayers are older than other respondents, the age gap is less dramatic than one would expect. Stayers are, on average, ten years older than other respondents (a mean of 57 for stayers vs. a mean of 47 for non-stayers). Stayers' income levels are also comparable to the income levels of other respondents. The median income for southern white stayers is between $50,000 and $60,000. The median income for other southern whites also in the $50,000 to $60,000 range. However, if we take the mean of the 12 ordinal-level codes for this CCES variable, the gap is very small, 6.1 for non-stayers and 6.0 for stayers. Overall, this indicates that stayers and non-stayers among southern whites are not significantly distinctive in income terms.

I find the same comparability on the education dimension. Stayers are slightly more likely to have failed to complete high school or to have only a high school education, and non-stayers are more likely to have college experience, a college degree, or a graduate degree. But the differences are relatively subtle. The modal category for both groups is a high school graduate, and the median category is "some college" for stayers and non-stayers alike.

From a partisan standpoint, stayers and non-stayers are also quite similar. A majority of both groups are attached to the Republican Party, either identifying specifically with the Republican Party or indicating that they "leaned" toward the Republican Party if they identified as independents. Stayers were slightly more likely to identify with the Republican Party than non-stayers. Non-stayers are slightly more likely to identify as independents.

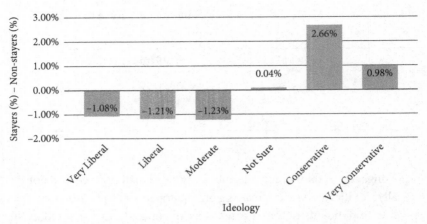

Chart 5.1. Stayers' Ideology vs. Non-Stayers' Ideology (Whites)

Stayers and non-stayers are also ideologically distinct. For both groups, "conservative" is the modal category, and "moderate" is the median category. But non-stayers are relatively more likely to characterize themselves as "moderate," "liberal," or "very liberal." As non-stayers tend to be younger than stayers—and would obviously include the group of movers—the relatively greater leftward lean of this group is not especially surprising. Although these differences are somewhat subtle, they are statistically significant.[16]

Finally, where do stayers live? And is there a distinction between the types of places stayers call home and the communities where the slightly (or substantially) more transient reside? Note that the comparison is not between movers and stayers. The comparison is between truly long-term residents and residents with some history in the community but without the long-term attachment of the stayers. Does the average 30-year resident live in a different place from more mobile residents? The answer is no. The average community size for white stayers in the South is nearly identical to the average community size for white non-stayers in the South.[17] Both tend to live in big places, stayers in slightly larger places than non-stayers. The mean adult population for stayers' counties is 462,620, and the mean adult population for non-stayers' counties is 419,202.[18] While the median county populations are significantly smaller for both groups (as would be expected), they are also quite similar. The median adult population in stayers' counties is 188,138, and the median adult population in non-stayers' counties is 188,812. One piece of data suggests that stayers live in more populous areas; the other piece of data suggests that non-stayers live in more heavily populated areas. Taken as a whole, the data suggest that stayers and non-stayers live in relatively similar places. There is no evidence that all stayers live in small towns and all non-stayers live in big cities (or vice versa).

Community income levels in the places stayers tend to reside are also comparable to the income levels in the communities where non-stayers tend to reside. For the sample of stayers, the community median household income is $55,699. For the sample of non-stayers, the figure is just slightly higher, $57,353. White stayers in the South live in predominantly white communities: whites make up 75% of the average stayer's community. The figure for the average non-stayer's community is almost identical: 77%. Community-wise, white stayers and non-stayers in the South live in remarkably similar communities.

For our purposes, the most important inference from the demographic, political, and geographic data presented above is the relative comparability of white stayers and white non-stayers.[19] Except in their length of residence in the city in which they currently live, they are not distinctive. This suggests that whatever lessons we learn about stayers and the way they respond to the growth or decline of their community may reasonably be applied to non-stayers—at least at the point when they will have lived in their current cities long enough to be considered "stayers."

How Movers Impact White Stayers

Movers impact stayers in one of two ways. They may join a stayer's community, or they may leave a stayer's community. Given the way we have defined "mover," they must, necessarily, have done one or the other. They may also do both (if they are moving from one southern community to another southern community). What we want to investigate here is the impact of the vector of migration on the partisanship and ideology of stayers. Movers and stayers theory predicts a relationship between migration patterns and white stayers' political orientations: greater population growth in stayers' communities should lead to more progressive political orientations (more liberal, more likely to identify as a Democrat, more likely to support Democratic candidates). Conversely, white stayers living in communities struggling with low population growth or even population decline should exhibit more conservative political orientations (more likely to identify as a Republican, more likely to support Republican candidates).

Remember, the relationship between population growth and political orientations is driven by distinctive dynamics present at the opposite ends of the population growth distribution. In areas with high growth, the influx of young, educated, progressive migrants in an economic environment that feeds on these migrants and provides substantial benefits for community members, I expect to see evidence of a contact hypothesis effect. As the community incorporates ever larger numbers of these young progressives, the increased contact between movers and stayers mitigates aversion to the newcomers and encourages the development of more progressive political orientations. Also, native residents who are most averse to the newcomers and their political attitudes are most likely to exit the community—a dynamic which also boosts the average progressivism among the remaining stayers.[20]

At the other end of the population growth continuum, in communities experiencing the slowest rates of population growth or even, in the most extreme cases, population decline, I expect long-term members of the local community to feel threatened (or react as if threatened). Given our national political environment, whites in these depressed areas are most likely have an attachment to the Republican Party. Remember that where white stayers are different from white non-stayers, it is consistently in the direction suggesting greater attachment to the Republican Party: slightly older, slightly less educated, slightly more conservative. In fact, the evidence indicates that stayers are slightly more likely to explicitly align themselves with the Republican Party.

In our polarized political environment, partisans respond to threat by increasing their attachment to the dominant party of their primary social group; in our current party system, race is the primary social group (see Lee 2020).[21] Rather than seeking redress through a shift of allegiance to another party (even a third party), I expect stayers to "double down" on their pre-existing partisan attachments, and for whites in these declining areas, those pre-existing attachments are likely to be to the Republican Party. Given the demographic character of the Republican Party in our polarized environment, the intensification of Republican Party attachment among *stayer* whites—often in rural areas—is likely to be encouraged by other stayers in their environment. By definition, there will be no influx of young, well educated, progressive movers, so we should not expect to see any of the "contact" effects that are present in high-growth areas. Not only are declining and low-growth areas *not* receiving an influx of young movers, these communities are actually losing many of their young, relatively well educated, relatively more progressive natives to high-growth areas. The workers on whom significant economic growth is most likely to be built are finding their ways to other communities, and they are taking their educations and their potential and their politics with them. Given these losses—the economic losses, the social losses, the personal losses—should we be surprised to find stayers in these declining areas feel threatened, or that they respond with increased conservatism and an even more intense attachment to the Republican Party? Two very different areas—one high growth, the other low growth, no growth, or decline—but both consistent with the hypothesized relationship between growth and stayer partisanship (at least among whites): more growth, more Democratic; less growth, more Republican.

If migration (and the concomitant growth in adult population) influences the political attitudes of long-term residents (stayers) how would we know? In this context, true experiments are unrealistic and unethical. Researchers can't control migratory patterns. Natural or quasi-experiments are at least a theoretical possibility. But finding an appropriate example—a natural or quasi-experiment which had the potential to fully assess the causal dynamics of movers and stayers theory *and* from which generalization might be reasonable—is not easy. I am not aware of any options in either of these experimental categories. Hopefully, future research will address this issue.

Apart from experimental or quasi-experimental settings, the most rigorous tests of the causal dynamics of movers and stayers theory would require detailed demographic, economic, and political data on a panel of respondents that (1) had been tracked across the 21st century and (2) would be sufficiently large to adequately represent the various growing and declining areas across the 11 southern states. Given the divergent theoretical expectations for whites and people of color, the sample would also need to include a sufficiently large number of whites and people of color. As it turns out, that is a very tall order. Rice and Pepper's 20-year-old assessment of the data limitations faced by researchers in this area still resonate:

> Panel interviews from long-term nationwide surveys would be ideal for examining the attitudes of Americans who move between regions. With

this type of information, we could track the attitudes of migrants over time and compare their attitudes with those of native southerners and nonsoutherners. Unfortunately, these data do not exist. (1997:85)

Nearly 25 years later, that sort of panel still does not exist.[22] As a next-best alternative to the unachievable ideal, I follow their lead, using cross-sectional opinion data gathered over more than a decade. While Rice and Pepper were limited to the relatively small samples available in the General Social Survey, I was able to leverage individual-level data—far more individual-level data than was available to Rice and Pepper—from the merged multi-year CCES (Kuriwaki 2018) and aggregate-level data from a variety of sources including the U.S. Census and the National Cancer Institutes. The analytical strategy centers on the assessment of the contextual impact of adult population growth on individual respondents' partisan attachments and ideological orientations while accounting for demographic factors associated with partisan alignment and ideological orientation. Because the CCES includes responses to questions relating to length of tenure in one's current city of residence, I am able to distinguish between relatively recent arrivals and long-term residents, between movers and stayers. This chapter (and the next) are about stayers.

To begin to assess the relationship between the prevalence of movers and the partisan attachments and ideological orientations of stayers, I calculated the county-level population growth (decline) for each of the southern counties for which there was a respondent in the cumulative 2006–2018 CCES file for the year in which the respondent participated in the survey. For example, the 10-year population growth (decline) difference for a respondent from Wake County, North Carolina, who participated in the 2012 survey would be: Wake County adult population in 2012 – Wake County adult population in 2002. After taking the natural log of these differences,[23] I determined the values of the 25th percentile and the 75th percentile of the distribution of logged adult population growth rates. I then distributed each respondent into one of the following categories:

1. High growth: Respondent resides in a county that had experienced adult population growth above the 75th percentile during the decade prior to the respondent's participation in the CCES.
2. Moderate growth: Respondent resides in a county that had experienced adult population growth at or above the 25th percentile but no more

than the 75th percentile during the decade prior to the respondent's participation in the CCES.

3. Low growth/decline: Respondent resides in a county that had experienced adult population growth below the 25th percentile during the decade prior to the respondent's participation in the CCES.

Then I determined which type of county each of the white stayers were living in. If population growth influences partisan attachment and ideological orientation, I should find that *stayers in the high-growth counties are more liberal and are more likely to align with the Democratic Party than stayers in the moderate-growth and low-growth or declining counties.* I should also see evidence that that *stayers in moderate-growth counties are more liberal and more likely to align with the Democratic Party than stayers in low-growth or declining counties.* Chart 5.2 illustrates the variation in partisan identification among stayers across declining and growing communities.

As the population of stayers we are currently focusing on is white (by construction) and somewhat beyond middle age (given a current life expectancy well short of 100), it is no surprise that a majority of respondents align with the Republican Party in each population growth category. Older, white, southerners are—in general—overwhelmingly Republican. The predominance of Republicans across the range of counties, however, does not obscure the clear differences in party attachment among the three categories

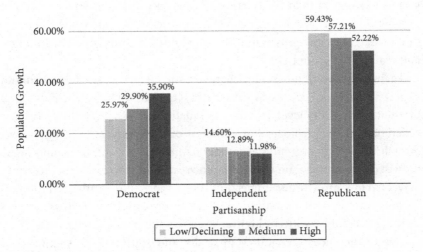

Chart 5.2. Population Growth vs. Partisanship (Whites)

of population growth. As expected, attachment to the Democratic Party is (easily) weakest among stayers in those counties with the lowest level of population growth (or population decline). Likewise, stayers in counties with a moderate level of population growth are rather less likely to identify with the Democratic Party than stayers in counties with the highest level of population growth.

The differences in partisan attachment across the different county-level growth patterns are both statistically significant[24] and substantively significant. The percentage of Democratic supporters in the moderate-growth counties is 15 percent higher than the percentage of Democratic supporters in the low-growth/declining counties. The percentage of Democratic supporters in high-growth counties is more than a third higher than in the low-growth/declining counties, and even the difference in Democratic attachment between the moderate-growth and high-growth counties is substantial. The prevalence of Democratic supporters among stayers in high-growth counties is more than 20 percent higher than the percentage of Democratic supporters among stayers in moderate-growth counties. At the most basic level, there is clear evidence in support of the hypothesized relationship between localized population growth and the partisan allegiances of stayers.

Analyses of the impact of localized population growth on the ideological orientations of stayers produce comparable results. In fact, the relationship between ideological orientation and population growth among stayers is stronger (slightly) than the relationship between partisan attachment and population growth. Chart 5.3 depicts the self-identified ideological orientation of stayers in low-growth/declining counties, medium-growth counties, and high-growth counties.

Again, given the demographic characteristics of our population, we should expect—and we do see—a conservative cant to the distribution of ideological orientations at every level of county population growth. Still, there are clear differences in the ideological orientations of those stayers residing in low-growth/declining communities, moderate-growth communities, and high-growth communities; and these differences are all in the expected direction. Stayers in low-growth/declining counties are more conservative than stayers in moderate-growth counties, who are more conservative than stayers residing in counties with the highest levels of adult population growth.

These differences are both statistically and substantively significant.[25] Well more than a majority, over 62% of all stayers residing in counties with

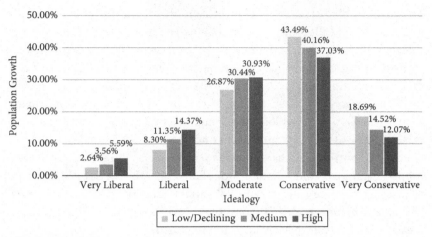

Chart 5.3. Population Growth vs. Ideology (Whites)

the lowest level of growth consider themselves to be some version of conservative, either "conservative" or "very conservative." Less than 12% of
stayers in low-growth/declining counties consider themselves "liberal" or
"very liberal." Stayers in moderate-growth counties are more likely to consider themselves "very liberal," or "liberal," or "moderate" than stayers in the
low-growth/declining counties, and the gap is substantial. The percentage of
"moderate" stayers in moderate-growth counties is 10% larger than the percentage of "moderate" stayers in low-growth/declining counties. Likewise,
the percentage of liberals (either "liberal" or "very liberal" respondents)
among stayers in moderate-growth counties is a third larger than the percentage of liberals in low-growth/declining counties. Stayers in high-growth
counties are the most liberal of all. There are slightly more moderates in
high-growth counties than in moderate-growth counties, and there are far
more liberals. Nearly 20% of the stayers in high-growth counties identify
as "liberal" or "very liberal," and this percentage of liberals is nearly double
the percentage of some type of liberal ("liberal" or "very liberal") in the de-
clining/low-growth counties.

In every respect, the descriptive data are consistent with my theoretical
expectations: stayers' liberalism and attachment to the Democratic Party
are directly related to population growth in the community. But I am not
claiming that geographic context is the only factor that influences partisan
attachments or ideological orientations. Even if we focus solely on whites,

other factors almost certainly play a role in the development of one's political attitudes and allegiances. If population dynamics truly play an important role in the development of political attitudes, it should be possible to demonstrate that relationship while accounting for other factors which might confound the relationship.

To more rigorously assess the connection between population growth and the partisanship and ideological orientations of stayers, I estimate a set of mixed level, ordered logit models. In one set of models I employ a common measure of partisanship as the dependent variable, and in the other set of models I employ a common indicator of ideology. The partisanship measure is an ordered, three-category ordinal variable in which Democrat is coded "0," Independent is coded "1," and Republican is coded "2."[26] The ideology measure is a five-category ordinal variable coded as follows:

1. Very Liberal = 0
2. Liberal = 1
3. Moderate = 2
4. Conservative = 3
5. Very Conservative = 4

The primary independent variable is based on the population growth measure constructed for the analyses above. Here, as the level of analysis is the respondent, the population growth measure is the logged population growth over the 10-year period immediately prior to the respondent's participation in the survey. For example, if the respondent is participating in the 2016 survey, the population growth figure would be based on the difference between the adult population in 2016 and the adult population in 2006. Based on the literature on individual partisan attachment and ideological orientation, I also include measures for age, gender, income level, and education in the analysis.[27] The coding of age is obvious. Gender is coded with "female" receiving the higher value ("1," as opposed to "0" for male). Income is a 12-category scale ranging from below $10,000 to $150k or more. The education variable is coded "1" if a respondent had no education beyond a high school diploma and "0" if she/he had any education beyond high school.

Finally, because of the dramatic nature of the population loss in New Orleans following Hurricane Katrina, Orleans Parish has been dropped from the analysis. Population loss in Orleans Parish following Katrina—a drop of nearly 30% from 2000 to 2010—was by far the largest in the sample, and outlier assessments consistently highlighted Orleans Parish as an extreme case. While New Orleans has experienced recent population growth, the city (and parish) is still well below its population in 2000. Movers and stayers theory is not intended to capture (or explain) migratory decisions driven by large-scale, time-specific natural disasters, so it has been dropped from the analysis.[28]

Many counties in the analysis have several respondents in the sample. Some counties have dozens of respondents in the sample, so respondents are clustered by county. And since we are focusing on stayers, these respondents have lived in these counties for many, many years (by definition). In the previous chapter, we were focusing on identifying the characteristics of movers, not understanding the role of contextual effects on their decisions to move.[29] Here, contextual effects are of central importance.

Due to the likely significance of contextual effects—a key aspect of movers and stayers theory—and the clustered nature of the data, I cannot reasonably assume that errors are independent across respondents; in fact, errors are likely to be correlated by the clustering variable (in this case, county of residence). If observations (and their related errors) are no longer independent, then we must account for this clustering to avoid inferential mistakes—especially the appearance of artificially high p-values on coefficient tests of statistical significance (Type 1 errors).[30] To avoid these inferential errors, I have estimated a multilevel model for both partisanship and ideology. The 2nd level (cluster) variable is county of residence (indicated by a FIPS, or Federal Information Processing Standard, code). In every case, the coefficient for the clustering variable is significant. The results for the model of partisanship are provided in Table 5.3.[31]

For the sample of stayers, we see evidence of the traditional demographic effects on partisanship. Older respondents are more likely to be Republicans, as are men and wealthier respondents. As we have recently come to expect among whites, education is inversely related to attachment to the Republican Party; respondents with no more than a high school diploma are more likely to identify as a Republican. Even when accounting for these demographic factors, we see that population growth is clearly associated with an increase in the likelihood that the respondent will identify with the Democratic Party (as hypothesized). Population *growth*—and the migration patterns which produce it—is the political driver.

Table 5.3. Understanding White Stayers' Partisanship

Partisanship	b	Robust SE	Z	p>|z|
Age	0.01	0.00	5.11	0.00
Gender	−0.35	0.04	−8.04	0.00
Income	0.06	0.01	8.06	0.00
High School Only	0.252	0.05	4.91	0.00
Ln (Δ Adult Population, 10-year)	−0.70	0.12	−6.02	0.00
cut1	−8.95	1.43		
cut2	−8.37	1.43		
Fips				
var(_cons)	0.32	0.04		

Table 5.4. Understanding White Stayers' Ideology

Ideology	b	Robust SE	z	p>|z|
Age	0.02	0.00	10.86	0.00
Gender	−0.37	0.04	−10.31	0.00
Family Income	0.03	0.01	4.11	0.00
High School Only	0.27	0.04	6.01	0.00
Ln (Δ Adult Population, 10-year)	−1.01	0.11	−8.93	0.00
cut1	−14.68	1.41		
cut2	−13.34	1.41		
cut3	−11.88	1.40		
cut4	−10.26	1.40		
Fips				
var(_cons)	0.27	0.04		

Results for the multilevel model of ideology are fully consistent with the partisanship model. Demographic variables behave as expected. Older respondents are likely to be more conservative, as are men. Income is positively associated with conservatism, and education level is inversely related to conservatism. More educated respondents are more progressive. Population growth is inversely related to conservatism. Population growth and population decline play much more important roles in the political dispositions of southern stayers—long-term community residents—than previously realized.[32]

In every respect, the data are consistent with a key novel feature of movers and stayers theory. The partisan attachments and ideological orientations of white stayers—long-term, multi-decade residents of their communities— are influenced by the migration patterns of movers. White stayers in areas attracting significant numbers of movers—those experiencing significant adult population growth—are more progressive (more Democratic, more liberal) than their nearly identical (in terms of age, income, time of residence) counterparts living in communities that have experienced population stagnation or even decline.

The county-level data presented in this chapter illustrate a key aspect of the process which is producing increasingly divergent political environments across the southern states. Not only are whites in fast-growing counties becoming increasingly politically distinct from whites in slow-growth or declining counties, states in which high-growth counties are dominating population dynamics are becoming more progressive than states where low-growth or declining counties predominate. To understand the fundamental difference between stagnating and growing states (Bullock et al. 2019 and Bullock 2020), we must focus on population dynamics at work at the sub-state level.

Movers are influencing the partisanship of stayers. Their migratory decisions appear to play an important role in creating a more progressive environment in those areas to which they are moving. Their emigration from areas experiencing little or no population growth produces exactly the opposite political effect. For whites, the regional impact of these key migratory dynamics is changing the shape of southern politics. A full accounting of the causal foundations for these changes in partisan attachment and ideology would require a region-wide panel for the first 20 years of this century, and that simply doesn't exist. All of the next-best empirical data imply that the movers and stayers narrative captures the shifting political orientations of southern whites to a surprisingly close degree.

But what about the impact of movers on stayers of color? What role does that dynamic play in the politics of the South? I now turn to these questions.

6

Migrant Magnets

How Movers Change the Politics of Their New Homes *and* the Places They Leave: The Cases of People of Blacks and Latinos

To this point, I have argued that we are in the midst of a sea change in southern politics. A region once dominated by one party (Democrats) and then controlled (if not dominated) by another party (Republicans) is in the process of becoming more Democratic again. The subtle progressive shift is evident in voting at the presidential level, in House elections and statewide contests, and in state legislative elections.

The extent of this shift has varied widely across the South. In some places the shift is substantial (e.g., Virginia); in other places, it is unclear that the shift has even begun (e.g., Tennessee). This variation does not, however, follow the outlines of the traditional sub-regions in southern politics: Deep South and Rim South. The locales where this progressive shift has made the greatest advances are neither all in the peripheral rim nor all in the core of the Deep South; note that both Virginia and Tennessee are Rim South states. Georgia and Mississippi are both in the Deep South, but Georgia's recent shift to the left easily exceeds what we see in Mississippi. At one time, location—Core/ Periphery, Deep/Rim—played a crucial role in state and sub-state politics. As the Solid South disintegrated during the middle of the last century, the Deep South and Rim South states began to exhibit important partisan differences, with Republican growth occurring more quickly in the Rim South states. As the 20th century wore on, the Deep South states became bastions of white Republicanism, and Democrats had greater success in the Rim South. In today's South, the key to the political future is *growth*—population growth to be specific, but also the economic growth associated with a growing work- force. And this growth is not limited to the Deep South or the Rim South.

Because population growth in the South is not a respecter of sub-regional location, political change is also no respecter of traditional sub-regional distinctions. Change comes to Rim South states and Deep South states alike.

As I highlighted in Chapter 2, the fastest-growing southern states aren't all in the Rim South, and the slowest growing southern states aren't all in the Deep South. There are fast-growing Rim South states (Texas, Florida, North Carolina, and Virginia); fast-growing Deep South states (South Carolina and Georgia); slow-growing Rim South states (Tennessee and Arkansas); and slow-growing Deep South states (Alabama, Mississippi, and Louisiana).

Historically, there were important political distinctions between the Deep South and the Rim South. The Deep South was more conservative; for much of the post-World War II era that did not mean it was also more Republican than the Rim South. The heightened Republicanism in the Deep South is a relatively recent—last 30 years—phenomenon. This sub-regional distinctiveness was based on the prevalence of African Americans along the "black belt" (Key 1949) that runs through the Deep South. As the relative size of the local black population grew, so did the racial conservatism of southern whites (Key 1949).[1]

Following the passage of the Voting Rights Act (VRA) in 1965—a broadly transformative legislative achievement, and nowhere more significant than in the southern states (Bullock and Gaddie 2009 and Davidson and Groffman 1994)—African American context drove the growth of the Republican Party. As the ballot box became available to blacks in the South, the political focus of conservative southern whites shifted from simple demographics (how large is the black population in my community) to the prevalence of black voters—how large is the *mobilized* black population in my community. Even after this significant shift in strategic orientation (detailed in Hood, Kidd, and Morris 2012a), racial context (*mobilized* racial context in the post-VRA era) in a local, geographic sense drove white attitudes on issues related to race and civil rights and, ultimately, partisan attachments and party identification.

Arguably, the most frequently cited paragraph from *Southern Politics in State and Nation* (Key 1949) is:

> In its grand outlines the politics of the South revolves around the position of the Negro . . . in the last analysis the major peculiarities of southern politics go back to the Negro. Whatever phase of the southern political process one seeks to understand, sooner or later the trail of inquiry leads to the Negro. (5)

But this paragraph can only be understood in the context of the following paragraph where Key writes:

The hard core of the political South—and the backbone of southern political unity—is made up of those counties and sections of the southern states in which Negroes constitute a substantial proportion of the population. In these areas a real problem of politics, broadly considered, is the maintenance of control by a white minority. . . . [T]hat white minority can maintain its position only with the support, and by the tolerance, of those outside . . . in the rest of the United States. . . . [T]he character of the politics of individual states will vary roughly with the Negro proportion of the population, [and] if the politics of the South revolves around any single theme, it is that of the role of the black belts. (1949:5–6)

Crucially, the argument Key makes is that localized racial context is *the* determining factor in the politics of place in the South. At one time, the "key" determinant of white political attitudes was the relative size of the local black population. In the post-VRA era, the relative size of the mobilized black population became the driving force for Republican growth as the Democratic Party staked out increasingly progressive positions on civil rights. And Republican growth fed the further mobilization of African Americans into the Democratic Party (Hood, Kidd, and Morris 2012a).

Over the course of the last 40 years, our politics have become more polarized and more *national*. In a recent book, Daniel Hopkins (2018) argues that the nationalization and polarization trends are causally related. As political parties have become more distinctive and voters have become more consistent in their party attachments, Hopkins contends that local variation in the political objectives and policy positions of the political parties has largely disappeared. As the extent of local, state, and regional variation in party positions declines, so too does the significance of local politics. In the case of the South, an increasingly nationalized politics has important implications for the *geographic* distribution of racial conservatism (among whites) and partisan attachment more generally. During Key's era, white conservatism was driven by black context. For most of the post-VRA era in the South, (mobilized) black context has driven Republican Party attachment in the South. In the era of polarized and nationalized political parties, the prominent direct relationship tie between black population and white conservatism has been severed. In fact, today, we might see evidence of the opposite relationship; we might see a hint of the "contact hypothesis" (Allport 1954) at work.

In attempting to provide a theoretically compelling rationale for the nascent party transformation currently occurring in the South, I have done the following in the preceding chapters:

1. Examined the relationship between population growth and Democratic Party support at the state level and the county level.
2. Assessed the distinctiveness of *movers* (recent migrants) to determine the direct effects of an influx of immigrants on their new homes and of the loss of emigrants on their native homes.
3. Evaluated the indirect effect of population change—from fast growth to decline—on the partisan attachments and ideological orientations of white *stayers*, the long-term natives, of these communities.

I now look to the indirect impact of population growth or decline on the partisan attachments and ideological orientations of non-white *stayers*, people of color who are long-term residents of the communities experiencing significant immigration, significant emigration, or something in between. More specifically, I focus on the indirect impact of migration dynamics on black stayers and Latino stayers.[2] In this chapter, I examine the impact of 21st-century migration patterns on long-term southern residents of color: African American stayers and Latino stayers.

I analyze white respondents and respondents of color separately because the movers and stayers theory has distinct expectations for the impact of migratory dynamics on white stayers and stayers who are people of color. Remember that the theoretical expectations for whites vary by rate of population increase. In those areas that are attracting a significant number of movers—recent migrants who tend to be younger, better educated, and, often, more likely to be people of color than non-migrants—I expect a contact hypothesis dynamic. As contact with these movers increases, *stayers* become more positively disposed toward them and the progressive political orientations they bring with them. To the extent that contact produces the expected effects in long-term natives, population growth should have a progressive influence on stayers.

I expect the impact of this progressive influence will be strongest among *white* stayers. Whites are significantly more likely to attach themselves to the Republican Party and significantly more conservative than people of color. The gap in political orientations of whites and Latinos is quite large; the gap between African Americans and whites is even larger. Data from

Table 6.1. Race and the Partisan Attachments of Stayers

	Democrat	Independent	Republican
White	0.30	0.13	0.57
Black	0.85	0.09	0.07
Latino	0.49	0.15	0.36

the 2006–2018 Cumulative CCES (Kuriwaki 2018) illustrates the vast political gaps between white, African American, and Latino stayers (see Table 6.1).

White stayers are overwhelmingly Republican. A majority of white stayers identify as Republicans; less than a forty percent identify as Democrats. Given the relatively advanced age of white stayers and their regional home, the relative strength of Republican attachment is no surprise. African American stayers are far, far more likely to identify as Democrats. In our sample, five out of every six black stayers aligned themselves with the Democratic Party. Of the remaining respondents, somewhat more identified as independents as identified as Republicans. As with the results for white stayers, the distribution of party support among black stayers is fully congruent with expectations. Nationally and in the South, African Americans are far more likely to identify as Democrats than as Republicans.

Our expectations are also borne out for Latinos, a group of stayers that sit between whites and African Americans on the party dimension. Nearly half of Latino stayers identified as Democrats; just over a third of Latinos identified as Republicans. The percentage of independents among Latinos is higher—15%—than the percentage of independents among the groups of white and black stayers. Independents are significantly more prevalent among Latino stayers than African American stayers.

Though not as stark as the partisan distinctions between black, Latino, and white stayers, there are also significant differences in ideological orientation across these racial and ethnic groups (see Table 6.2). Large percentages of every group of stayers identify as "moderate." For blacks and Latinos, the number of moderates is a plurality of stayers, and in both cases the percentage is well more than a third. Among whites, 30% identify as "moderate." Whites are, again not surprisingly, significantly more likely to consider themselves "conservative" or "very conservative" than Latino or African American stayers, and white stayers are nearly *four*

Table 6.2. Race and the Ideology of Stayers

	Strong Liberal	Liberal	Moderate	Conservative	Strong Conservative
White	0.04	0.11	0.30	0.40	0.15
Black	0.08	0.21	0.48	0.18	0.05
Latino	0.05	0.15	0.41	0.31	0.08

times more likely to identify as some type of conservative ("conservative" or "strong conservative") than some type of liberal ("liberal" or "very liberal"). Latino stayers are also more likely to identify as some type of conservative than some type of liberal, though the ratios are more comparable than they are for white stayers. Black stayers are significantly more likely to identify as some type of liberal than some type of conservative—with liberal blacks (of both varieties) being relatively more prevalent than liberal Latinos.

The movers and stayers theory is predicated on a stayers' perception of threat associated with declining population in their community.[3] As the perceived threat to a local community increases with population decline or stagnation, long-term residents (stayers) should respond in a politically meaningful fashion. In a far less polarized time (i.e., the 1960s or 1970s), stayers might plausibly have responded to this type of community threat by switching parties; frustrated with the status quo and prospects for the future, Democrats could switch to the Republican Party or Republicans could switch to the Democratic Party. This is actually what we see among white southerners during the 1960s and 1970s—Democrats switching, albeit relatively slowly, to the Republican Party—and among African Americans in general, with the overwhelming majority of those still remaining in the Republican Party exiting to the Democratic Party during this time period.[4]

But in our time, the 21st century, the nature of our partisan environment promotes the escalation of partisan attachments in the wake of economic, political, or social threat. When people are threatened, rather than switching to the other party in disgust and frustration with their current party, they tend to align themselves more closely with their party. Attachment to one's current party is intensified in reaction to the economic, social, political—in some cases, existential—threats their community faces. And this threat is intimately tied to population loss or stagnant growth.

Those not already intimately tied to a political party look to their friends and family, the people with whom they have the most in common, for partisan cues. Their response to threat will mirror that of fellow community members with whom they have the most in common. White southern stayers who are long-time Republicans become even more rabidly Republican in response to the threats posed by population loss. Independents who lean Republican among this group become more likely to identify as Republicans in the wake of community threat, and white stayers who were independents begin to lean Republican or identify as Republicans. Even the "unsure" among white southern stayers should begin to move into the Republican camp. We might even see some cross-pressured Democrats—those who also consider themselves conservative—shifting into the independent or Republican camp. Hardcore Democrats—especially those who also consider themselves liberal or very liberal—should realize an intensification of their attachment to the Democratic Party in response to community threat, even among whites in the South. But the group of liberal Democrats among white southern stayers is extremely small.[5] Southern white stayers who are overwhelmingly Republican should respond to the threat of population loss by becoming even more Republican, even more conservative. Broadly, speaking that is exactly what we see happening in the data presented in Chapter 5. Population decline is clearly associated with increased conservatism and an increased likelihood of identifying with the Republican Party.

I expect to see a similar dynamic among African Americans, though the response to threat should result in an increased attachment to the *Democratic* Party rather than the *Republican* Party. As discussed above, the Democratic and Republican coalitions have become more demographically and ideologically aligned over the course of the last half-century (Abramowitz 2018); African Americans' and Latinos' attachment to the Democratic Party has increased over time; and whites have (generally) grown closer to the Republican Party. This is the causal argument underpinning this aspect of movers and stayers theory—that political responses to threat will be (1) toward pre-existing partisan and ideological orientations, and in cases where those are weak or non-existent (i.e., independent identifiers, respondents who do not identify as a partisan or independent), (2) toward the predominant partisan and ideological dispositions of similar community members.[6]

Theoretically, there is reason to expect that the response to threat will be more consistent (and stronger) for African Americans than for whites. Scholars have argued that long-standing social, economic, and political forces have forged a collective orientation to public policy issues and the broader political environment. Dawson argues that "the historical experiences of African Americans have resulted in a situation in which group interests have served as a proxy for self-interest" (1994:74). He refers to the perception among African Americans that their individual self-interest is linked to the broader interest of their race as "linked fate" (1994:77). The conceptualization of linked fate is not without its critics (see Beltran 2010, Price 2009, and Simien 2006), but the idea has had extraordinary staying power.

In a very thoughtful recent work focused on explaining the now long-standing African American attachment to the Democratic Party, White and Laird (2020) argue that black social networks reinforce African Americans' attachment to the Democratic Party. They refer to this cultivation of Democratic attachment as *"racialized social constraint"* (2020:26), a process involving the development and promulgation of group norms associated with support for the Democratic Party. These norms and related social pressures are powerful. According to White and Laird:

> . . . because black Democratic Party identification consolidated under the heightened group consciousness of the Civil Rights Movement, supporting the Democratic Party became defined as a well-understood norm with the African American community . . . . Those who may have ideological or self-interested reasons to defect from the in-group norm of supporting the Democratic Party (e.g., black conservatives or black business owners who might want lower taxes) nonetheless maintain their support for the Democratic Party in pursuit of social acceptance or approval from other group members or in an effort to avoid negative social sanctions for defection. (2020:27)

White and Laird's explanation for the extraordinary consistency of African American support for the Democratic Party—and its particular emphasis on community pressure—is fully consistent with the movers and stayers theory of southern partisan change. We should expect to see threat (resulting from population decline or stagnation) to redound to the benefit of the Democrats, by far the most popular party among African Americans.

High population growth may also lead to higher Democratic support among African Americans. However, the extent and consistency of African American support for the Democratic Party over time mitigates against the manifestation of a statistically significant population effect. The partisan ratio for African Americans is already so skewed toward the Democrats that even a strong effect is unlikely to substantially change the distribution of party support. Subtle effects, even when substantively significant, are difficult to adequately assess with the available survey data.

What we are more likely to see is a change—in the progressive direction—of African American *ideology* in response to population growth. Increased interaction with new community members—the progressive *movers* from Chapter 4—may well produce "contact hypothesis" effects that lead to greater ideological progressivism among African American stayers. Population growth might also lead to more progressive opinions—particularly on local policy issues—if the influx of movers leads to a level of gentrification that threatens long-term community residents. As in the case of population decline, threats associated with population growth should also lead to greater progressivism among African Americans. And this increased ideological progressivism may lead to a slight leftward shift on the partisan scale, but more than that is unlikely (and unrealistic).

Based solely on the partisan attachments of Latinos, we should expect to see results that fit somewhere between those for African Americans and those for whites. We should expect results more similar to those for whites in areas of population decline or stagnant growth, though instead of threat redounding to the benefit of the Republican Party, the perception of threat should boost support for the Democratic Party. In high-growth areas, the expectations are more akin to those for African Americans. The contact hypothesis effect we see in the white sample is less likely to obtain for Latinos for several reasons. First, Latinos are already predominantly Democratic, so even a substantively significant effect is likely to produce a much smaller increase in Democratic support than a similar effect among whites. Second, Latinos may also face negative ramifications from the gentrification which might occur when movers flocking to areas with long-standing Latino communities put significant upward pressure on the cost of housing. Third, if Latino stayers are in communities that are predominantly Latino, an influx of movers might alter the demographics of the locale in such a way as to produce a non-Latino majority population. As with African Americans, growth is rather more of a mixed blessing for Latinos than it is for whites.

In the case of Latinos, we have two key complicating empirical factors. First, the CCES cumulative data file does not provide information on national origin identity (i.e., if an individual identifies as a Mexican-American, Cuban-American, Puerto Rican, etc.). While there is evidence of the development of a pan-ethnic orientation among Latinos, the extent to which this attitude is widespread, the political substance of the orientation, and the extent to which it mitigates traditional political differences are open questions (see Beltran 2010, Escaleras et al. 2019, and Vidal 2017). Second, and perhaps more significantly, Latinos—overwhelmingly—live in relatively high-growth areas. As we will see below, half of Latino stayers reside in the top quarter of counties ranked according to population growth. Not surprisingly, Latino stayers also tend to live in relatively large communities. Among Latino stayers, the correlation between county-level adult population (in the year in which the respondent participated in the survey) and the log of the adult population growth rate (over the 10 years prior to survey participation) is 0.88.

These two issues—an inability to account for distinctions in political orientation associated with national identity groups (especially the inability to account for the distinctive conservatism and Republican attachment of Cuban Americans) and the high concentration of Latino stayers in one particular type of community (relatively large, high-growth locales)—make it difficult to assess the extent to which Latino stayers are influenced by population growth patterns in their community. The relatively small sample of Latinos living in declining communities makes it especially difficult to draw firm conclusions regarding the effects of community threat on the partisanship and ideology of Latino stayers. The results presented below should be considered in that light.

Now, I turn to the data.

Who are the Stayers of Color, and How Do Movers "Move" Them?

Stayers Versus Non-Stayers in the Black Community

Who are the long-term community natives, the *stayers*, among blacks in the South? More specifically, how do black stayers differ from non-stayers in the black community?[7] And how do black stayers differ from white stayers?

One of the more interesting comparisons between African American stayers and white stayers is the relative size of the group within the broader racial group. As in the case of whites, stayers in the black community are a smaller percentage of the population than non-stayers. In fact, the relative percentage of stayers in both communities is nearly the same, 26% among whites and 23% among blacks.[8] Given the dramatic differences in the political orientations of whites and African Americans, the comparability of the proportion of stayers across both racial groups suggests that migration (or the decision to remain in a community) has sources other than politics or ideology. This is fully consistent with an economics-oriented understanding of migration patterns and the movers and stayers theory more generally.

On the age dimension, African American stayers are significantly younger than their white counterparts: the average age of a white stayer is 52, while the average age of an African American stayer is 39. Although there is a significant age gap between white stayers and the much younger black stayers, black stayers are still older than the more transient members of the black community. The difference in average age (and median age) is four years.[9] In both cases, black stayers are older than black non-stayers.

The more mobile members of the African American community appear to be better off than the stayers in the African American community, though the difference is relatively small. For both stayers and non-stayers in the African American community, the median family income is in the $30,000 to $40,000 category. Non-stayers have a slight income advantage when we compare the averages of the income variable for both black stayers and black non-stayers. However, because the income variable is an ordinal variable, the mean may not be the best point of comparison (even though the income variable has a dozen categories).

If we look at the distribution of income by stayer category, we see a similar result: a subtle but discernable difference in income that favors the more mobile members of the African American community. The modal category is the same for both groups ($20k–$30k), but the upper end of the distribution is slightly larger for the group of non-stayers, with nearly 8% of the sample earning $100k or more. Among the stayers, the percentage earning $100k is less than 6% or 25% lower. Likewise, the lower ends of the income distributions for both stayers and non-staryers are comparable.

As stayers within the African American community tend to be older and to have a smaller percentage of high earners, we might also expect black non-stayers to be slightly more educated than black stayers. And that is exactly what we see. Stayers are less likely to have finished high school and less likely to have gone to college. They are also less likely to have earned a four-year degree or a postgraduate degree. But these differences are very small, and in at least one case—the two-year degree category—the percentage of stayers is higher than the percentage of non-stayers. These subtle, and not always consistent differences, are not statistically significant. Among African Americans the demographic differences between stayers and non-stayers—except in the category of age—are quite small if they are present at all (see Chart 6.1).

Given the fact that more mobile African Americans are so demographically similar to more stationary African Americans, their partisan allegiances and the ideological orientations should be relatively similar. Given the slight income advantage of non-stayers, we might expect them to be slightly less attached to the Democratic Party and slightly less conservative. In terms of partisanship, black stayers are more likely to align with the Democratic Party than black non-stayers (see Chart 6.2).

First, any partisan differences between stayers and non-stayers within the African American community must be interpreted in light of the fact that African Americans—regardless of their level of mobility—are far more likely to identify with the Democratic Party than they are to identify with the Republican Party. In both groups of African Americans, stayers and

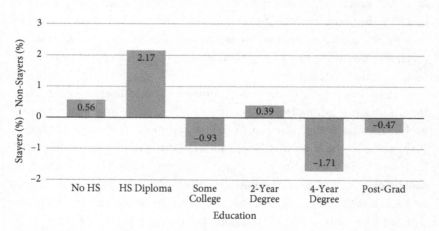

Chart 6.1. Stayers' Education vs. Non-Stayers' Education (African Americans)

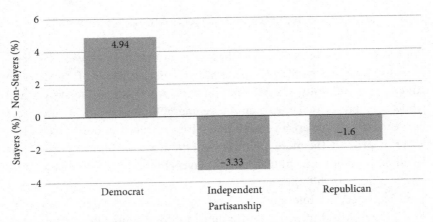

Chart 6.2. Stayers' Partisanship vs. Non-Stayers' Partisanship (African Americans)

non-stayers, 80% of respondents identified with the Democratic Party and fewer than 10% of respondents identified with the Republican Party. With that caveat, there is still a significant difference between the partisan attachments of stayers and non-stayers within the African American community, and it is the stayers that are more closely tied to the Democratic Party.[10] Nearly 85% of stayers identify with the Democratic Party, and among stayers who identify with one of the two major political parties, 93% identify with the Democratic Party. Non-stayers are slightly less attached to the Democratic Party: 80% of the more mobile African Americans identify as Democrats, and among respondents who identified with either the Democratic or Republican Party, just less than 91% identified with the Democratic Party. These are substantively and statistically significant differences between stayers and non-stayers. And they suggest that expecting any leftward movement among stayers—regardless of the level of localized population growth—may not be realistic.

Ideologically, African American stayers and non-stayers are indistinguishable. Differences in the ideological orientations of black stayers and black non-stayers are very small, and even these small differences have no obvious directionality. For example, non-stayers are more likely to identify as strong conservatives, moderates, and strong liberals than non-stayers. Though we see very subtle differences in the ideological distribution of black stayers and black non-stayers, the differences are statistically insignificant.

How Do Movers Impact African American Stayers?

We see from the analysis above that African American stayers are demographically quite similar to the more mobile members of the African American community. Clearly, the differences between white stayers and white non-stayers are larger than the demographic and political differences between African American stayers and African American non-stayers. This is not surprising. The more important question, at least for our purposes, is whether or not movers influence black stayers in the same ways that movers clearly influence white stayers.

As expected, I found a strong (and significant) direct relationship between the influx of migrants and support for the Democratic Party among white stayers. We see the opposite among white stayers in communities that have faced significant population decline or particularly meager population growth. White stayers in those areas tend to be more conservative and more closely aligned to the Republican Party—just as the movers and stayers theory predicts. If movers and stayers theory also provides an accurate depiction of the role of migration patterns on the partisan attachments and ideological orientations of the most geographically stable members of the African American population, we should expect to find a subtler *and* more complex relationship between population growth and black partisanship and ideology—if we find any relationship at all.

Movers and stayers theory suggests two options regarding the relationship between local (county-level) population growth and black partisanship and ideology:

1. Black stayers respond to threat—population decline or very low (well below average) population growth—with increased attachment to the Democratic Party. High population growth also encourages increased attachment to the Democratic Party due to greater contact with an increasingly socially diverse population in a growing economic environment. This implies the presence of a curvilinear relationship between population growth and black stayers' support for the Democratic Party. Due to the very high levels of pre-existing support for the Democratic Party among African Americans in general—and stayers in particular—the effects of population growth are likely to be marginal, if they manifest at all.

2. Black stayers respond to an increased perception of threat due to population decline or very low (well below average) population growth by increasing their attachment to the Democratic Party. But high population growth *fails* to encourage increased attachment to the Democratic Party due to (1) the limited impact of increased social diversity in local communities due to population growth, and/or (2) the very high levels of pre-existing support for the Democratic Party among African Americans in general. Remember, the overwhelmingly strong pre-existing attachment of African Americans to the Democratic Party mitigates against a significant additional increase in Democratic Party support.

Black stayers are expected to respond to threat in either case, and, as discussed above, the response to threat should be in the direction of their pre-existing partisan attachments. In those cases where they have no pre-existing attachments (i.e., independents), any shift will be in the direction of the preponderance of their racial community. In the case of African Americans, movers and stayers theory predicts that threatened independents shift toward the Democratic Party.[11]

Based on movers and stayers theory, the strongest expectations for change in the political orientations of African American stayers are for those living in areas that have experienced the greatest population decline (or most meager population growth), and the expectation is that in these areas, relative support for the Democratic Party will be greater than it is in other, faster growing areas. To evaluate this aspect of movers and stayers theory, I divide southern counties (and independent cities) into three categories based on the relative extent of their population growth: counties below the 25th percentile in population growth, counties between the 25th and 75th percentiles in population growth, and counties above the 75th percentile in population growth—the same categorization scheme used for the analysis of migratory impacts on white stayers.[12]

I divide African American stayers into these categories based on the population growth in the county of residence for each respondent. Because African Americans overwhelmingly identify with the Democratic Party regardless of their city of residence, differences across the growth category are quite small, but they are in the expected direction: attachment to the Democratic Party among blacks is most prevalent in the areas experiencing population decline and the slowest level of growth. As growth levels increase, we see slight shifts into the independent category and the Republican Party. Again, these are subtle differences. In every category, African American Democrats outnumber African American Republicans by nearly ten to one or more. In fact, in every growth category, the number of black independents is larger than the number of black Republicans. Overall, these differences are not statistically significant. In terms of ideology, African American stayers in declining or low-growth areas are indistinguishable from African American stayers in moderate-growth or high-growth areas. The first-order results suggest the possibility of an impact of population decline (and the concomitant community threat) on partisanship that is consistent with movers and stayers theory, but nothing more.

Because of the potential for a non-linear relationship between population growth and the change in political orientations among African Americans—greater progressivism at the ends of the growth distribution (declining counties *and* high growth)—I alter the multivariate estimation strategy employed with the white sample. To examine the distinctive impact on black partisanship and ideology of declining/low population growth, moderate population growth, and high population growth, I include two dummy variables based on the ordinal population growth variable employed in the bivariate analysis above. *Low Growth* is coded "1" for all counties in the lowest quarter of the population growth distribution and "0" otherwise. *High Growth* is coded "1" for all counties in the highest quarter of population growth distribution and "0" otherwise.[13]

Results from multivariate models of partisanship and ideology among blacks paint slightly different pictures (see Table 6.3). I find no evidence of a contextual effect in high-growth areas for African Americans. Long-term black residents of high-growth areas in the South are not more likely to identify as Democrats than southern blacks who are long-term residents of communities that have experienced moderate population growth. In both areas, African Americans are overwhelmingly supportive of the Democratic Party; there is simply no evidence that black stayers in high-growth areas have an even more extreme attachment to the Democratic Party.

Population dynamics are at the core of movers and stayers theory. An equally important facet of movers and stayers theory is the distinctiveness of the responses of whites and people of color to population decline and, to a lesser extent, population growth. Among whites, population decline is hypothesized to engender greater attachment to the Republican Party. Among African Americans, if there is a partisan effect of population decline,

Table 6.3. Population Growth and the Partisanship of African American Stayers

Partisanship	b	Robust SE	z	p>|z|
Age	–0.02	0.00	–5.05	0.00
Gender	–0.49	0.14	–3.60	0.00
Family Income	0.06	0.02	2.76	0.01
High School Only	0.43	0.14	3.02	0.03
Low Growth	–0.11	0.16	–0.70	0.48
High Growth	0.40	0.22	1.79	0.07
cut1	0.39	0.41		
cut2	1.49	0.43		
Fips				
var(_cons)	0.65	0.28		

we would expect it to redound to greater support for the Democratic Party.[14] But even if the overwhelming pre-existing support for the Democratic Party precludes an additional contextual effect, movers and stayers theory tells us not to expect the white response to community decline among African Americans. This is one of the reasons we see different partisan trajectories in majority-minority counties with little or no population growth and majority-white counties with little or no population growth. While overwhelmingly white counties like Tazewell and Buchanan in Virginia have veered hard to the right over the past 20 years; majority-minority counties like Scotland and Northampton in North Carolina—both of which were more heavily populated at the turn of the century—are still bastions of Democratic support in a largely purple state.

The diametrically opposed partisan responses to population loss among white stayers and black stayers also demonstrates that local-level partisan dynamics are not simply a function of the direct effect of the loss of progressive movers. If the loss of movers had no effect on stayers' partisanship—if changes in stayers' partisanship were solely a function of emigration patterns rather than altered partisan attachments among those who aren't going anywhere—why does population loss affect whites and blacks so differently? Movers do have an effect on stayers' partisanship just as movers and stayers theory predicts.

Movers and stayers theory also tells us to expect whites who are long-term residents of high-growth areas to lean more toward the Democratic Party. While a shift in the same direction is possible for African Americans, the nature of their overall partisan attachments—heavily Democratic—makes a substantively and statistically significant effect much less likely. In this context, movers and stayers theory provides a compelling rationale for the partisan behavior characterized by the available data.

Just as in the case of partisan attachment, we find no evidence of a relationship between varying levels of population growth on the ideological orientations of African American stayers is greatest among those living in the fastest-growing areas. There is no evidence that counties with declining populations are ideologically distinct from counties with more moderate growth. The same is true for black stayers in counties with the fastest growing populations; the overwhelming attachment to the Democractic Party remains unchanged.

In sum, movers and stayers theory provides a compelling explanation for the distinctiveness of black and white responses to localized population growth and decline. Given the distinctive natures of their pre-existing partisan attachments, we should not expect comparable partisan vectors when population change alters their communities. Blacks facing the threat of population loss in declining communities maintain their attachment to the Democratic Party, the dominant political party in the African American community. This pattern of behavior is also fully consistent with a generation or more of research flowing from the conceptualization of "linked fate" within the black community (Dawson 1994; Tate 1994; White and Laird 2020). Movers and stayers theory also explains why blacks in communities experiencing significant growth contribute to the growing progressivism of these areas by remaining steadfast in their support for Democratic Party and its progressive agenda. Increased contact and interaction with 21st-century movers—younger, more educated, and more progressive migrants—encourages inclusive attitudes (particularly on issues of social policy) that are more consistent with those of the migrants themselves. And, to the extent gentrification places undue economic pressure on blacks, continued attachment to the Democratic Party can be understood as support for more progressive land use and urban development policies (including increased support for affordable housing, investment in mass transit, etc.). Where African American stayers are concerned, movers and stayers theory helps us understand the consistent character of their political attachments and orientations in a changing environment; it also helps us understand this aspect of their contribution to the growing strength of the Democratic Party in the South. I now turn to a description of Latino stayers and how they compare to the more mobile members of the Latino community.

Comparing Latino Stayers and Non-Stayers

Just as in the case of blacks (and to a somewhat lesser extent, whites), Latino stayers are comparable to the more mobile members of the Latino community.[15] The largest distinction between stayers and non-stayers in the Latino community is in age. This is also a significant demographic distinction between Latino stayers and white stayers. The average Latino stayer is 50 years old, but the average non-stayer in the Latino community is only 39.[16] Latino stayers and African American stayers are comparably aged, but as we know from the data presented in Chapter 5, white stayers are significantly older (with an average age of 57).

As in the case of African Americans, the income levels of Latino stayers and non-stayers are very similar. The median income for Latino stayers is in the $40,000 to $50,000 range, as is the median income for non-stayers.[17] The more mobile members of the Latino community are slightly better off than Latino stayers, but the difference is quite small—smaller even than the gap between stayers and non-stayers in the African American community (where the gap is also quite small).

Non-stayers in the Latino community have somewhat more education than Latino stayers, but as in the case of African Americans, the differences, while not dramatic, slightly favor the more mobile segment of the Latino population (see Chart 6.3). Less than 30% of stayers have a college degree. Over 32% of non-stayers have a college degree (including two-year degrees), and nearly a quarter of non-stayers have a four-year degree (assuming those with a graduate degree all have a four-year degree). Among the sample of stayers, less than 21% have a four-year college degree. Though it is a small difference, the postgraduate degrees are also less common in the sample of stayers than in the sample of non-stayers. So while there are subtle differences indicating a slightly higher level of education among the more mobile members of the Latino population, those differences are relatively small.[18]

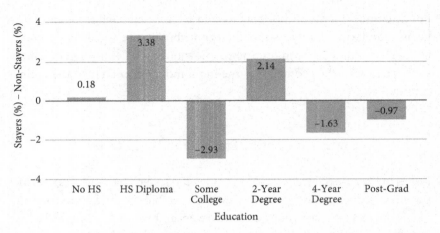

Chart 6.3. Stayers' Education vs. Non-Stayers' Education (Latinos)

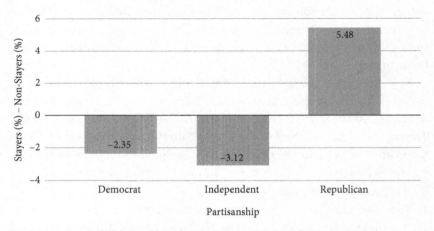

Chart 6.4 Stayers' Partisanship vs. Non-Stayers' Partisanship (Latinos)

Party differences among Latino stayers and non-stayers are statistically and substantively significant.[19] The differences are not, however, consistent with the pattern we see in African Americans. Among Latinos, stayers are more likely to be Republicans and less likely to be Democrats. On the other hand, and like African Americans, non-stayers are more likely to be independent than stayers (see Chart 6.4). The same dynamic holds true for ideological differences between Latino stayers and the more mobile members of the Latino community. Latino stayers are more likely than Latino non-stayers to identify as strong conservatives and conservatives. Latino non-stayers are more likely to identify as moderates, liberals, or strong liberals, than stayers within the Latino community. The modal ideological category for both groups—by far (i.e., over 40% among stayers and non-stayers)—is moderate. The differences are highly significant.[20]

Except in age, Latino stayers are demographically and comparable to the more mobile members of the Latino community. But the age gap is substantial, and in the Latino community this age gap coincides with a substantive differences in party attachment and ideological orientation. Latino stayers are clearly more Republican than more mobile Latinos, and they are more conservative than more mobile Latinos as well.

Given the expectations of movers and stayers theory, the Republican and conservative lean of stayers within the Latino community is particularly important. As stayers within the African American community are the more Democratically-oriented segment of that community, the absence of a population growth effect has little impact on their overall role in the growing progressivism of high growth areas. They are a key component of the growing Democratic constituency. But if we also find no population growth effect among the more conservative-minded Latino stayers—this could prove to be an obstacle for the overall expansion of progressivism movers and stayers theory predicts in areas with high population growth. Time to consider the evidence. Just what impact does population growth (or decline) have on Latinos who are long-term community residents?

How Do Movers Impact Latino Stayers?

How do migrants and migration patterns influence the partisan attachments and ideological orientations of long-term community residence? How do Latino stayers deal with or respond to an influx of movers? Or maybe even more importantly, how do stayers within the Latino community respond when their communities decline and friends and family members leave for other counties, states, regions, or beyond? Given the key political differences between stayers and non-stayers in the Latino community, what we learn about the behavior of stayers—the truly long-term residents—may very well help us understand the political impact of the broader community on areas experiencing significant population growth (or decline).

Remember also that we are trying to understand the emerging partisan transformation in the South. If population growth affects Latinos as movers and stayers theory suggests, we have identified a mechanism whereby the more conservative Republican members of the Latino community are pulled to the left. If they can be pulled to the left by migratory forces, we may reasonably expect similar effects among somewhat more mobile Latinos. In both cases, it is simply another movers and stayers dynamic working on a distinctive population group that has as its primary effect a progressive shift in partisan attachments and ideological orientations.

Movers and stayers theory suggests the following regarding the relationship between local (county-level) population growth and Latino partisanship and ideology:

- Latino stayers respond to threat—population decline or very low (well below average) population growth—by increasing their attachment to their existing party of choice. Among Democrats and Democratic-leaning independents, attachment to the Democratic Party increases. Among Republicans and Republican-leaning independents, attachment to the Republican Party increases. For independents—a more popular category among Latinos than among African Americans or whites—the shift depends on a variety of factors—national identity, partisan disposition of local Latino population, ethnic group consciousness, national political dynamics—for which Democrats tend to be advantaged. For this reason, the vector of partisan shift for Latinos in declining or very low-growth areas, *if one exists*, would likely be in the Democratic direction. As far as the impact of threat on the ideological orientation of Latinos, movers and stayers theory does not imply a directional prediction. What is most likely, given the overall conservatism of Latinos and the distribution of partisan attachments—less Democratic than African Americans and more Democratic than whites—is a result somewhere between the strong conservative tilt for whites and the non-result for African Americans. A subtle conservative shift in the context of population decline would not be a surprise.
- High population growth may also encourage increasing attachment to the Democratic Party due to greater contact with an increasingly socially diverse population in a growing economic environment. While Latinos do not support the Democratic Party at the same level as African Americans, the average level of support is much higher than

among whites, so the manifestation of partisan "contact" effects—in an environment in which the Democratic Party is already dominant—may be quite subtle. If there is an ideological shift among Latinos in high-growth areas, it should be in the progressive direction.

What do the data say about the relationship between migratory patterns and the partisan attachments and ideological orientations of Latino stayers? At first glance, it would appear that population growth has little or no impact on the partisanship of Latinos who are long-term community residents. Latino stayers are more likely to identify as Republicans in high growth communities and low growth/decline communities than they are in moderate growth communities. Democratic identification is also more common in moderate growth communities than in areas growing at a higher or lower rate. The same is true for those identifying as independents.[21]

The ideology of Latino stayers is another matter. Latino stayers in high-growth communities tend to be more liberal than Latino stayers in declining or low-growth communities (see Chart 6.5). The difference between the two population-growth extremes is most dramatic in the "liberal" category; stayers in high-growth areas are almost twice as likely to be identify as a liberal than stayers in the declining/low-growth category. Differences in the expected direction are manifest in all of the other categories except "strong liberal," where, by a very small margin, stayers in the high-growth category are the least prevalent. These differences are statistically significant.[22]

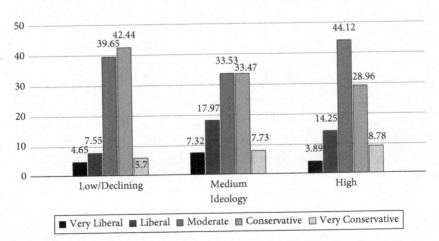

Chart 6.5. Population Growth and Stayers' Ideology (Latinos)

The complexity of the relationship between population growth and the political attitudes of Latinos is highlighted by the results presented in Chart 6.5. Stayers in high-growth areas are clearly more liberal than stayers in areas with the least growth, but in some cases, stayers in areas of moderate growth are as liberal (if not more so) than the stayers in high-growth areas. The most consistent results involve the stayers from the low-growth areas: the only deviation from a pattern of greater conservatism when compared to both the moderate- and high-growth areas is the slight advantage among strong liberals. Otherwise, population decline or stagnation is associated with greater conservatism among Latinos.

In the case of ideology, the multivariate results provide little support for a context effect among Latino stayers. There is no evidence that population growth has a significant impact on the ideological orientations of stayer's Latino stayers. In an ordered logit models analogous to that estimated for African Americans—one including controls for age, income, gender, and education (a dummy variable coded "1" if a respondent had no more than a high school diploma) and dummy variables for low population growth areas and high population growth areas, there is no evidence of a population growth effect on the ideological orientations of Latino stayers.

However, there is some evidence of a context effect on the partisanship of Latino stayers in high growth areas. Again, in an ordered logit models analogous to that estimated for African Americans, there is evidence that stayers

Table 6.4. Population Growth and the Partisanship of Latino Stayers

Partisanship	b	Robust SE	z	p>|z|
Age	0.01	0.00	3.03	0.00
Gender	−0.37	0.14	−2.69	0.01
Family Income	0.06	0.02	3.046	0.01
High School Only	0.12	0.09	−0.13	0.89
Low Growth	−0.02	0.20	−0.09	0.93
High Growth	−0.17	0.11	−1.51	0.131
cut1		0.30	0.36		
cut2		0.92	0.36		
Fips				
var(_cons)	0.04	0.06		

in high growth areas are more likely to be Democrats than stayers in areas where the population growth is more limited (if there is population growth at all). This effect obtains in the context of controls for age, gender, income, and education, and it is significant at .10-level (one-tailed test) (see Table 6.4).

Though the partisan result for Latino stayers only manifests in high-growth areas—there was no evidence of a threat effect among Latinos—this finding is more important than it might appear at first glance. Remember, Latino stayers are more likely to identify as Republicans than more mobile Latinos. Thus, stayers are an important potential *growth* constituency for the Democratic Party. But this result is also particularly important for a reason that is not immediately obvious. Why? Because of where Latino stayers live in the South.

The distribution of stayers, by race, across low-growth, moderate-growth, and high-growth counties in the South is instructive. Chart 6.6 depicts the percentages of stayers in specific racial groups living in each type of community: low growth (including declining communities), moderate growth, or high growth. So, 31% of white stayers live in low-growth communities. Nearly half (47%) of white stayers live in moderate-growth communities, and 22% of white stayers live in high-growth communities. The distributions of whites and African Americans across communities growing (or declining) at different rates are quite comparable. Whites are slightly more likely to live in moderate-growth communities than African Americans (47% vs. 43%) and slightly more likely to live in low-growth/declining communities (31% of white stayers vs. 36% of African American stayers).

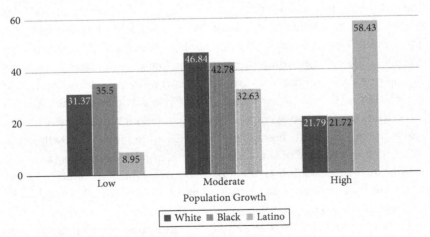

Chart 6.6 Population Growth and the Race of Stayers

The distribution of Latino stayers is completely distinctive. Less than half of all Latino stayers live in low-growth or moderate-growth communities; under 10% live in low-growth communities. Nearly 60% of Latino stayers live in the top quartile of communities based on population growth—a percentage that is nearly triple the relative percentage of African American stayers or white stayers who live in these communities. In short, Latino stayers are a very small proportion of the communities suffering through declining or stagnating population. That population decline appears not to impact their partisanship or ideology matters relative less because so few live in affected areas.

Of far greater significance is the prevalence of Latinos—and Latino stayers in particular—in the fastest-growing communities in the South. Not only are Latinos moving to these areas; in many cases, they have been living in these areas for years. Many of the fastest-growing communities in the South (e.g., Houston, Orlando, and San Antonio) have significant Latino populations—some for many years. Given their tendency to become more Democratic in high growth communities and striking prevalence in these high growth communities, Latino stayers are likely to play a key role in the growth of the Democratic Party in the South.

Given the enormous gaps in the population trajectories where a majority of Latinos live compared to those where a majority of whites (and a majority of African Americans) live, it should be no surprise that the *growing* states have far larger Latino populations—and far higher percentages of Latinos—than *stagnating* states (see Bullock et al. 2019). According to the 2017 American Community Survey, Hispanics (of any race) make up 16.5% of the population of the set of six high population growth states in the South: Florida, Georgia, North Carolina, South Carolina, Texas, and Virginia. The corresponding number in the low-growth states is 5%—the Latino population of the high-growth states is more than triple the Latino population of the low-growth states. As a point of comparison, African Americans make up, on average, 23% of the population in the fast-growing states and only a slightly higher percentage (27%) in the slow-growth states. While the relative size of the African American population was (and is) a significant distinguishing characteristic between the Rim South and the Deep South, the same is not true for the slow-growth/high-growth sub-regional distinction.

If we were to order the states by size of the Latino population, the first five would be high-growth states (in order, Texas, Florida, Georgia, North

Carolina, and Virginia). Ironically, South Carolina, the most Republican of the high-growth states, also has the lowest percentage of Latinos (5.7%). So as Latinos in high-growth areas become more Democratic, their influence on the partisan balance in these growing states will only be magnified.

Discussion and Conclusions

Movers and stayers theory is a tool for understanding how a fundamentally non-political activity—migration patterns in the South—is driving the present (and the future) of southern partisan politics. In simplest terms, southern migrants—those moving from other countries to the South, those moving from other regions to the South, those moving from one southern state to another southern state, and those moving from county to county (or city to city) within a single southern state—are doing so for two primary reasons: economics (new job opportunities) and family connections.[23] Often, these two are related.

Movers are different from non-movers demographically and politically. When they move to new places, they *alter* the political environment of their new homes *and* the communities they have exited. In Chapter 4, we saw how migrants (movers) were different from non-movers. In Chapter 5, we learned how movers influenced white stayers, both those in the places where movers were congregating and those in the places movers had left. In this chapter, we see that movers also have an impact on people of color, but only in the Latino community. As movers and stayers theory predicts, the impact of population decline on blacks and Latinos is distinct from its impact on whites. While population decline does not produce a progressive impact on stayers of color, it also does not foster the increase in conservatism and Republicanism we see among whites.

Population growth, on the other hand, does foster increased attachment to the Democratic Party among Latino stayers (just as it does among white stayers). And while we do not see the same partisan effect among African American stayers, it is hardly shocking given the overwhelming support for the Democratic Party among blacks and the particularly high Democratic attachment among African American stayers regardless of level of population growth manifest in their communities. Again, we see how the migration dynamics manifest in the 21st-century South—migration dynamics driven primarily by economics and family ties—have significant political implications that favor the continued expansion of support for the Democratic Party and progressive ideological orientations more generally.

Putting all of these pieces of the partisan puzzle together, we can see how the Democratic Party has begun to turn the tide of Republican growth in the South. As movers and stayers theory predicts, whites, blacks, and Latino stayers respond distinctively to the pressures and opportunities of population growth and decline based on their pre-existing partisan attachments and ideological orientations. And, in a South in which the distinctions between high-growth and low-growth states have overtaken the traditional distinction between Rim South and Deep South, the dramatic disparity between the relative size of the Latino population in high-growth states relative to low-growth states takes on additional importance. Racial dynamics are still a defining feature of southern politics, but they have shifted over the past two decades. Today, southern politics revolves around Latinos (at least in the fast-growing states) like never before. In Key's time, the politics of the South did revolve around the position of blacks; today, southern politics revolves around the positions of blacks and Latinos. Where there was once a single sun, now there are two.[24]

7

The Special Case of Retirees

When the Elderly Move

When I began to think about the impact of mobile retirees on the geography of southern politics, I considered my own family's experience with relocations at or beyond retirement age. When my dad retired, my parents moved to a new city within the same southern state they had lived in since I was four. They moved to a retirement community where my mom had been on the board for years, to a house a few minutes' drive from a large public university. Years after retirement, my father's mother, Grandma Morris, moved to an apartment in a new city and then to a retirement home in a different city.[1] Gran, my mother's mother, moved from one southern state to another southern state. Both of my grandfathers passed away before they could move. My wife's parents, now retired for some time, still live in the southern city where she grew up (though not in the same house). My father-in-law's parents never left the small southern town in which he was raised, but my mother-in-law's parents moved from a big city in North Carolina to a medium-sized city in South Carolina to be nearer to her.

As my family's experience suggests, retirees—particularly those from generations before the Baby Boom—often left home when they moved on from their jobs and careers. Baby Boomers are somewhat less transient. Those of retirement age today are significantly less likely to move to a new city than those of retirement age a generation ago (Rogerson 2018). But there are still movers among all the retirement generations. And as our country ages, the older generations make up an ever-increasing segment of our population and, most apt for my purposes, our voting population.[2]

Even if retirees don't move like they used to, they make up such a significant component of our electorate that their mobility can have potentially dramatic effects on the partisan and ideological trajectories of the places they leave and the places they move to. If the mobility patterns of retirees were random—or could be treated as random—then their impact might be less significant, but their mobility patterns are clearly not random. Retirees tend to congregate; they tend to move to the same places.

Retirees also don't mirror the politics (or the demographics) of younger generations. Members of the Baby Boom generation and the Silent Generation are more likely to be white, more likely to be religious, more likely to be conservative, and more likely to identify with the Republican Party than younger Americans (Pew Research Center 2018a). Politically, retirees are distinctive. The growing numbers of retirees—bolstered by the early Baby Boomers reaching retirement age, their political distinctiveness, and their relatively focused migration to certain locales—makes this group an important player in the recent and future political trajectory of the South. In this chapter, I investigate the impact of their mobility on the future of the South's partisan character and its political geography.

I begin by assessing the demographic distinctiveness of movers and non-movers among the most senior generations. I have already demonstrated that movers are, *in general*, younger, better educated, more liberal, and more likely to identify with the Democratic Party. But if those generalities—particularly the ideological and partisan generalities—are not reflective of the differences between movers and stayers in older generations, then the effect of movers, in general, on the politics of the South—on the politics of the communities they leave and the politics of the communities they are drawn to—may be more limited than the preceding analyses suggest.

This may be particularly true if elderly movers tend to congregate in certain types of southern locales. We know that elderly movers do tend to be drawn to southern climes—whether they start out in the South or not—but to what extent are certain southern states and localities magnets for retirees seeking new homes? Florida is obviously the stereotypical southern setting for retirees, particularly the northern "snow birds." But what portion of the elderly movers end up in Florida? How big is this effect (really)?

And are there other southern states (and other southern settings) that attract retirees as well? Certainly. In Chapter 5, I highlighted Brunswick County, one of the fastest growing counties in North Carolina, and increasingly a magnet for retirement-age movers. As Brunswick County has grown in population, the average age has increased as well. The beaches and the warm, vacation lifestyle are clearly attractions for those who have finished their careers.

Other areas—very different areas hundreds of miles away from Brunswick County but still in North Carolina—have also drawn retirees. Retirees are also attracted to the cooler parts of North Carolina, such as the western mountains near Asheville. Buncombe County, for which Asheville is the county seat, has also grown substantially over the past two decades (though not as fast as Brunswick County). However, this increasingly popular retirement locale, and home to the University of North Carolina at Asheville, has steadily shifted in the progressive direction since the early Bush years. Not all retiree magnets become bastions of conservatism.

To grasp just how population growth affects southern political geography, we must understand just who retirees are—especially politically—and where they congregate If retirees are politically distinctive and they tend to congregate in certain areas in large numbers, then the implications of movers and stayers theory laid out in previous chapters should be revised accordingly.

Distinguishing Between Movers and Stayers in the Retirement Generation

Retirees have a significant impact on the communities in which they live. They provide a significant source of support for a variety of community organizations—both in terms of time and resources. Depending upon the nature of the tax structure, they may also provide significant support for local and state government activities. At the same time, they are high demanders in the health care arena, and the oldest members of the retiree generation often require additional types of support, components of which are provided by nonprofits and government programs (too often stretched to their limits).

Beyond the economic and social impacts of large numbers of retirees on their communities, how do retirees influence the political dynamics of communities in which they live? Generationally speaking, retirees are the most consistent voters, and their interests are represented by effective, well-resourced interest groups (e.g., AARP), so we should fully expect them to have an impact on local politics. As I have focused on the role of migration in the changing politics of the South, we must now take a look at the impact of the migration of the oldest members of our communities. Movers and stayers theory helps us understand how and why we should expect to see a growing progressive shift (which has already begun) in southern politics. And while the data provides strong support for movers and stayers theory, the migration of some of the most conservative members of our community (at least from a generational standpoint) could alter our expectations regarding the broader partisan and ideological implications of migratory dynamics in the 21st-century South.

Retirees are most likely to disrupt the progressive partisan and ideological trajectory predicted by movers and stayers theory if the following is true:

1. Mobile retirees tend to concentrate in particular states and communities, *and*
2. mobile retirees are *at least as* conservative as those who retire in place.

If the migration of retirees does not result in a congregation or concentration in certain areas, then retiree-specific migratory dynamics are unlikely to influence the geographical distribution of partisans or ideologues. If relatively equal numbers of retirees leave and enter any given community— the precondition for the absence of migration-driven concentrations of retirees—then the movement of retirees would not contribute to a shift in community-specific, state-specific, or region-wide partisan attachment or ideological orientation.

If, however, migrant retirees did congregate in particular communities (and particular states), we should expect to see an effect on community-level (and by extension state-level) partisan attachment and ideological disposition, because older southerners tend to be more likely to be Republicans and to be more conservative than younger southerners. Focusing solely on the generational differences in party attachment and ideology, we would expect those places where retired migrants congregate to be relatively more Republican and relatively more conservative than we would predict from the migration numbers alone. However, this effect depends on the conservatism and extent of support for Republicans among migrant retirees. We should see an effect if mobile retirees are as likely to be Republicans and as likely to be conservative as those who are aging in place. If mobile retirees were significantly more likely to be conservative and Republican, then their movements would mitigate the effects of population growth on political progressivism. If declining communities were bleeding their oldest, most conservative residents, that should dampen the increased Republicanism predicted by movers and stayers theory. Likewise, if these conservative retirees make up a significant portion of the population growth in a particular area, the progressive shift predicted by movers and stayers theory is less likely to manifest.

If, on the other hand, mobile retirees are more likely to be Democrats or are more progressive in their ideological orientation, this migratory effect dissipates, if it does not disappear entirely. The two key empirical questions are:

1. Do mobile retirees ("movers" in the retirement generation) tend to congregate or concentrate in certain southern cities, southern counties, and/or southern states?
2. Are mobile retirees politically distinctive from retirees who are aging in place?

In the next section, I discuss the demographic distinctiveness of migrant retirees. In the section following, I focus on the geographic distribution of migrant and non-migrant retirees, and in the final section, I assess the political distinctiveness of migrant retirees.

Who are the Migrant Retirees?

To understand the impact of retiree migration on southern partisanship and southern ideology, we first need to understand how the migration of retirees alters the age distribution in communities in the South. If there were no 21st-century retiree migration at all, the percentage of retirees would still vary significantly across counties and across states. This is true for several reasons. The migration of pre-retirement adults in the late 20th century has an impact on the geographic distribution of retirees today. Likewise, variation in life expectancy (which is considerable across the South) impacts the relative size of the retiree population in any particular county or community. At the other end of the age continuum, differences in family size and the relative prevalence of infant births—also a factor that varies across the South—influence the *relative* size of the retiree population in any particular community, county, or state. If migrating retirees tend to move to the same places (or the same sorts of places), it makes a difference politically. We begin by describing just who migrant retirees in the South are.

I operationalize migrant retirees as movers who are at least 66 years of age. Remember that movers are individuals who migrated from one city to another city—so a politically significant move—within the last four years. Clearly, retirees may be much younger than 66. Police officers and school teachers who started working right after school and have spent their entire careers in a particular locale may often be able to retire after 30 years of service. In that context, retirement in one's early to mid-fifties is a clear possibility. However, with significant constraints on the earliest age that retirees can receive Social Security or register for Medicare, retirements before these age limits are a very small portion of the total. And retirees in their early 50s are likely to be quite different from retirees of a more conventional age. To avoid the complications associated with an overly broad conceptualization of migrant retirees, I have defined this group so as to limit it to individuals who would, at least, be eligible for Social Security at the time they move. Movers who are 66 must have been at least 62 when they moved. With 62 as the age limit for (reduced) Social Security retirement benefits, this operationalization captures the overwhelming majority of retirees that share the demographic and political characteristics that distinguish this generational group.

The data indicate that migrant retirees tend to be in their early 70s, with an average age of 72 and a median age of 70. In age, migrant retirees and non-migrant retirees are fully comparable. Based on our sample of southerners, women make up a significantly larger proportion of the group of migrant retirees than do men. Women make up a larger proportion of the migrant retiree population than they do of the group of retirees who age in place.[3] The median migrant retiree has income in the $50,000-$60,000 range, exactly the same median income range as that of non-migrant retirees. The percentage of whites among migrant retirees is fully comparable to the percentage of whites among retirees who age in place. The percentage of whites is actually slightly higher among non-migrant retirees, but the difference is statistically and substantively insignificant.

Over half of all retirees—migrant and non-migrant—have no more than a high school diploma, and just less than a third have a college degree of any type. Again, there are no significant differences between migrant retirees and non-migrant retirees. In educational attainment these two groups of retirees are statistically indistinguishable.

Given the average age and general level of education, we should expect migrant retirees to be more likely to identify as Republicans and conservatives than members of the general adult population. In fact, that is exactly what we find. Southerner movers of retirement age are significantly more likely to be Republicans than to be Democrats or independents.[4] Among the pre-retirement cohort, those under retirement age, Democrats are slightly more common than Republicans (and significantly more common than independents).

We see a similar pattern in the ideological dispositions of migrant retirees. The modal ideological orientation among migrant retirees is "conservative," and nearly half of all migrant retirees self-identify as some type of conservative (either "conservative" or "very conservative"). Moderates are significantly more common than any types of liberal (either "liberal" or "very liberal"), and less than 20% of migrant retirees identify as some type of liberal—a figure that is far less than half of the percentage of migrant retirees who identify as some type of conservative. Among the pre-retirement generations, liberals are slightly more common, moderates are much more common, and conservatives are significantly less common.

Clearly, migrant retirees are politically distinctive from younger respondents. When compared to the broader (and younger) sample of adults, they are more likely to identify with the Republican Party than the Democratic Party and more likely to identify as a conservative than identify as a liberal (or a moderate). But are migrant retirees different from retirees who age in place (or at least age in their long-term community if not in the same residence)? As we saw above, the only demographic distinction between mobile retirees and those who are aging in place is their gender; women of retirement age are more likely to move. Given the similarities—albeit with one key difference—between movers and stayers of retirement age, are there important political differences between the groups? I address that question later in the chapter.

But first, we need to know whether retirees tend to congregate in locales in a way that might significantly impede the progressive trend resulting from migratory patterns more generally. If they are widely dispersed, or they disperse to areas that lean strongly in the Democratic direction, their impact on the politics of their new communities may not be as significant as the disparity between their own partisanship and ideology and younger generations would suggest. In the next section, we examine the question of geographic clustering.

Do Elderly Migrants Congregate? If Yes, Where?

When discussing the concentration of retirees, we must begin by understanding that significant concentrations of retirees—to the extent they are a function of retiree migrations—only develop over an extended period of time. Only a small portion—less than 2%—of retirees cross state lines when they retire; the vast majority remain in their cities of pre-retirement residence or make shorter in-state moves.[5] There is little evidence that this attachment to one's home (or one's home state) is likely to change any time soon. According to a recent survey of members of the American Association of Retired Persons (AARP), over 75% of prospective retirees hoped to age in place in *their current homes*.[6] These results are fully consistent with the CCES data. Migrant retirees may have moved at any time during the four years prior to their participation in the survey, and they make up slightly less than 10% of our sample of retirees.[7] With an annual rate of migration of approximately 2%, our percentage of migrants is just over four times the population average—just what one would expect when the operationalization of migration is based on a four-year time range.

Given the relatively limited geographic mobility of the overwhelming majority of retirees, significant concentrations of retirees depend upon a consistent net stream of retirees over an extended period of time: years, if not decades. That doesn't preclude the congregation of retirees in particularly attractive locales, but it does suggest that the impact of retiree migration patterns on politics take both (1) consistent patterns and (2) long timeframes to develop.

At the state level, some locales are clearly more attractive to retirees—especially mobile retirees—than others. Florida has long been a magnet for retirees, and the CCES data reflect this geographic dynamic. Table 7.1 depicts the number (and overall percentage) of retirees in each of the southern states by migrant status, so for each state we have an estimate of the percentage of southern retirees who reside in that state, an estimate of the percentage of migrant retirees who reside in that state, and an estimate of the percentage of non-migrant retirees who reside in that state. Note that in a majority of states, the relative percentage of non-migrant retirees is higher than the percentage of migrant retirees. Only in Arkansas, Florida, Georgia, and Tennessee is the percentage of migrant retirees higher than the percentage of non-migrant retirees, and the in the case of Arkansas and Tennessee, the differences are less than a percentage point. In Florida and Georgia, the proportion of migrant retirees is more than 10% higher than we would expect based on the state-level proportions of non-migrant retirees.

Table 7.1. Prevalence of Retirees by State and Migration Status

State	Non-migrant Retirees	Migrant Retirees	All Retirees
Alabama	4.18%	2.99%	4.03%
Arkansas	3.41%	4.13%	3.50%
Florida	30.28%	34.69%	30.84%
Georgia	8.15%	10.07%	8.39%
Louisiana	3.77%	2.76%	3.589%
Mississippi	2.01%	1.06%	1.897%
North Carolina	9.18%	7.88%	9.01%
South Carolina	4.68%	4.40%	4.65%
Tennessee	6.09%	6.37%	6.13%
Texas	21.00%	18.72%	20.71%
Virginia	7.31%	6.92%	7.27%

Because of the relatively small numbers of migrant retirees in the sample, we must be cautious about any generalizations we make at the state level.[8] We have fewer than 200 migrant retirees from Tennessee and just over 200 migrant retirees in Georgia and North Carolina—and fewer than 100 migrant retirees in five states—so any conclusions must be viewed in that light.[9] But it is still worth noting that the states which draw the largest percentages of the migrant retiree population—Florida, Texas, Georgia, and North Carolina—are also four of the fastest growing states. This is true if we focus solely on the CCES sample data, and it is true if we focus on census data.[10] These are also the states experiencing faster and more extensive liberalization of their voting populations. Differences in state size may also play a role in the distribution of the migrant retiree population, but the relationship is far from perfect. Texas is significantly larger than Florida, but it has received a substantially smaller percentage of the migrant retiree population. Arkansas is home to a larger percentage of the migrant retiree population than Alabama, Louisiana, and Mississippi—all larger states.

Are migrant retirees slowing the pace of political change in these growing areas? To get a clearer picture of the political effects of retiree migration, let's look at the county-level data. If we focus on those counties with a significant proportion of the migrant retiree sample—namely, those counties which have at least 1% of the migrant retiree sample—we see, not surprisingly, that they are clustered in a very small number of states. A majority of the counties that satisfy this criterion are in Florida. Given the criterion of selection, all of these counties are quite large from the standpoint of population. All would have more than 200,000 registered voters, approximately 10 times the number for an average-sized county in the South. Some of these Florida counties, however, are much larger than the others. Lake County has fewer than 250,000 registered voters, while Broward and Miami-Dade have over a million registered voters.[11] More than half of these Florida counties have Republican majorities (based on voter registration rolls). That suggests that migrant retirees are having a conservative effect on their new communities. But there is also a clear size effect. The larger counties—and the counties with the largest migrant retiree populations—tend to be majority Democrat. Often, the Democratic advantage in these larger counties is overwhelming. This is true in Broward, Miami-Dade, and Palm Beach, easily the three largest counties in Florida. If migrant retirees tip the political scales in the conservative direction, that effect is, at best, very small in Florida.

The remaining "retiree magnet" counties are in South Carolina and Texas. We see conflicting evidence in South Carolina and Texas. The retiree magnet county in South Carolina, Horry County, is one of the most Republican counties in the state (based on the vote in the 2016 election). Horry County, South Carolina, is an analog to Brunswick County, North Carolina. An overwhelmingly white county in a state with a large African American population, it is also a coastal county, largely sustained by tourism. But in Texas, the retiree magnet counties tend to be more likely to be Democratic. Of the four retiree magnet counties in Texas—Bexar, Dallas, Harris, and Tarrant— only Tarrant went for President Trump in 2016. Secretary Clinton won each of the other counties by more than 10 percentage points. If migrant retirees are counteracting the progressive effects of the broader migratory dynamic, their impact is quite limited.

The relatively small number of migrant retirees mitigates against their having a significant region-wide political impact. Likewise, even though they do tend to congregate in certain states (like Florida) and certain counties (like Broward), they tend to move to those areas that are large and growing more generally. This also limits their particular effect on the partisan character of the locales to which they are moving. But a full consideration of the effect of migrant retirees on their communities must assess their political attributes as well. Even if they are a small portion of the population in their new homes, if their political orientations are sufficiently distinctive, especially if they are significantly more Republican and more conservative than the less mobile members of their generation, they could stem the progressive tide we otherwise associate with population growth. The next section includes an analysis of the political distinctiveness of migrant retirees within the retirement generation.

Movers and Stayers in the Elderly Generations: Are They Different?

In subtle but politically noteworthy ways, the movers among the retiree generation differ from the stayers (and other non-movers) in the same generation.[12] First, we know that migrant retirees are more likely to be women than retirees who age in place. Second, and related to the gender distinction, movers in the retirement generation are more likely to align themselves with the Democratic Party than non-movers from the same generation (see Chart 7.1).

Republicans are far more prevalent among retirees who are long-term residents of their community than among migrant retirees. Though the gap is smaller, independents are also more common among retirees who

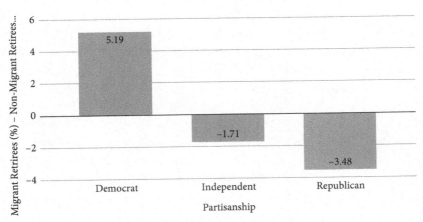

Chart 7.1. Migrant Retirees' Partisanship vs. Non-Migrant Retirees' Partisanship

are long-term residents of their communities. Democrats, on the other hand, are significantly more prevalent among migrant retirees than those who are aging in place or those who migrated to their current home many years earlier. From a generational standpoint—though not from a gender standpoint—migrant retirees may be relatively more likely to align with the Republican Party, but when compared with their less mobile generational peers, they are significantly stronger supporters of the Democratic Party.

We see a similar ideological distinction between the movers and the non-movers in the retirement generation: more mobile retirees are more liberal than other retirees (see Chart 7.2). More mobile retirees are much less likely to self-identify as "conservative" or "very conservative" than their generational peers with longer residences in their current communities. By the same token, migrant retirees are significantly more likely to self-identify as "liberal" or "very liberal," and they are slightly more likely to consider themselves moderate.

The differences in partisan attachment and ideological orientation within the retirement generation are robust. In a logistic regression predicting migrant status among retirees, we see a clear relationship between attachment to the Democratic Party and the likelihood of migration (at least among white retirees).[13] In a logistic regression including age, gender, income, a dummy variable for no education beyond a high school diploma, and partisanship, on the sample of whites over 65 only age and partisanship are close

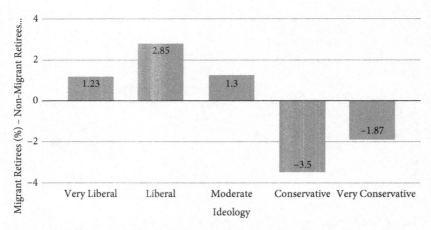

Chart 7.2. Migrant Retirees' Ideology vs. Non-Migrant Retirees' Ideology

to statistical significance.[14] In a supplemental regression including only these terms, only partisanship was significant.[15] Democrats of retirement age are more likely to be migrants. Clearly, on party attachment, migrant retirees are distinct from retirees who age in place.

There is even stronger evidence for the hypothesized result in the case of ideology (see Table 7.2). Gender, income, and education have no significant impact on the likelihood that a retiree is a recent migrant; only age and ideology makes a difference. Liberals and strong liberals are significantly more likely to be migrants than conservatives and strong conservatives. Ideology matters; as retirees lean increasingly to the progressive side of the ideological spectrum, they are more likely to be movers than stayers. Among the retiree population, movers are clearly more progressive—whether in terms of partisanship or ideology—than the more stationary members of their cohort.[16] This is simply additional evidence for the tie between a progressive outlook and one's migratory experience. It bears repeating that what we see here for ideology and for partisanship is what we see in the broader, multi-generational sample. On average, movers are more progressive than stayers.

When comparing across generations, retirees tend to have a more conservative orientation to politics. Among whites, retirees also tend to be more likely to align with the Republican Party than those in younger generations, and this generational gap has been expanding.[17] However, when comparing within the retirement generation, we see important political differences between retirees who move and those who are aging in place (and have been for some time). As is true in the broader sample encompassing all generations of adults, migrants are more progressive—in both their partisanship and their ideology—than those who have

Table 7.2. Ideology and Migration among White Seniors

Migrant Retiree	b	Robust SE	z	p>|z|
Age	−0.02	0.01	−2.05	0.04
Gender	0.09	0.12	0.77	0.44
Family Income	−0.00	0.02	−0.19	0.85
High School Only	−0.04	0.11	−0.40	0.69
Ideology	−0.12	0.04	−2.70	0.01
_cons	−0.09	0.90	−0.10	0.92

long periods of residence in the same community. Migratory dynamics among the retired clearly contribute to, rather than detract from, the progressive shift of southern politics over the last 20 years. To assume those areas which draw large numbers of retirees from other states and regions are going to be as conservative as communities with similar age demographics populated by elderly stayers, one would have to ignore the empirical record.

8

Movers, Stayers, and the End of
Southern Politics?

How do you oversell the role of migration—both from abroad and internally—in the grand story of American history? You can't. Whatever your personal perspective on immigration policy today, one can't get around the fact that we are a country of immigrants. We have come from other places, and once we got here, we often moved somewhere else. And we tend to move a lot; "[d]ecades of data . . . characterizes the United States as *one of the most geographically mobile countries* in the world" (Chandler 2016, emphasis in the original). The average American is likely to move more than 10 times during their life; in comparison, the average European is likely to move less than half that number of times (Chandler 2016).

Since we move so much, it should come as no surprise that migratory patterns play an important role in our politics. Demographers and political geographers have paid considerable attention to the impact of international immigrants on U.S. politics, and students of southern politics have been sensitive to the impact on the South of migrants from other regions. Scholars have recognized the impact of migration on southern politics for decades. This research focused on the role of regional immigrants—what Brown (1988:16) refers to as "internal migration": U.S. residents moving from the "North,"—that is, anywhere outside the South—to the South. Until recently, the primary storyline was that (white) in-migrants from the North were significantly more likely to identify with the Republican Party and support the candidates of the Republican Party than native southerners (see Scher 1992 for a description of this literature).

Over the past two decades, however, it has become clear that in-migrants are not more Republican or more conservative than native southerners. Even if we limit our consideration to white in-migrants, the evidence increasingly shows that they are more likely to align with the Democratic Party (or identify as independents) than native southerners (McKee 2010; McKee and Teigen 2016; and Hillygus, McKee, and Young 2017). One reason for the change in the partisan impact of in-migrants is the shift in the partisan orientation of the South (and native southerners). In the 1970s, the South was an overwhelmingly Democratic region; even if migrants from other regions were drawn at random from those regional populations, they would have been more Republican than the average southern resident. But as the region became staunchly Republican more quickly and more consistently than any other region in the country, in-migrants were no longer more likely to be Republicans than native southerners. As native southerners shifted to the Republican Party, in-migrants actually became more Democratic, as racial and ethnic minorities made up a growing percentage of in-migrants. During this time, in-migrants became an increasingly large portion of the southern electorate. The proportion of in-migrants in the southern electorate is nearly twice what it was in the years immediately after the publication of Key's *Southern Politics* (McKee 2019).

One of the interesting aspects of this literature is its preoccupation with the numerical impact of cross-regional migration to the exclusion of consideration of the impact of in-migrants on the political environment of their new neighbors. So, what impact do in-migrants have on the communities to which they move? Brown (1988) examines the potential impact *on* in-migrants of the political context to which they have moved, but what of the impact of in-migrants on their new communities? The literature also ignores the impact of *internal* migrants on the political communities to which they move. The presumption has long been that to the extent change occurs, it is subtle and it manifests in the changing attitudes and behaviors of the *movers*: "they are influenced by the political environments in which they have moved" (Brown 1988).

Much is lost in the translation of this body of research—primarily developed during a different century and a much less polarized era—to the 21st-century South. Movers and stayers theory is an effort to address this gap in the literature and to explain why we have begun to see signs of a progressive resurgence in a region that has trended to the right as long as people have been studying southern politics. Movers and stayers theory begins with the proposition that *movers* are distinctive, and they have an impact on the communities they are joining *and* the communities they have left behind. This is true for all movers—those coming from other countries or other states, as well as those native southerners moving from state to state or city to city within a state. Movers in the 21st century are younger, more educated, more liberal, and more likely to align with the Democratic Party than non-movers. As

I have shown, this is true both nationally and in the South specifically. These results are fully consistent with and expand on the recent literature which demonstrates that in-migrants from other regions are more likely than native southerners to align with the Democratic Party. Movers and stayers theory asserts that movers—whether from outside the South or not—are more progressive, and thus more likely to align with the Democratic Party than less mobile southerners. Again, rather than comparing new southerners to existing southerners, movers and stayers theory compares mobile southerners (whether new to the South or not) to less mobile southerners.

A key contribution of movers and stayers theory is its treatment of the impact of movers on their new communities (and in the case of native southerners, those communities that they have left behind). Existing research on southern politics has ignored the impact of migration on the long-term residents of communities where movers find their new homes and the long-term residents of communities from which the movers have exited. For *stayers* in movers' new homes and those in movers' old homes, migration has political implications. In general, movers and stayers theory presumes that long-term residents (*stayers*) in declining communities perceive a threat to their communities, their way of life, their families, and themselves. In our racialized (and polarized) political environment, the perception of threat induces a political response; stayers identify more strongly with the dominant party in their racial or ethnic group. White Republicans become strong Republicans. White Republican "leaners" become Republicans, and white independents start to lean toward the Republican side. White Democrats are likely to weaken their attachment to the party; some will become independents, and others may even shift to the Republican Party. Comparable effects will occur in the realm of ideology. Just as threatened whites will shift toward the Republican Party, they will also shift toward the conservative end of the ideological spectrum.

The dynamics of movers and stayers theory is identical for blacks and Latinos, but because their typical partisan attachments and ideological orientations are distinctive, so are the results we would expect. While white southerners respond to threat by increasing their attachment to the Republican Party, black southerners respond to community threat by maintaining or increasing their attachment to the Democratic Party. Among Latinos in the South, with partisan allegiances split between those of whites and African Americans, any partisan shift we see should be in the Democratic direction.

For two important reasons, we should expect the partisan and ideological shift to be subtler among minorities. First, because the partisan distribution of blacks and Latinos is already so skewed toward the Democratic Party, the magnitude of the shift in partisan attachment due to the threat from community decline will be less dramatic than in the case of whites. As the overwhelming majority of Latinos and African Americans already identify as Democrats, fewer minorities are in a position to shift partisanship in reaction to community decline, and those minorities who have remained Republican in the face of overwhelming support for the Democratic Party among other members of their racial or ethnic group may be particularly difficult to influence under any circumstances (even dramatic community decline). However, given the strong conservatism among southern Latinos, community threat—in the form of declining or stagnating population—should lead to greater conservatism. Population growth, on the other hand, should lead to a shift to the left among whites, African Americans, and Latinos. The extent to which that shift will manifest empirically varies by the existing partisan attachments and ideological orientations of the three racial groups. Specifically, we should see the largest partisan effects—"contact hypothesis" effects—among the most Republican group (whites). Among African Americans and Latinos, movers and stayers theory suggests smaller effects, and that is generally what we see.

Stayers in the vibrant, growing areas to which movers flock will also be influenced by this migratory pattern. Stayers in these towns and cities will come into greater contact with a younger, more educated, more diverse, and more progressive population. Stayers that are least amenable to the changing nature of their neighborhoods and communities will exit. Stayers who remain will experience the effects of the "contact hypothesis"; existing prejudices will tend to break down, and a more inclusive and progressive orientation will develop among these long-term residents. As this happens, they will tend to identify more closely with the Democratic Party.

As in the case of responses to threat, reactions to increased contact with new community members will vary across racial groups. The greatest effects will be seen among whites in these growing communities. As Latinos and African Americans (especially) are already overwhelmingly attached to the Democratic Party, partisan (or ideological) shifts manifesting in these racial groups in growing communities will be subtle (if such shifts manifest at all).

The predictions of movers and stayers theory are largely borne out by the data. Specifically, we see the following:

1. *Population growth produces more progressive politics. Population decline produces more conservative politics among whites and in largely white areas.*
2. *Movers are different. They are younger, better educated, more liberal, and more likely to attach to the Democratic Party. There is also some evidence that movers are more racially and ethnically diverse than non-movers.*
3. *Except in age and residential stability, stayers are generally similar to non-stayers. This is true for each racial group. It strongly suggests that the results for today's stayers will generalize to non-stayers who remain in their communities in the future.*
4. *White stayers in declining communities become more Republican and more conservative. Whites in fast-growing communities become more progressive.*
5. *African American stayers in declining communities maintain their attachment to the Democratic Party.*
6. *Latino stayers in declining communities tend to maintain their attachment to the Democratic Party. Latino stayers in high growth areas tend to become more Democratic. As the overwhelming majority of Latinos live in the fastest growing communities and the fastest growing states, and their presences in these fast-growing areas plays a key role in the related increase in Democratic attachment.*
7. *Mobile retirees are more progressive than retirees who are aging in place. Given this, it is easy to overestimate the conservative shift in communities that attract significant numbers of retirees.*

Taken as a whole, movers and stayers theory and the empirical record consonant with it provide the answers to the following key questions:

1. Why are we seeing significant recent (and why might we see future) growth in identification with the Democratic Party and support for Democratic Party candidates in the South as a whole? Because population growth in the 21st-century South engenders progressivism in the manner outlined in the movers and stayers theory.
2. Why is the Democratic Party growing quickly in some places while the Republican Party is growing quickly in other places? Not everywhere in the South is growing, and we should expect to see increased attachment to the Republican Party in declining and low-growth areas that are predominantly white.

3. Why aren't all rural areas overwhelmingly Republican? Because there are rural areas in the South that have large African American populations, and African Americans do not respond to community threat by becoming more Republican.

4. Why aren't huge cities the only bastions of Democratic support? Because huge cities aren't the only places in the South that are growing.

For students of southern politics in the 21st century, these are all big questions. Movers and stayers theory provides compelling answers.

A great deal of work remains to be done. Movers and stayers theory posits that places become more progressive as population grows because (1) movers, the new residents, are more progressive than non-movers, and (2) stayers (primarily white stayers) become more progressive due to their contact with new residents. It is easy to see how an influx of progressives— whether from outside the South or from another state (or county) in the South—would influence an area's political orientation. The change in stayers' partisan attachments and ideological orientations is more difficult to rigorously assess. While this characterization of stayers' responses to population growth is fully consistent with the data presented above, what is really required is panel data—ideally over a significant span of time (at least a decade)—with a large enough southern sample to allow for the assessment of the hypothesized distinctions between white, black, and Latino stayers. This sort of panel data would also enable researchers to assess (with precision) the relative impact of (1) changing racial and ethnic demographics, and (2) the changing partisan attachments and political orientations within racial and ethnic groups on the overall progressivism (or conservatism) of communities throughout the South as they grow (or decline).

The contact hypothesis dynamic also depends upon the interaction between movers and stayers—particularly white stayers and movers of color. The extent to which these interactions occur are at least partly a function of the level of racial segregation in the communities where population growth is occurring. Future research could profitably expand the empirical record associated with the movers and stayers theoretical landscape by assessing the extent to which residential racial segregation in the South varies according to population growth over the course of the first 20 years of this century. This research would also allow for a more rigorous assessment of Key's (1949) "black belt" hypothesis in areas where the population is growing (and in areas where the population is declining). One of the central features of movers and stayers theory is that in the 21st century, white Republicanism often develops in contexts where few African Americans live; local black context simply isn't the driving force of white conservatism that it was during the middle of the last century. Likewise, mobilized black context (Hood, Kidd, and Morris 2012a) no longer plays the central role in the expansion of white Republicanism that it did during the last 35 years of the 20th century.

Finally, there are no theoretical obstacles to the generalization of movers and stayers theory to the United States more generally. As long as movers are distinctive in the ways we see here—younger, better educated, more progressive—we should expect to see similar outcomes. Future work could very profitably determine if we do.

Of Time and the River and Sub-Regional Distinctiveness

Even when Key (1949) was writing, the Rim South was larger (more states and more populous) than the Deep South, but the differences were significantly smaller than they are today. In 1950, the population of the Deep South was nearly 40% of the South; today it is a little over a quarter of the region. In 1950, Florida was, by population, the median southern state. Today, it's second only to Texas, and it is twice as large as the next most populous state (Georgia, which is just ahead of North Carolina). Texas actually has slightly more residents than all of the states in the Deep South.

Given these changes, maybe it is no surprise that the characteristic region of the South—the Deep South—is no longer the distinctive, dominant force in southern politics it once was. Key's black belt was not limited to the Deep South, but it was a constitutive facet of the Deep South in a way that it was not in the Rim South. Key's contention—that "if the politics of the South revolves around any single theme, it is that of the role of the black belts" (1949:5-6)—no longer reflects the underlying political dynamics of the broader region. In fact, as I have shown above, the Deep South/Rim South distinction is no longer the principal dividing line in southern politics. That is not to say that no sub-regional differences exist between the southern states; important sub-regional differences do exist. The simple fact is that the sub-regional differences do not cleave along the traditional borders; they cleave according to population growth, just as movers and stayers theory would predict.

Population growth is one of the drivers of southern progressivism—along with, though not unrelated to, increasing racial and ethnic diversity. There are fast-growing states in the Rim South (Florida, Texas) and the Deep South (Georgia and, to a lesser extent, South Carolina). Likewise, there are states where population growth is much more pedestrian in the Rim South (Arkansas and Tennessee) and in the Deep South (Louisiana and Mississippi in particular). Growth varies across the sub-regions, so partisan change varies as well. With the rather dramatic weakening of the relationship between white partisanship and local racial context as our partisan politics becomes more polarized and more nationalized, the political significance of one of the characteristic differences between the Rim South and the Deep South—the prevalence of black belt counties in the Deep South and their relative rarity in the Rim South—has waned. Today, racial conservatism is prevalent in areas where hardly any African Americans live, so the contextual substructure upon which earlier partisan distributions depended are no longer necessary. As I noted earlier, we have learned to hate at a distance. In that context, one of the important implications of movers and stayers theory is the waning significance of the distinction between the Deep South and the Rim South. There are still important sub-regional differences in southern politics; it's just that the sub-regions are no longer defined in terms of a core (Deep South) and a periphery (Rim South).

Whither Party Polarization in the South

Barring a significant disruption in the core dynamics of movers and stayers theory—more on that eventuality below—party polarization in the South, particularly as it manifests geographically, should increase. A dramatic increase is not out of the realm of possibility. The question of the future of partisan polarization is fundamentally a question of the future geographic character of income inequality.

Movers and stayers theory—and the wealth of evidence that supports it—shows us how migration is driving the 21st-century partisan transformation in the South. Movers are distinctive—distinctively young, educated, and progressive. When they arrive in their new homes, they influence the behavior and the political attitudes of long-term residents (stayers). Some portion (likely on the conservative end of the ideological spectrum) will exit. The size of the exiting population will vary, but in those places where the adult population is experiencing significant growth, the number of movers entering the community obviously exceeds the number of long-term migrants who are leaving. Long-term migrants who remain respond to increased contact with the distinctive population of movers with a greater acceptance of the lifestyle and political attitudes of the new community members. Long-term migrants tend to become more progressive (and more attached to the Democratic Party) as these new migrants join their community. Because African Americans and Latinos tend to be so much more likely to identify with the Democratic Party in the first place, new migrants' effects on their political attitudes are more muted than the effects on the political attitudes of whites.

Movers also influence the political attitudes of the communities they leave or exit. White stayers in declining communities—communities experiencing the most extensive and widespread emigration—respond to the multiple threats implied by declining population (economic malaise, family disintegration, the weakening of community organizations, the loss of government services) by aligning themselves more closely with the partisan home of their primary social group—the Republican Party. Among Latinos and African Americans, I find no such rightward shift. While there is no evidence of increased attachment to the Democratic Party in response to threat among African Americans and Latinos, they do maintain their already strong preexisting attachments. As expected, the party-shifting effects are greater among whites than among minorities.

A central feature of movers and stayers theory is that all of these political dynamics flow initially from the decisions of movers, and these migratory decisions are rarely driven by politics.[1] This is an important distinction between movers and stayers theory and the "Big Sort" dynamic championed by Bishop (2009). Rather than viewing migrants as primarily driven by politics—Republicans seeking Republican communities, Democrats seeking Democratic communities—movers and stayers theory sees migrants as primarily driven by economics and family relations. Demographic research on the self-reported reasons for moving provides significantly more support for the movers and stayers perspective than the "Big Sort" dynamic.[2] So the driving force of southern partisan change is, fundamentally, geographic variation in economic growth or, more accurately but somewhat less concretely, economic opportunity.[3]

If economic growth and economic opportunity were the same everywhere, we would see far less migration. We will always have some level of migration—such as for family reasons—but since the preponderance of migration is job-related, if economic opportunity is constant across communities, that primary impetus for migration is eliminated. Alternatively, as the geographic component of economic inequality grows—the gap between the most prosperous communities and the least prosperous communities grows—we should expect migration, and the political implications of migration, to increase. In that case, declining communities that are primarily white would become increasingly conservative and increasingly Republican. Majority-minority communities in decline will become more Democratic; vibrant, growing locales will become more progressive and more Democratic. As this happens, geographic polarization will increase. Growth will breed progressivism, and decline will foster a reactionary response (see Gervais and Morris 2018). Parties (and politics more generally) will become more racialized. This will occur within states and across states.

Population growth will underpin this geographic polarization. It bears repeating that the high-growth states and the low-growth states do not follow the outlines of the traditional southern sub-regions, the Rim South and the Deep South. Some Rim South states are high growth; some are low growth. Some Deep South states are high growth, some are low growth. As the politics of the southern states are variably altered by their levels of population growth, the political (and economic) distinctiveness of the Rim South and the Deep South will fade away.

Do We Still Have a "Southern" Politics?

Not really, no.

Key was extremely careful in his characterization of the South and in his explanation of the methodological rationale for defining the South as the 11 states of the former Confederacy. He wrote that "[m]uch labor could be expended on a definition of the South" (1949:11). Key based his operationalization of the South on political behavior; more specifically, the inordinate and very distinctive level of support for the Democratic Party. He writes, in fact, "no better delimitation can be devised than one based on political behavior" (1949:11). As it happened, the list of states that exceeded Key's standards for the consistency and extent of Democratic Party support were also the 11 states of the former Confederacy. While the states Key defined as southern were those states which had seceded from the Union (and *only* those states), he makes it clear that he had not based his definition on the historical decisions associated with secession. He writes:

> Incidentally—and not without importance—it may be noted that the eleven states that meet the test of partisan consistency also are the eleven states that seceded to form the Confederacy. (1949:11)

One of Key's extraordinary insights was the way in which local politics could drive national politics. While the phrase is most closely associated with Tip O'Neill, Key realized (likely earlier than O'Neill did) that local conditions may create dynamics that drive politics far beyond the immediate boundaries of the city, county, or state where those conditions exist. In Key's South, the black belt drove politics in the Deep South states, and those states, in turn, dominated the political dynamics of the South as a whole. Then the distinctive politics of the South played a crucial role in national-level politics from the end of Reconstruction to the present day. That powerful relationship between black context and white political behavior was, for Key, distinctively southern. Movers and stayers theory (and the extensive evidence consistent with it) suggests that defining dynamic is no longer a central aspect of southern politics.

In the wake of that realization, we must seriously reconsider whether or not "the South" even exists. In a recent article, Springer (2019) problematizes the concept of a "South." She writes:

> ... much of the literature has portrayed it [the South] as a central feature of American political development. This work, however, centers on the slipperiness of the concept; on the problem of treating "the South" as a fixed geographic region rather than as a set of political traits or patterns, or as a more fluid, continuous variable that might shift over time. (1101)

Springer catalogs the various definitions of the South, from two distinct definitions of the "Deep South" to definitions of "the South" that include 10 additional variations. The definitions range from 10 states to 17 states. A few states are always included: Alabama, Georgia, Louisiana, Mississippi, and South Carolina—the traditional characterization of the "Deep South." Beyond that it is a grab bag of inclusion. Springer goes on to demonstrate that the use of substantive criteria for defining the South—size of the African American population, voter turnout, and voting on civil rights legislation—imply several different versions of "the South." States that satisfy one criterion often fail to satisfy another. In the case of voting on civil rights legislation, there are even key differences depending upon which type of civil rights legislation the criteria are based on.

Springer (2019) also highlights the *temporality* of our definitions of the South. As I indicated above, Key's definition of the "South" was firmly founded on the distinctiveness of the voting behavior of southerners. In 1949, this distinctive voting behavior happened to be both a necessary *and* sufficient condition for inclusion in the southern category; and as it happened, that group of states were also *exactly* the same states that seceded from the Union. Movers and stayers theory helps us understand a set of political dynamics that are occurring in the southern states (as we have defined them in this volume). But these political dynamics are producing mass-level behaviors and attitudes—votes, party attachments, and ideological orientations— which are increasingly varied. If the criteria for inclusion is political behavior and attitudes, then at this point in the 21st century we don't even have a distinctive "Deep South" (regardless of which of the two definitions you use), let alone a distinctive (and consistent) "South."

As I suggest above, it's possible that movers and stayers theory only holds true for the "South." If that were the case, then that could be a substantive basis for defining this region. But that is also unlikely. Population growth may not also bolster progressivism—consider, for example, those areas in the United States where population growth is primarily (if not exclusively) driven by the influx of workers in the energy industry. Those individuals are less likely to be as progressive as our movers, and so their effect on stayers in those areas may well be different (if there is any effect at all). But most population growth in the United States is not driven by oil and/or natural gas extraction. And in those cases, movers and stayers theory is a reasonable tool for understanding the relationship between population change and political change. Further examination of that thesis is work for another time.

Preempting Movers and Stayers Theory

What sort of politics (or economics) might disrupt the movers and stayers dynamics? I see two serious political options and two, not unrelated, economic scenarios. The distinction between "options" and "scenarios" is one of choice. We view options in instrumental terms; we choose our politics (albeit imperfectly) in a way that we are not able to choose our economic circumstances. But economics and politics are not unrelated. The political options might be chosen in the absence of the economic scenarios; what is more likely is that one or the other political option will be chosen because of the realization of one (or both) of the economic scenarios.

There was a time when the key distinguishing features between the Democrats and the Republicans were their positions on issues related to the economy and economic policy. Republicans were the "small" government party. Focused on limiting the size of government and its role in the marketplace, Republicans wanted low taxes and balanced budgets. They feared inflation and sought to manage monetary policy accordingly—think of the extent to which Volcker's Fed pushed interest rates to squeeze inflation out of the economy during Reagan's first term (Greider 1987). And they were free-traders. Democrats, on the other hand, were much more accepting of government expenditures (particularly for social programs)—consider the expansion of social programs during FDR's administration and Lyndon Johnson's administration. They were more concerned about the damage caused by unemployment than inflation, and they were willing to trade higher inflation for lower unemployment when it seemed that it was possible to manipulate those macroeconomic variables with fiscal and monetary policy. For much of the 20th century, the "party differences" model of macroeconomic politics was the primary tool for understanding the central differences between Democrats and Republicans (see, e.g., Hibbs 1987).

This was a much less politically polarized time. Not coincidentally, it was also an era in which the parties were far less demographically distinctive than they are today. In particular, they were far less racialized. As the parties have become more demographically distinct, and as they have become more racialized, the economic policy distinctiveness which was fundamental to partisan politics in the 20th century eroded. If the central facets of any comprehensive economic policy regime are fiscal policy (managing deficit and debt), monetary policy, and trade policy, then distinguishing between Democrats and Republicans is far more difficult that it once was. Which is the party of small government (i.e., balanced budgets and declining debt)? Which party (ever) seeks tighter monetary policy? Is there a free trade party? In an extraordinarily polarized time, the dividing lines do not cleave on the traditionally important economic issues.

Today's divisions, the divisions that feed the movers and stayers dynamic, are in the realm of social policy and civil rights policy (see Gervais and Morris

2018). The Republican Party has staked out conservative positions in both of these policy areas (e.g., anti-abortion policy, opposition to gay marriage and the full extension of civil rights to members of the LGBTQ community, and increasingly restrictive immigration policies). The Democratic Party has taken more progressive positions on all of these issues. Some scholars have even suggested that the distinction between the Democratic Party and the Republican Party has gone beyond ideological differences. Grossman and Hopkins (2016) view the Democratic Party as a collection of social groups rather than a political organization with a detailed ideological agenda. The Republicans, on the other hand, are viewed as clearly focused on socially and racially conservative ideological agenda (Gervais and Morris 2018 and Grossman and Hopkins 2016).[4]

As long as these are the dividing lines between the parties—and Mason's (2018) recent work suggests there will be for the foreseeable future—we have every reason to think the movers and stayers dynamics will continue to drive southern politics (and, potentially, national politics). But in politics, nothing is forever. The two most plausible (and significant) disruptions to the movers and stayers dynamics are (1) the development of a *class*-based politics or (2) the development of a *generational* cleavage within our political system. The two are not unrelated.

Even during the period of party differences in macroeconomic politics, the United States never developed a class-based politics comparable to those that were common in Western Europe during the same time period. Historically, class-based cleavages have played a relatively smaller role in American politics than in the politics of many other industrial democracies. But that does not preclude the future development of a system in which a party representing the working class and a party representing the upper class compete for middle class voters.

Likewise, we have no experience with a party system organized along generationally based political differences, but a future in which a party representing rather younger voters faced a party with a much more senior membership is not outside the realm of possibility. Given our current demographics, an age-based politics would have a class component as well. Older Americans hold significantly more wealth than younger Americans, and by far the most expensive federal programs are primarily geared toward providing income support and health care for the elderly. So conflicts between generations are likely to have class-based implications.

What scenarios might lead to one of these political scenarios, a class-based politics or an age-based politics? One possibility is a dramatic economic downturn that inordinately effected fast-growing, high-income communities. To the extent that financial benefits are associated with migratory decline, the class-based political pressure which migration had tempered would intensify. As class pressures intensify, they have the potential to overwhelm the other demographic distinctions that are currently reinforcing our polarized politics. I'm obviously talking about an extraordinary downturn. The Great Recession failed to produce a class-based politics. In that case there were the obvious complications of the Obama election and the conservative response to that (see Gervais and Morris 2018), but still, it was a window to a party system transformation that did not materialize. A more dramatic downturn might produce different results.

An age-based politics might result from a substantial increase in the frequency and severity of environmental disasters. Since environmental degradation plays out over a span of decades, younger voters pay a far higher total cost for this degradation than do older voters. Because they pay a higher cost, they have reason to care much more about current environmental policy. They also have a much stronger incentive to invest resources in those policies most likely to mitigate the worst effects of past and current environmental policies. Theoretically, these differences on environmental policies could form the foundations of our political parties—and thus generate an age-based politics. But they have not done so to this point. A series of serious environmental catastrophes might open a window to this new politics.

These are dark and troubling scenarios that lead to partisan change. Serious partisan change might result, however, from a much more pedestrian (and less apocalyptic) process. Movers and stayers theory might simply run its course. At some point, as movers move and stayers respond to their growing or declining communities, Democratic attachment and attitudes will become more progressive. At some point, the Republican Party, as currently constituted from a demographic *and* ideological standpoint, will find it difficult to compete. And this is in the South. When that time comes, southern Republicans will need a new plan. If southern Republicans need a new plan, national Republicans will need a new plan. Class-based politics, anyone?

COVID-19 Coda

A full draft of this manuscript was at Oxford ready to go out for review before the end of December 2019—before the identification of the COVID-19 virus in the United States. In important respects, we live in a different world. And just what that different world will look like a month from now—let alone six months from now or a year from now—is still very much up in the air. In this unsettled environment, projections are always suspect. But from my vantage point in May 2020, there is every reason to believe that the COVID-19 crisis has the potential to *accelerate* the movers and stayers dynamics that are already in place.

To this point, perceptions of the seriousness of the pandemic, assessments of federal responses to the pandemic, and attitudes toward social distancing and various local, state, and national sheltering requirements have been highly partisan. To the extent the pandemic reinforces existing partisan attachments, it is unlikely to disrupt the movers and stayers' dynamics. Consider the impact on movers' demographics. Will the elderly begin to move at much higher rates than younger adults? In *this* public health environment? Not likely. Are urban minorities—one of the demographic groups suffering most during the pandemic—likely to shift their allegiance to a party dominated by a national leader whose crisis management skills they consistently give extraordinarily low marks? Would we expect any different from younger voters, many of whom are (or will) be dealing with what is potentially the worst job market of their lives? Are whites in declining areas—many of which have to this point escaped the full wrath of the virus—likely to leave the Republican fold while their impressions of the President are so much more positive than residents of higher growth areas? Again, probably not.

There are a few caveats. Early polling suggests that COVID-19 has generated a surprising amount of fear and frustration in one of the President's strongest vote demographics: the elderly. Those over 60 are significantly more likely to see the pandemic as a serious health risk—whether or not they see it as a serious economic risk—than those under 60. The elderly are also a disproportionate share of those focused solely on the health risks associated with the pandemic; a full quarter of this group is 70 or older.[5] If this result solidifies, it may suggest less Republican attachment among the characteristically older white populations in declining areas in the South. Given the region-wide trend toward the left driven by movers and stayers theory, this age-specific dynamic—while not an aspect of movers and stayers theory—is, nonetheless, an accelerant of the process it outlines.

If the economic fallout associated with the pandemic reaches Depression-level proportions, then I still expect growing areas to tilt toward the left, and stagnating or declining areas to tilt toward the right. That does not mean that the future geographic patterns of growth and decline will remain the same; but where there is growth (and where there is decline) the same processes will engender equivalent political ramifications. *Were the President a Democrat*, history suggests a plausible alternative to the political path delineated by movers and stayers theory: imminent, wholesale realignment to the Republican Party in response to the abject failure of the sitting president to manage the health crisis *or* the national economy.

But the President is not a Democrat. The one plausible alternative path available to him involves a dramatic and permanent decline in the severity of the virus, a V-shaped economic recovery that takes root well in advance of the fall, and something quite close to a return to a pre-COVID lifestyle before the November elections. Even all of that is unlikely to disrupt the long-term effects of movers and stayers simply doing what they do. But for a season, it might win the President and his party a reprieve. Failing this sort of dramatic and unlikely epidemiological and economic turnaround, the President may be facing a loss of historic proportions. If this occurs, don't be surprised if fast-growing southern states like Virginia, and North Carolina, and Georgia, and Texas, and Florida are in the vanguard.

Notes

Chapter 1

1. The Rim South includes the states of Arkansas, Florida, North Carolina, Tennessee, Texas, and Virginia. The remainder of the South, often referred to as the Deep South, includes Alabama, Georgia, Louisiana, Mississippi, and South Carolina.
2. As Gaddie candidly writes, "Was 1994 the year of realignment? Yes" (2012: 309).
3. Throughout the manuscript, "South" refers to the eleven states of the former Confederacy: Alabama, Arkansas, Florida, Georgia, Louisiana, Mississippi, North Carolina, South Carolina, Tennessee, Texas, and Virginia. In common parlance, the group of southern states is often more extensive, sometimes including Delaware, Kentucky, Maryland, Missouri, and/or Oklahoma. However, research focused on the *politics* of the southern region focuses almost exclusive on the 11 former Confederate states, though Springer (2019) presents an interesting counterpoint.
4. Respondents indicating a "lean" toward one party or the other are counted as identifying with the party toward which they are leaning.
5. Though there is evidence of a rural–urban divide in partisan attachment (and support for Trump), it is not uncomplicated. In particular, not all rural areas—such as those which are majority minority—are strong Republican (Trump) supporters. See Scala and Johnson (2017) and Scala, Johnson, and Rogers (2015) for extensive treatments of this dynamic.
6. See Cox (2016) for additional information.
7. Maxwell and Shields' (2019) recent work is an example of a cultural theory of partisan change that is founded on racially focused politics.
8. And the role of race in southern politics—and American politics more broadly—remains substantial (see, e.g., Knuckey and Kim 2015 and 2016).
9. Though locally oriented, the broader partisan shift at the elite level—Republicans to the right and Democrats to the left—on issues related to civil rights, and the central role civil rights and issues related to race played in the trajectory of public opinion (and "public mood"), also played important contextual roles in the transformation of southern politics (Carmines and Stimson 1989).
10. Some scholars have suggested (see, e.g., Voss 2000) that Key's "black belt" referred to an arc of counties in the Deep South with particularly dark soil. The discussion of the black belt on pp. 4–6 of *Southern Politics* (1949) makes it clear that Key was referring to those areas that had large black populations. Key writes, "It is the whites of the black belts who have the deepest and most immediate concern about the maintenance of white supremacy. Those whites who live in counties with populations 40, 50, 60, and even 80 percent Negro share a common attitude toward the Negro" (1949: 5).

This description makes little sense in a context in which the term "black belt" refers to communities distinctive only for the color of their soil.

11. Thus, the title of the most prominent work from this perspective is *The End of Southern Exceptionalism* (Shafer and Johnston 2006).

12. White and Laird (2020) and Philpot (2017) provide compelling explanations for African Americans' historically strong attachment to the Democratic Party despite their social conservatism.

13. The trajectory of the Democratic Party in the South depends at least as much, if not more, on success at the state legislative level than at the national presidential level. Though a number of states use independent commissions to draw legislative districts, that's not true for any of the southern states. Following the 2020 census, it is the state legislatures that will draw the congressional and legislative districts for the next decade (subject, of course, to judicial challenge and review and, in some cases, gubernatorial approval). Barring an ideological reorientation of the parties—for more on this, see Chapter 8—the results of the election of 2020 may impact the *speed* of the partisan shift in the South, but they will not influence its direction. The speed of the partisan transition will be a function of the extent of Democratic success at the state legislative (and gubernatorial) levels in 2020: greater success will lead to a faster transition. A victory by Trump in 2020 simply makes a Democratic victory at the presidential level in 2024 more likely. As Abramowitz's (2016) "time-for-change" model demonstrates, fellow partisans (with George H.W. Bush the singular modern example), find it extremely difficult to win elections in the wake of a two-term president.

14. See Hood, Kidd, and Morris 2012a and 2012b and Scher 1992 for descriptions of this vein of research.

15. Demographers have viewed economic circumstances as a key factor in internal (i.e., within-country) migratory patterns for over a century (see, e.g., Greenwood's 2019 treatment of the significance of E.G. Ravenstein's seminal work in the 19th century). Recent U.S. data reinforces the preeminence of economic factors in migratory decisions (Maciag 2018).

16. Obviously, this won't always be the case. They may arrive at their destination and find that the professional opportunities are more limited than they had imagined, a la *The Grapes of Wrath,* Steinbeck (1939). In general, however, we expect migrants' expectations to be warranted. Otherwise, the flow of migrants—the vector of migration—ceases or is redirected.

17. Knowles and Tropp (2018) provide a useful overview of what is a burgeoning literature.

18. Whites who respond to increased contact with movers by exiting cease to be stayers (or long-term community residents). I expect this to be a relatively small portion of the white population. In the rare cases where an inordinately large portion of the white population respond with exit, community-level population growth will be greatly inhibited. In cases where population growth is still substantial in the face of significant white (conservative) exit, the replacement of white voters by African American and Latino voters (or progressive white movers) implies a shift in the progressive direction for the community as a whole.

19. The source for the population growth data is the Surveillance, Epidemiology, and End Results Program of the National Cancer Institute. Because of the intercensal estimates generated for a wide range of relevant demographic and economic variables, this is a particularly valuable resource that I will describe in detail in Chapter 3.

Chapter 2

1. If we replace population growth with lagged population growth, we see a similar (and stronger) relationship.
2. For the sake of exposition, we are assuming that all residents are white or African American.
3. Note that in most cases, county-level analyses also include the small set of independent cities in Virginia.
4. It might also suggest that the difference between the average likelihood of voting Democrat among whites and African Americans was quite small. Even as early as 1996 or 2000, that was simply not the case.
5. In fact, individual-level analyses based on data from relevant years of the Cooperative Congressional Election Study (CCES) suggest that whatever relationship between black context and white conservatism/Republican support existed years ago, today the relationship might actually be inverted: as the relative size of the African American population grows, whites tend to be more likely to support Democratic candidates. Without the mobilized African American populations for much of the 21st century, it is difficult to assess the change in the impact of racial context on white votes at the individual level, but it is telling that in 2006 there appears to be no relationship between the relative prevalence of African Americans in the local population (though not, necessarily, in the mobilized local population), while in 2018, there is a strong positive relationship between the likelihood that a white respondent aligns themselves with the Democratic Party and the relative size of the African American population in the county in which they reside. Clearly, the old rules have changed.
6. Also see David Brooks' *Bobos in Paradise* (2001) and *On Paradise Drive* (2004).
7. Again, Monnat and Brown (2017) provide a useful overview of the literature.
8. See Hood and McKee's (2010) analysis of in-migration and voting in the 2008 presidential election in North Carolina.
9. In fact, disagreements over the prevalence of polarization among the mass public focused specifically on the variation in policy preferences (or lack thereof) between Democrats and Republicans (see Fiorina et al. 2005 and 2008).
10. Due to the greater partisan diversity among Latinos than African Americans, the pull of the Democratic Party for Latino independents under threat will be weaker than for African Americans under threat.
11. See Population Reference Bureau (2011). A related report produced by the DC Policy Center (Rusk 2017) simply concludes that, among U.S. cities, "The faster the rate of [population] growth, the lower the level of racial segregation."

12. I will also provide evidence that the same sort of demographic distinctiveness is true for migrants across the United States (not just in the South).

13. Allport (1954) is the canonical exposition of this phenomenon, including the conditions for its manifestation. Pettigrew et al. (2011) provides a useful description of the literature, particularly as it relates to the role of the conditions in producing the contact effect.

14. Abramowitz (2018) provides a thorough description of the alignment and polarization of the parties over the last several decades.

15. Philpot's (2017) discussion of this ideological and partisan pattern with the African American community is particularly insightful.

Chapter 3

1. Note that the cut-off points for the age cohorts in the NIH data are such that our sample of adults excludes those under 20. Eighteen- and 19-year-olds were included in a younger age cohort from which they could not be isolated.

2. These population figures aggregate the effects of immigration, emigration, and the net effects of births and mortality.

3. Significantly, both counties are in the same southern state, Texas.

4. Orleans County was obviously not the only county affected by Hurricane Katrina, but it had by far the most significant population loss.

5. A more complete discussion of related methodological issues may be found at Blackwell, Honaker, and King (2017a and 2017b).

6. https://www.census.gov/prod/cen2010/briefs/c2010br-01.pdf.

7. These are the fifteen counties with the highest logged difference between the adult population in 2016 and the adult population in 1996.

8. Note that relative rate of growth is based on the percentage change in population from the two most recent census years, 2000 and 2010.

9. As it happens, Buchanan County bordered the county I grew up in, Tazewell, itself a locale that has experienced significant population loss.

10. These are quartiles of the log of adult population growth from 1996 to 2016. If we use the quartiles of percent of adult population growth, the substantive results are quite similar.

11. Based on ANOVA results (not reported), these differences are statistically significant.

12. Based on ANOVA results (not reported), these differences are statistically significant.

13. Based on ANOVA results (not reported), these differences are *not* statistically significant.

14. See Monnat and Brown (2017), Scala and Johnson (2017), and Scala, Johnson, and Rogers (2015).

15. At the national level, the partisan distinctiveness of white and minority voters is quite dramatic. In a recent report produced by the Pew Charitable Trust (Bump 2019), approximately 57% of whites identified as Republicans. Among Asian Americans and

Hispanics, nearly 70% identified as Democrats, and among African Americans, nearly 90% identified as Democrats.

16. The negative value log corrections for the multivariate model were based on 1996–2016 population change.

17. This is the one variable where the 2000-base year results are significantly distinct from the 1996-base year results. In the case of the 2000-base year results, there is evidence of a positive relationship between the change in unemployment and the change in Democratic support. Given the inconsistencies manifest in the results related to the impact of changing economic contexts on changing partisan fortunes, no firm conclusions may be drawn.

18. See Aistrup (1996) on "creeping realignment."

19. See Gervais and Morris (2018) for a fuller discussion of this dynamic in a national context.

Chapter 4

1. Quote attributed to John Gardner by David Long (1986). According to Long, Gardner contended that all stories fit into one of two categories: (1) a man [or woman] goes on a journey, or (2) a stranger comes to town. In the context of movers and stayers theory, I would argue there is a third category—a member of the community leaves. Those three narrative structures cover a lot of ground—and can tell us a lot about southern politics.

2. See Hillygus, McKee, and Young (2017) for a description of this literature.

3. This is in comparison to the states in the other U.S. census regions (the Northeast, the Midwest, and the West). Technically, the Census Bureau defines the South in broader terms than the 11 states of the former Confederacy. Regardless of whether the non-Confederacy states included in the Census Bureau's definition of the South are reallocated to the Northeast or the Midwest, the South was, and likely still is, the most Republican region.

4. Brown (1988) is an important exception here. Rather than focusing on the direct effect of migrants on the political character of their new homes, he evaluates the impact of existing residents (whom I refer to as *stayers*) on the partisan attachments of the newcomers (*movers*). He concludes that migrants tend to modify their political orientations to fit their new surroundings. This is dynamic obviously reinforces the pre-existing political environment. Though the mechanism is different, the net effect is similar to that produced by the "Big Sort" dynamic: red states/communities growing redder, blue states/communities growing bluer. Remembering the "redness" of the southern states in the early 21st century—two straight presidential elections in which neither Democratic candidate (one a southerner) won a southern state—there was no blue to get "bluer." What we see in current southern politics is partisan change; theories predicting stasis and reinforcement aren't consistent with the empirical record.

5. Note the contrast with Brown's argument regarding the influence of existing residents on the political orientations of new migrants (1988).

6. And to be clear, "migrants" are internal movers, not "immigrants" from other countries.

7. A recent Pew report on the demographic characteristics of Democrats and Republicans provides an excellent overview of each of the distinctions listed below. See https://www.people-press.org/2018/03/20/1-trends-in-party-affiliation-among-demographic-groups/.

8. See Fisher (2020) for a thoughtful and extensive analysis of the changing generational character of partisan attachment.

9. Most significantly, I got a dog.

10. The average American moves 11 times during their lifetime (U.S. Census Bureau).

11. At least one previous study of the impact of migration on southern politics (Hillygus, McKee and Young 2017) uses this CCES question as an indicator of *inter*-regional migration. Given the limited number of data options, this is not an unreasonable strategy. But the wording of the question makes no reference to crossing state or regional boundaries; that is an inference of the researchers. Nothing about the actual wording of the question excludes *intra*state migrants, and so I interpret participants' responses in that light.

12. As distinct from patterns of *immigration* or international migration.

13. These nominal distinctions between types of migrations should not be taken to imply any ordinal ranking of distances associated with the types of migrations. It is easy to think of examples in which migrants move between neighborhoods many miles apart that are in the same city, county, state, and region (think about moving from the Beaches area in Jacksonville, FL to far Westside of the same city). It is equally easy to think of very short migrations—say from Prince George's County, MD, to Alexandria, VA, just across the Potomac—in which the movers are living in a new neighborhood, a new voting precinct, a new city, a new state, and a new region (given the traditional definition of the South). While the number of political boundaries crossed is often associated with the geographic distance moved, the relationship is far from perfect.

14. Analyses in this chapter are based on a sample weighted by the *weight-cumulative* variable provided for the 2006–2018 cumulative CCES dataset. This variable is a transformation of the weight variable, which accounts for the considerable variation in sample sizes across the CCES surveys included in the cumulative dataset.

15. It is important to remember that this graphic is based on joint responses to the following questions from the CCES:

    "How long have you lived in your current city of residence? (Years)"
    "How long have you lived in your current city of residence? (Months)"

    Due to the nature of the questions, certain types of moves—those within the same city—would not be reflected in the migration data.

16. Note that the composition of the "native" group changes when the comparison group changes from one-year migrants to four-year migrants. In the overwhelming majority of cases, a native in one context is a native in the other context. However, when the comparison is between one-year migrants and all others, some portion of the native

population will be four-year migrants—individuals who have lived in their current cities at least a year but less than four years.

17. Again, the South refers to the states of the former Confederacy: Alabama, Arkansas, Florida, Georgia, Louisiana, Mississippi, North Carolina, South Carolina, Tennessee, Texas, and Virginia.

18. This does not mean that the elderly do not move; clearly they move, often when they reach retirement age, and that is reflected in Figures 4.1–4.4. It is too easy, however, to overestimate the relative size of the group of elderly migrants. Whether in the South or the rest of the United States, elderly migrants are on the tail of the distribution; they are not the central tendency.

19. See https://www.people-press.org/2003/11/05/part-1-party-affiliation/.

20. See https://www.people-press.org/2018/03/20/1-trends-in-party-affiliation-among-demographic-groups/.

21. Some college, 2-year degree, 4-year degree, and Post-grad would all be included in the "beyond" high school designation.

22. This difference is significant at the $p < .01$ level. The same is true for all other bivariate results presented in this chapter except where indicated.

23. This result is only significant at the $p < .1$ level (one-tailed test).

24. Note that these income figures are necessarily based on the sample from the Cumulative CCES file covering the 2006–2018 time period. The income figures reflect the data from that time period and are thus somewhat lower than the current income figures.

25. There is even some evidence suggesting that the arrival of international immigrants who do not go on to become naturalized citizens benefits the Republican Party. The argument is that natives react negatively (as group conflict theory would predict) to the influx of new migrants, and because of the Republican Party's conservative position on immigration policy, these natives become more aligned with the Republican Party (see Mayda, Peri, and Stengress 2016). Evidence of a reactionary effect of undocumented migration on natives has been an aspect of the literature on migratory politics for years (see Hood and Morris 1998).

26. The only category of respondents with a longer average residency is "Other."

27. Results generated from unweighted samples are statistically and substantively consistent with results generated from weighted samples. In those few situations in which there were differences, the weighted sample tended to produce results with larger standard errors. Taking a conservative approach, I have chosen to focus on the results based on the weighted sample.

28. One-year migrants are also more likely to identify as independents. Given their demographics, this is not especially surprising.

29. The specific operationalization of migrant plays a somewhat more important role in determining the relative prevalence of independents among movers and stayers. When focusing on the most recent category of movers, independents appear to be ever so slightly more common among stayers. The opposite is true—and the effect is larger—if we extend the time period for migration to anything short of four years.

Chapter 5

1. Population figures based on data from the U.S. Census.
2. Population figures based on data from the U.S. Census.
3. Except in a trivial sense. If rural areas that experience significant population growth attain urban/suburban status, then we will see a rural–urban divide on politics, but it will be the result of population growth.
4. However, as we'll see in Chapter 7, movers of retirement age are politically distinctive in an important way from those of retirement age who are stayers, and this distinctiveness cautions against overestimating the anti-progressive impact of migrant retirees.
5. I want to thank Michael Hardison, one the students in my recent Southern Politics class, for bringing the unusual character of Brunswick County to my attention.
6. All of which I have vacationed on.
7. 2000 figures are based on actual U.S. Census data. The 2018 figures are U.S. Census estimates.
8. As an example of this dynamic, consider the exit of whites from Houston in response to the migration of African Americans following Hurricane Katrina (see Anastasopoulos 2019).
9. Metzel (2019) provides a useful discussion of these and related issues.
10. For descriptions of group conflict theory and related references see Giles and Hertz 1994; Glaser 1994; Hutchings and Valentino 2004; and Oliver and Mendelberg 2000.
11. The residence question was asked in the following years: 2006, 2007, 2009, 2010, 2011, 2014, 2015, 2016, 2017, and 2018.
12. Respondents who (1) gave inconsistent responses to the residential longevity questions (i.e., number of months did not agree with number of years) and/or (2) gave highly implausible responses (i.e., time of residence in excess of 150 years) were excluded from the analysis.
13. Note that many respondents participated in the CCES during the first decade of this century.
14. As before, results are based on weighted data.
15. The difference in the mean time in residence for whites and non-whites is statistically significant at the .05 level.
16. At the .001 level.
17. These averages were calculated by taking the mean of the adult population estimate for the county of residency for each respondent satisfying the residency criteria (stayer or not) during the year in which the respondent was surveyed.
18. The difference in means is insignificant at the .05 level.
19. We will examine the demographic, political, and geographic distinctiveness of stayers and non-stayers of color in Chapter 6.
20. Note that this "exit" dynamic should be consistent across whites and people of color. To the extent it contributes to the increased progressivism of high-growth areas, the stayers who exit—regardless of race—should be conservatives (and Republicans). If this effect is not consistent across races, then the exit effect plays a much smaller role

in the political transition of high-growth areas than the role played by the political transformation of stayers (who, by definition, remain).

21. The dramatic decline in partisan cross-pressuring through identification with an array of groups with distinctive political identities (see Mason 2018) reinforces the impact of racial or ethnic identity on partisan choice.

22. The panel data gathered through the General Social Survey and the American National Election Study—which are often considered the standards for national panel data—are simply far too limited both in size and in temporal scope. And in the case of the General Social Survey, the migration queries—focusing on region of residence when respondent was 16 and migration activity since age 16—do not allow us to identify recent migrants (at all), migrants from other states (but the same region), or migrants from the same state. Given these limitations—and the others already referenced—the GSS is simply insufficient for my analytical purposes.

23. After adding a constant term sufficient to ensure all calculations were positive (to enable the subsequent calculation of the natural log for each term).

24. Pearson $X^2 = 115.57$, p=.000.

25. Pearson $X^2 = 248.56$, p=.000.

26. Remember that "leaners"—independents who indicate that they lean toward one party or the other—are counted as identifying with that party toward which they lean. For example, if a respondent identifies as an independent in response to the initial party ID question and then in response to a subsequent question indicates a lean toward the Republican Party, that respondent is coded as a Republican.

27. The literature on the relationship between age, education, and income—particularly as it relates to the southern context—is discussed extensively in Chapters 2, 3, and 4. Research on the partisan gap between males and females is now decades long; females have tended to identify as Democrats and support Democratic candidates at a significantly higher rate than men—particularly among whites. See Box-Steffensmeier, et al. (2004) for a description of the early canonical literature and Ondercin (2017) for a treatment of more recent work. Note that there is a distinctive flavor to the gender gap among southern whites (see Maxwell and Shields 2019).

28. If we expand the set of "Katrina-affected" parishes/counties to those in Louisiana and Mississippi that were widely considered to have suffered the most severely beyond Orleans Parish—St. Bernard Parish, Jefferson Parish, Hancock County, Harrison County, and Jackson County—we obtain fully comparable statistical and substantive results.

29. Data on the locations from which movers emigrated is unavailable. Future research with additional data might very profitably examine the local contextual effects associated with emigration. That is beyond the scope of the current project.

30. See Garson (2019) for a full discussion of the methodological rationale for modeling clustered variables in a multilevel framework.

31. Note that the multilevel model results presented below are based on the unweighted sample. To avoid biased coefficients, the proper weights must be available for each level of analysis. For the cumulative CCES data file, only two weights are available: the original by-survey weights and cumulative weights (which have been applied

throughout the foregoing analysis). The cumulative weights are simply a transformation of the original survey weights based on the relative sizes of the survey samples. Unfortunately, this provides no information regarding the proper weighting of responses at the fips or county-level, and given the serious inferential issues associated with improper weighting at any level of a multilevel analysis, the estimates are based on the unweighted sample.

32. This is true even in the face of static population controls—a tough standard given the high correlation between different measures of population and population growth which consistently range between .7 and .9.

I evaluated the impact of three static population controls in both multivariate models: (1) current (2018) adult population, (2) adult population in the survey year, and (3) the log of adult population in the survey year. Population growth consistently outperformed current adult population in both partisanship and ideology models. Population growth also consistently outperformed logged survey year adult population. In a subset of models, adult population in the survey year outperformed population growth. The results in the models where adult population in the survey year outperformed population growth appear to be driven by the earliest surveys in our sample—surveys in which the respondents' experience of growth included years from the previous century. In models limited to respondents from the 2011 survey forward, population growth and population perform comparably. In estimates from the most recent surveys—since 2011 forward—population growth clearly outperforms population (i.e., growth is signed correctly and highly significant, and population is not close to any traditional standard of significance). In sum, even in the face of strong controls, there is substantial evidence that population growth (and population decline) have a substantial impact on white stayers. If we focus specifically on the population dynamics of the last 15+ years—the time period in which population growth and decline are influencing the political orientations and attitudes of the more recent survey respondents—the empirical support for the predicted relationship between population growth/decline and partisanship is overwhelming.

In the case of ideology, the support for a population growth/decline dynamic is even stronger. In some cases, the population control and population growth performed at comparable levels. In other cases, population growth outperformed one or more of the population controls. Throughout the range of ideology models estimated, population growth performed consistently well.

Chapter 6

1. See McKee (2012) for a full description of the literature on the impact of African American context on white racial conservatism and white partisanship.

2. Unfortunately, even with the combined data from multiple iterations of the CCES, we do not have a large enough sample of Asian American (or Middle Eastern) stayers from which to draw generalizable inferences.

3. The focus on "perceived" threat is not meant to suggest the absence of a real threat to the local economy, the viability of the social community, or the long-term maintenance of relationships with family and friends. But the perception of threat is instrumental in eliciting a political response, and while the perception of threat is likely to be closely tied to the broad range of negative effects associated with population, it may also be associated—in a more complex manner—with certain effects related to population increase (particularly for people of color). I explain this in more detail below.

4. Farrington (2016) provides an insightful treatment of the transition of African Americans out of the Republican Party during this era.

5. The percentage of white southern stayers who are Democrats (or Democratically leaning independents) *and* liberal or very liberal (13%) is more than the number of true independents in the same population.

6. For white stayers, the "similar community members" would be other white stayers in their community. As the extent of the similarity increases—similar age, similar religious orientation, comparable education, same economic class—the strength of the effect of the partisanship and/or ideology of the "similar community members" increases.

7. Remember that "stayers" and "movers" are mutually exclusive groups, but they are not exhaustive. A significant portion of every racial/ethnic group fails to satisfy the criteria for either the stayer group or the mover group. These respondents have lived too long in their current cities to be considered movers but not long enough to be considered stayers. The non-stayer group includes these individuals and movers. The stayer group and the non-stayer group (which includes, but is not limited to, movers) are mutually exclusive and exhaustive.

8. As throughout, unless otherwise indicated, results are for the South.

9. As one would expect, the difference in median ages between the groups (40 vs. 52) is comparable to the difference in means (39 vs. 50).

10. $X^2 = 44.2023$, $p = 0.002$.

11. This is also consistent with the group-based dynamic outlined in White and Laird (2020).

12. Note that all counties are categorized a single time, and their category designation remains constant regardless of the focal population (white, African American, Latino) of the analysis.

13. In both cases, the population growth distribution is based on the logged population growth for each respondent's county for the decade prior to the year of survey participation.

14. Just as Latinos' partisan attachments fall between those of African Americans and whites, the partisan impact of population decline on Latino stayers is also likely to fall between that of African Americans and whites.

15. As in the case of whites and African Americans, it is important to remember that our target population is potential voters or citizens. While some of the migrant/non-migrant distinctions among citizens may also manifest among the larger population of Latinos (including non-citizens)—i.e., migrants tend to be younger than

non-migrants—because I am interested in variations in partisan attachment and voting, the specific focus is potential voters.

16. The difference between the median ages for the stayer and non-stayer groups among Latinos is somewhat larger, 52 vs. 37.

17. If we compare the means from the 12-category family income variable for Latino stayers and Latino non-stayers, they are statistically indistinguishable.

18. Note that "High School Grad" is the modal category for stayers and non-stayers. Educational differences between stayers and non-stayers are significant at the .10 level.

19. $X^2 = 35.0826$, $p = 0.0139$.

20. $X^2 = 57.4988$, $p = 0.0028$.

21. $X^2 = 22.7786$, $p = 0.1798$.

22. $X^2 = 61.7368$, $p = 0.0082$.

23. All of these moves cross substantial political boundaries—national boundaries, state boundaries, county borders, and/or city limits. That these sorts of migration are driven primarily by economic incentives and/or familial ties does not preclude the possibility that shorter, neighborhood to neighborhood moves are made primarily for political purposes (à la the "Big Sort") (see Bishop 2009).

24. Science fiction fans of my generation will no doubt be reminded of Tatooine.

Chapter 7

1. Grandma Morris was not a southerner. She lived in the Midwest, Ohio and Pennsylvania specifically.

2. See Jonathan Vespa's (2018) *The Graying of America: More Adults Than Kids by 2035* for a comprehensive look at the aging of the American population.

3. This difference is statistically significant at the .05 level.

4. Again, for the purposes of this analysis, retirees are those who are over 65.

5. https://www.investopedia.com/articles/retirement/020117/most-popular-states-retire-us.asp.

6. https://www.aarp.org/retirement/planning-for-retirement/info-2018/retirees-age-in-place-aarp-study.html.

7. Remember that these figures are based on the weighted sample.

8. This is true even with a reasonable weighting scheme.

9. For example, other analyses suggest that South Carolina and Texas draw larger migrant retiree numbers than our survey data suggest. See https://smartasset.com/retirement/where-are-retirees-moving.

10. https://smartasset.com/retirement/where-are-retirees-moving.

11. https://dos.myflorida.com/elections/data-statistics/voter-registration-statistics/voter-registration-monthly-reports/voter-registration-by-county-and-party/.

12. Remember that the "movers" and "stayers" categories are mutually exclusive but not exhaustive. A sizable number of respondents—and older adults more generally—have

not yet lived long enough in their current cities of residence to qualify as "stayers" nor have they moved so recently as to qualify as "movers."

13. There does not appear to be a relationship between migrant status and partisanship among people of color. The same is true for migrant status and ideology for people of color; migrant retirees are neither significantly more progressive or significantly less progressive than their less mobile peers. Given the strong progressive lean of non-whites in general—and African Americans, the largest minority group in the South, in particular—expecting to find an even more dramatic partisan and/or ideological slant among groups that are so similar (particularly in age) was unrealistic.

14. Both age and partisanship are significant at the .10 level (two-tailed test).

15. At the .05 level, two-tailed test.

16. Again, this result is based on the weighted sample of *whites* of retirement age.

17. See Fisher (2020) for a recent assessment of the literature on the growing generational divide in American politics.

Chapter 8

1. Remember that the focal point here is migration that involves the crossing of significant political boundaries (state lines and county lines). Local moves—especially those that do not involve a change in jobs, different schools for the kids, etc.—are in a different category, and they may well involve significant political considerations—just as the "Big Sort" argument suggests.

2. In the context of *politically* significant moves, those moves which cross one or more politically significant boundaries (state line, county line, or municipal border), I am concerned about those moves which have the potential to change the politics of a local community through new entry or exit. If an individual (or family) is moving to a different residence in the same community, that is not a politically significant move. These politically significant moves are the contexts in which I believe the "Big Sort" is most likely to manifest.

3. Ironically, Shafer and Johnston (2006) were correct about the significance of economic growth in modern southern politics, but by the time they were writing, the relationship between economic growth and political change was the mirror image of the one which they were describing. Economic Growth = Republican Growth had actually become Economic Growth = Democratic Growth.

4. This characterization of the Republican Party is fully consistent with Maxwell and Shield's (2019) argument in *The Long Southern Strategy*.

5. https://www.pewresearch.org/fact-tank/2020/04/07/younger-americans-view-coronavirus-outbreak-more-as-a-major-threat-to-finances-than-health/.

Bibliography

Abramowitz, Alan I. 1994. "Issue Evolution Reconsidered: Racial Attitudes and Partisanship in the U.S. Electorate." *American Journal of Political Science*. 39: 1–24.

Abramowitz, Alan I. 2018. *The Great Alignment: Race, Party Transformation, and the Rise of Donald Trump*. New Haven, CT: Yale University Press.

Abrams, Samuel T. and Morris P. Fiorina. 2012. "'The Big Sort' That Wasn't: A Skeptical Reexamination." *PS: Political Science and Politics*. 45(2): 203–210.

Adams, Greg. 1997. "Abortion: Evidence of an Issue Evolution." *American Journal of Political Science*. 41: 718–737.

Aistrup, Joseph. 1996. *The Southern Strategy Revisited: Republican Top-Down Advancement in the South*. Lexington, KY: University of Kentucky.

Allport, Gordon. 1954. *The Nature of Prejudice*. Reading, PA: Addison Wesley Publishing.

Anastasopoulos, L. Jason. 2019. "Migration, Immigration, and the Political Geography of American Cities." *American Politics Research*. 47(2): 362–390.

Bass, Jack and Walter DeVries. 1995. *The Transformation of Southern Politics: Social Change and Political Consequence Since 1945*. Athens, GA: University of Georgia Press.

Beltran, Cristina. 2010. *The Trouble with Unity: Latino Politics and the Creation of Identity*. New York: Oxford University Press.

Bishop, Bill. 2009. *The Big Sort: Why the Clustering of Like-Minded America Is Tearing us Apart*. Boston, MA: Mariner Books.

Black, Earl and Merle Black. 1987. *Politics and Society in the South*. Cambridge, MA: Harvard University Press.

Black, Earl and Merle Black. 1992. *The Vital South*. Cambridge, MA: Harvard University Press.

Black, Earl and Merle Black. 2002. *The Rise of Southern Republicans*. Cambridge, MA: Harvard University Press.

Black, Earl and Merle Black. 2012. "Deep South Politics: The Enduring Racial Division in National Elections." In *The Oxford Handbook of Southern Politics* edited by Charles S. Bullock and Mark J. Rozell, pp. 401–422. New York: Oxford University Press.

Blackwell, Matthew, James Honaker, and Gary King. 2017a. "A Unified Approach to Measurement Error and Missing Data: Overview and Applications." *Sociological Methods and Research*. 46(3): 303–341.

Blackwell, Matthew, James Honaker, and Gary King. 2017b. "A Unified Approach to Measurement Error and Missing Data: Details and Extensions." *Sociological Methods and Research*. 46(3): 342–369.

Blizzard, Brittany and Jeanne Batalova. 2019. "Naturalization Trends in the United States." *Migration Information Source*. Migration Policy Institute. https://www.migrationpolicy.org/article/naturalization-trends-united-states#.

Box-Steffensmeier, Janet M., Suzanna De Boef, and Tse-min Lin. 2004. "The Dynamics of the Partisan Gender Gap." *American Political Science Review*. 98(3): 515–528.

Brooks, David. 2001. *Bobos in Paradise*. New York: Simon and Schuster.

Brooks, David. 2004. *On Paradise Drive: How We Live Now (And Always Have) in the Future Tense*. New York: Simon and Schuster.

Browder, Glen. 2009. *The South's New Racial Politics: Inside the Race Game of Southern History*. Montgomery, AL: New South Books.

Brown, Thad A. 1988. *Migration and Politics: The Impact of Population Mobility on American Voting Behavior*. Chapel Hill, NC: UNC Press.

Bullock, Charles S., III. 2020. "Growth Versus Stagnation and Partisan Change." Paper presented at the Citadel Symposium of Southern Politics. March 5-6. Charleston, SC.

Bullock Charles S., III and Ronald Keith Gaddie. 2009. *The Triumph of Voting Rights in the South*. Norman, OK: University of Oklahoma Press.

Bullock, Charles S., Susan A. MacManus, Jeremy D. Mayer, and Mark J. Rozell. 2019. *The South and the Transformation of U.S. Politics*. New York: Oxford University Press.

Bump, Philip. 2019. "The Simple Math that Should Keep Republicans Up at Night." *Washington Post*. July 30, 2019. https://www.washingtonpost.com/politics/2019/07/30/simple-math-that-should-keep-republicans-up-night/.

Campbell, Angus, Philip E. Converse, Warren E. Miller, and Donald E. Stokes. 1960. *The American Voter*. New York: John Wiley & Sons.

Carlson, Caroline and James G. Gimpel. 2019. "Political Implications of Residential Mobility and Stasis on the Partisan Balance of Locales." *Political Geography*. 71: 103–114.

Carmines, Edward G. and James A. Stimson. 1982. "Racial Issues and the Structure of Mass Belief Systems." *Journal of Politics*. 44(1): 2–20.

Carmines, Edward G. and James A. Stimson. 1989. *Issue Evolution: Race and the Transformation of American Politics*. Princeton, NJ: Princeton University Press.

Caughey, Devin. 2018. *The Unsolid South: Mass Politics and National Representation in a One-Party Enclave*. Princeton, NJ: Princeton University Press.

Center for Immigration Studies. 2017. "Record 44.5 Million Immigrants in 2017: Non-Mexico Latin America, Asian, and African Populations Grew Most." https://cis.org/Report/Record-445-Million-Immigrants-2017?gclid=EAIaIQobChMIqpia8ri15gIVB8DICh3QEw3kEAAYASAAEgJYM_D_BwE.

Chandler, Adam. 2016. "Why Do Americans Move So Much More Than Europeans? How the National Mythos and U.S. Labor Laws Influence Geographic Mobility." *The Atlantic*. October 21, 2016.

Cox, Daniel, Jacqueline Clemence, and Eleanor O'Neill. 2019. "The Decline of Religion in American Family Life: Findings from the November 2019 American Perspectives Survey." Washington, D.C.: American Enterprise Institute. https://www.aei.org/research-products/report/the-decline-of-religion-in-american-family-life/.

Cox, Wendell. 2016. "America's Most Urban States." *Newgeography*. https://www.newgeography.com/content/005187-america-s-most-urban-states.

Crespino, Joseph. 2007. *In Search of Another Country: Mississippi and the Conservative Counterrevolution*. New York: Oxford University Press.

Davidson, Chandler and Bernard Grofman, eds. 1994. *Quiet Revolution in the South: The Impact of the Voting Rights Act, 1965-1990*. Princeton, NJ: Princeton University Press.

Dawson, Michael C. 1994. *Behind the Mule: Race and Class in African-American Politics*. Princeton, NJ: Princeton University Press.

Drutman, Lee. 2016. "Democrats are Replacing Republicans as the Preferred Party of the Very Wealthy." *Vox*. June 3. https://www.vox.com/polyarchy/2016/6/3/11843780/democrats-wealthy-party.

Edsall, Thomas B. 2019. "Red and Blue Voters Live in Different Economies." *New York Times.* September 29. https://www.nytimes.com/2019/09/25/opinion/trump-economy. html?action=click&module=Opinion&pgtype=Homepage.

Escaleras, Monica, Dukhong Kim, and Kevin M. Wagner. 2019. "You Are Who You Think You Are: Linked Fate and Vote Choices Among Latino Voters." *Politics & Policy.* 47(5): 902–930.

Farrington, Joshua D. 2016. *Black Republicans and the Transformation of the GOP.* University of Pennsylvania Press: Philadelphia, PA.

Fiorina, Morris, Seth Abrams, J. Pope. 2005. *Culture War? The Myth of a Polarized America.* New York: Pearson-Longman.

Fiorina, Morris, Seth Abrams, J. Pope. 2008. "Polarization in the American Public: Misconceptions and Misreadings." *Journal of Politics.* 70(2): 556–560.

Fisher, Patrick. 2020. "Generational Cycles in American Politics, 1952-2016." *Society.* 57: 22–29.

Florida, Richard. 2008. *Who's Your City? How the Creative Economy Is Making Where to Live the Most Important Decision of Your Life.* New York: Basic Books.

Frendreis, John P. 1989. "Migration as a Source of Changing Party Strength." *Social Science Quarterly.* 70(1): 211–220.

Gaddie, Ronald Keith. 2012. "Realignment." In *The Oxford Handbook of Southern Politics* edited by Charles S. Bullock and Mark J. Rozell, pp. 289–313. New York: Oxford University Press.

Garson, George David. 2019. *Multilevel Modeling: Applications in STATA, IBM SPSS, SAS, R, & HLM.* Los Angeles, CA: Sage Publications.

Gervais, Bryan T. and Irwin L. Morris. 2018. *Reactionary Republicanism: How the Tea Party in the House Paved the Way for Trump's Victory.* New York: Oxford University Press.

Giles, Michael W. 1977. "Percent Black and Racial Hostility: An Old Assumption Revisited." *Social Science Quarterly.* 58(3): 412–427.

Giles, Michael W. and Kaenan Hertz. 1994. "Racial Threat and Partisan Identification." *American Political Science Review.* 88(2): 317–326.

Giles, Michael W. and Melanie A. Buckner. 1993. "David Duke and Black Threat: An Old Hypothesis Revisited." *Journal of Politics.* 58(4): 1171–1180.

Gimpel, James G. 1999. *Separate Destinations: Migration, Immigration, and the Politics of Places.* Ann Arbor, MI: University of Michigan Press.

Gimpel, James G. and Jason E. Schuknecht. 2001. "Interstate Migration and Electoral Politics." *Journal of Politics.* 63(1): 207–231.

Glaser, James M. 1994. "Back to the Black Belt: Racial Environment and White Racial Attitudes in the South." *Journal of Politics.* 56(1): 21–41.

Glaser, James M. 1996. *Race, Campaign Politics, and the Realignment in the South.* New Haven, CT: Yale University Press.

Green, John C., Lyman A. Kellstedt, Corwin E. Smidt, and James L. Guth. 2009. "The Soul of the South: Religion and Southern Politics in the New Millennium." In *The New Politics of the Old South*, 4th ed. edited by Charles S. Bullock III and Mark J. Rozell, pp. 283–304. Lanham, MD: Rowman & Littlefield.

Greenwood, Michael J. 2019. "The Migration Legacy of E.G. Ravenstein." *Migration Studies.* 7 (2): 269–278.

Greider, William. 1987. *Secrets of the Temple: How the Federal Reserve Runs the Country.* New York: Simon and Schuster.

Grossman, Matt and David A. Hopkins. 2016. *Asymmetric Politics: Ideological Republicans and Group Interest Democrats*. New York: Oxford University Press.

Hibbs, Douglas A., Jr. 1987. *The American Political Economy: Macroeconomics and Electoral Politics*. Cambridge, MA: Harvard University Press.

Hillygus, D. Sunshine and Todd G. Shields. 2008. *The Persuadable Voter: Wedge Issues in Presidential Campaigns*. Princeton, NJ: Princeton University Press.

Hillygus, D. Sunshine, Seth C. McKee, and McKenzie Young. 2017. "*Polls and Elections*: Reversal of Fortune: The Political Behavior of White Migrants in the South." *Presidential Studies Quarterly*. 47(2): 354–364.

Honaker, James, Gary King, and Matthew Blackwell. 2011. "Amelia II: A Program for Missing Data." *Journal of Statistical Software*. 45(7): 1–47.

Hood, M.V., III and Seth C. McKee. 2010. "What Made Carolina Blue? In-migration and the 2008 North Carolina Presidential Vote." *American Politics Research*. 38(2): 266–302.

Hood, M.V., III and Irwin L. Morris. 1997. "*Amigos o Enemigos?*: Racial Context, Racial Attitudes, and White Public Opinion Towards Immigration." *Social Science Quarterly*. June 78(2): 309–323.

Hood, M.V., III and Irwin L. Morris. 1998. "Give Us Your Tired, Your Poor, . . . But Make Sure They Have a Green Card: The Effects of Documented and Undocumented Migrant Context on Anglo Opinion Towards Immigration." *Political Behavior*. March: 1–15.

Hood, M.V., III and Irwin L. Morris. 2000. "Brother, Can You Spare a Dime: Racial/ Ethnic Context and the Anglo Vote on Proposition 187." *Social Science Quarterly*. 81(1): 194–206.

Hood, M.V. III, Quentin Kidd, and Irwin L. Morris. 2004. A Report on the Reintroduction of the *Elephas maximus* in the Southern United States: Explaining the Rise of Republican State Parties, 1960–2000. *American Politics Research*. 32: 68–101.

Hood, M.V. III, Quentin Kidd, and Irwin L. Morris. 2008. Two Sides of the Same Coin? A Panel Granger Analysis of Black Electoral Mobilization and GOP Growth in the South, 1960–2004. *Political Analysis*. 16(3): 324–344.

Hood, M.V., Quentin Kidd, and Irwin L. Morris. 2012a. *The Rational Southerner: Black Mobilization, Republican Growth, and the Partisan Transformation of the American South*. New York: Oxford University Press.

Hood, M.V., Quentin Kidd, and Irwin L. Morris. 2012b. "Partisan Change in the American South: From Radical Fringe to Conservative Mainstream." In *Oxford Handbook on Southern Politics* edited by Charles Bullock III and Mark Rozell, pp. 330–354. Oxford: Oxford University Press.

Hopkins, Daniel J. 2018. *The Increasingly United States: How and Why American Political Behavior Nationalized*. Chicago, IL: University of Chicago Press.

Huddy, Leonie, Lilliana Mason, and Lene Aaroe. 2015. "Expressive Partisanship: Campaign Involvement, Political Emotion, and Partisan Identity." *American Political Science Review*. 109: 1–17.

Hutchings, Vincent L. and Nicholas A. Valentino. 2004. "The Centrality of Race in American Politics." *Annual Review of Political Science*. 7: 383–408.

Iyengar, Shanto, Yphtach Lelkes, Matthew Levendusky, Neil Malhotra, and Sean J. Westwood. 2019. "The Origins and Consequences of Affective Polarization in the United States." *Annual Review of Political Science*. 22: 129–146.

Jurjevich, Jason R. and David A. Plane. 2012. "Voters on the Move: The Political Effectiveness of Migration and its Effects on State Party Competition." *Political Geography*. 31(7): 429–443.

Kellstedt, Lyman A., James L. Guth, John C. Green, and Corwin E. Smidt. 2007. "The Soul of the South: Religion and Southern Politics in the Twenty-first Century." In *The New Politics of the Old South*, 3rd ed. edited by Charles S. Bullock III and Mark J. Rozell, pp. 301–320. Lanham, MD: Rowman & Littlefield.

Key, V.O. 1949. *Southern Politics in State and Nation*. New York: A. A. Knopf.

Kimball, David C., Matthew Owings, and Michael Artime. 2010. Paper presented at the Annual Meeting of the Midwest Political Science Association. Chicago, IL.

Knowles, Eric D. and Linda R. Tropp. 2018. "The Racial and Economic Context of Trump Support: Evidence for Threat, Identity, and Contact Effects in the 2016 Presidential Election." *Social Psychological and Personality Sciences*. 9(3): 275–284.

Kuriwaki, Shiro. 2018. "Cumulative CCES Common Content (2006-2018)." https://doi.org/10.7910/DVN/II2DB6. Harvard Dataverse, V4.

Kuziemko, Ilyana and Ebonya Washington. 2018. "Why Did the Democrats Lose the South? Bringing New Data to an Old Debate." *American Economic Review*. 108(10): 2830–2867.

Lang, Corey and Shanna Pearson-Merkowitz. 2015. "Partisan Sorting in the United States, 1972–2012: New Evidence from a Dynamic Analysis." *Political Geography*. 48(2015): 119–129.

Layman, Geoffrey. 2001. *The Great Divide: Religious and Cultural Conflict in American Party Politics*. New York: Columbia University Press.

Lee, Frances E. 2020. "Populism and the American Party System: Opportunities and Constraints." *Perspectives on Politics*. 18(2): 370–388.

Long, David. 1986. "Notes from a Contest Judge." *Coda: Poets & Writers Newsletter*.

Levendusky, Matthew. 2009. *The Partisan Sort: How Liberals Became Democrats and Conservatives Became Republicans*. Chicago, IL: University of Chicago Press.

Lublin, David. 2004. *The Republican South: Democratization and Partisan Change*. Princeton, NJ: Princeton University Press.

Maciag, Michael. 2018. "Why Are So Many People Moving Out of the Northeast?" *Governing*. https://www.governing.com/topics/urban/gov-migration-northeast-population-trend.html.

Mangum, Maruice. 2013. "The Racial Underpinnings of Party Identification and Political Ideology." *Social Science Quarterly*. 94: 1222–1224.

Martin, Gregory J. and Steven W. Webster. 2018. "Does Residential Sorting Explain Geographic Polarization." *Political Science Research and Methods*. X: 1–17.

Mason, Lilliana. 2018. *How Politics Became Our Identity*. Chicago, IL: University of Chicago Press.

Mathews, Donald R. and James W. Prothro. 1966. *Negroes and the New Southern Politics*. New York: Harcourt.

Maxwell, Angie and Todd Shields. 2019. *The Long Southern Strategy: How Chasing White Voters in the South Changed American Politics*. New York: Oxford University Press.

Mayda, Anna Maria, Giovanni Peri, and Walter Steingress. 2016. "Immigration to the U.S.: A Problem for the Republicans or the Democrats?" NBER Working Paper No. 21941.

McCarty, Nolan, Keith Poole, and Howard Rosenthal. 2006. *Polarized America: The Dance of Ideology and Unequal Riches*. Cambridge, MA: MIT Press.

McGhee, Eric and Daniel Krimm. 2009. "Party Registration and the Geography of Party Polarization." *Polity*. 41(2009): 345–367.

McKee, Seth C. 2010. *Republican Ascendancy in Southern U.S. House Elections*. Boulder, CO: Westview Press.

McKee, Seth C. 2012. "Demanding Deliverance in Dixie: Race, the Civil Rights Movement, and Southern Politics." In The Oxford Handbook of Southern Politics edited by Charles S. Bullock and Mark J. Rozell, pp. 153–178. New York: Oxford University Press.

McKee, Seth C. 2019. *The Dynamics of Southern Politics: Causes and Consequences.* Washington, DC: CQ Press.

McKee, Seth C. and Jeremy M. Teigen. 2009. "Probing the Reds and Blues: Sectionalism and Voter Location in the 2000 and 2004 U.S. Presidential Elections." *Political Geography.* 28(8): 484–495.

McKee, Seth C. and Jeremy M. Teigen. 2016. "The New Blue: Northern In-Migration in Southern Presidential Elections." *PS: Political Science and Politics.* 49(2): 228–233.

Metzel, Jonathan M. 2019. *Dying of Whiteness: How the Politics of Racial Resentment Is Killing America's Heartland.* New York: Basic Books.

Monnat, Shannon M. and David L. Brown. 2017. "More Than a Revolt: Landscapes of Despair and the 2016 Presidential Election." *Journal of Rural Studies.* 55(2017): 227–236.

Moreland, L.W. and Robert P. Steed. 2012. "The South and Presidential Elections." In *The Oxford Handbook of Southern Politics* edited by Charles S. Bullock and Mark J. Rozell, pp. 470–483. New York: Oxford University Press.

Myers, Adam S. 2013. "Secular Geographical Polarization in the American South: The Case of Texas, 1996-2010." *Electoral Studies.* 32(2013): 48–62.

Nadeau, Richard and Harold W. Stanley. 1993. "Class Polarization in Partisanship among Native Southern Whites, 1952-1990." *American Journal of Political Science.* 37: 900–919.

Nadeau, Richard, Richard G. Niemi, Harold W. Stanley, and Jean-Francois Godbout. 2004. "Class, Party, and South/Non-South Differences: An Update." *American Politics Research.* 32: 52–67.

Oliver, J. Eric and Tali Mendelberg. 2000. "Reconsidering the Environmental Determinants of White Racial Attitudes." *American Journal of Political Science.* 44: 574–589.

Ondercin, Heather L. 2017. "Who Is Responsible for the Gender Gap? The Dynamics of Men's and Women's Democratic Macropartisanship, 1950-2012." *Political Research Quarterly.* 70(4): 749–761.

Perlstein, Rick. 2001. *Before the Storm: Barry Goldwater and the Unmaking of the American Consensus.* New York: Hill and Wong.

Pettigrew, Thomas F., Linda R. Tropp, Ulrich Wagner, and Oliver Christ. 2011. "Recent Advances in Intergroup Contact Theory." *International Journal of Intercultural Relations.* 35: 271–280.

Pew Research Center. 2016. *2016 Party Identification: Detailed Tables.* https://www.people-press.org/2016/09/13/2016-party-identification-detailed-tables/.

Pew Research Center. 2018a. *The Age Gap in Religion Around the World: By Several Measures, Young Adults Tend to be Less Religious Than Their Elders; The Opposite Is Rarely True.* https://www.pewforum.org/2018/06/13/the-age-gap-in-religion-around-the-world/.

Pew Research Center. 2018b. *Wide Gender Gap, Growing Educational Divide in Voters' Party Identification: College Graduates Increasingly Align with Democratic Party.* https://www.people-press.org/2018/03/20/1-trends-in-party-affiliation-among-demographic-groups/.

Phillips, Kevin. 1969. *The Emerging Republican Majority.* New York: Arlington House.

Philpot, Tasha S. 2017. *Conservative but Not Republican: The Paradox of Party Identification and Ideology among African Americans*. New York: Cambridge University Press.

Population Reference Bureau. 2011. "Least Segregated U.S. Metros Concentrated in the Fast-Growing South and West." https://www.prb.org/us-residential-segregation/.

Porter, Eduardo. 2019. "Can a Coal Town Reinvent Itself?" *New York Times*. December 6. https://www.nytimes.com/2019/12/06/business/economy/coal-future-virginia.html.

Radford, Jynnah. 2019. "Key Findings about U.S. Immigrants." *Fact Tank: News in the Numbers*. Pew Research Center. https://www.pewresearch.org/fact-tank/2019/06/17/key-findings-about-u-s-immigrants/.

Rice, Tom W. and Meredith L. Pepper. 1997. "Region, Migration, and Attitudes in the United States." *Social Science Quarterly*. 78(1): 83–95.

Richman, Jesse T., Guishan A. Chatta, and David C. Earnest. 2014. "Do Non-Citizens Vote in U.S. Elections." *Electoral Studies*. 36: 149–157.

Rodden, Jonathan. 2019. *Why Cities Lose: The Deep Roots of the Urban-Rural Political Divide*. New York: Basic Books.

Rogerson, Peter. 2018. "Mapping America's Aging Population." Citylab. https://www.citylab.com/life/2018/05/mapping-americas-aging-population/561200/.

Rozell, Mark J. and Mark Caleb Smith. 2012. "Religious Conservatives and the Transformation of Southern Politics." In *The Oxford Handbook of Southern Politics* edited by Charles S. Bullock and Mark J. Rozell, pp. 133–152. New York: Oxford University Press.

Rusk, David. 2017. "*Suburbia: The Promised Land?*" D.C. Policy Center. https://www.dcpolicycenter.org/publications/suburbia-promised-land/.

Scala, Dante J. and Kenneth M. Johnson. 2017. "Political Polarization along the Rural-Urban Continuum? The Geography of the Presidential Vote, 2000-2016." *Annals of the American Academy of Political and Social Science*. 672(1): 162–184.

Scala, Dante J., Kenneth M. Johnson, and Luke T. Rogers. 2015. "Red Rural, Blue Rural? Presidential Voting Patterns in a Changing Rural America." *Political Geography*. 48(2015): 108–118.

Scher, Richard K. 1992. *Politics in the New South: Republicanism, Race and Leadership in the Twentieth Century*. New York: Paragon House.

Shafer, Byron E. and Richard Johnston. 2001. "The Transformation of Southern Politics Revisited: The House of Representatives as a Window." *British Journal of Political Science*. 31(October): 601–625.

Shafer, Byron E. and Richard Johnston. 2006. *The End of Southern Exceptionalism: Class, Race, and Partisan Change in the Postwar South*. Cambridge, MA: Harvard University Press.

Simien Evelyn M. 2006. *Black Feminist Voices in Politics*. Albany, NY: SUNY Press.

Smith, Gregory A., Anna Schiller, and Haley Nolan. 2019. "In U.S., Decline of Christianity Continues at Rapid Pace: An Update on America's Changing Religious Landscape." Washington, D.C.: Pew Research Center.

Springer, Melanie J. 2019. "Where Is 'the South'? Assessing the Meaning of Geography in Politics." *American Politics Research*. 47(5): 1100–1134.

Stonecash, Jeffrey M. 2000. *Class, Party, and American Politics*. Boulder, CO: Westview Press.

Stonecash, Jeffrey M. and Brewer. 2001. "Class, Race Issues, and Declining White Support for the Democratic Party in the South." *Political Behavior*. 23(2): 131–156.

Suro, Roberto, Richard Fry, and Jeffrey S. Passel. 2005. "Hispanics and the 2004 Election: Population, Electorate and Voters." *Hispanic Trends*. Washington, DC: Pew Research Center. https://www.pewresearch.org/hispanic/2005/06/27/iv-how-latinos-voted-in-2004/.

Tate, Katherine. 1994. *From Protest to Politics: The New Black Voters in American Elections*. Cambridge, MA: Harvard University Press.

Thee-Brenan, Megan. 2014. "Asian-Americans Have Had the Sharpest Shift Toward Democrats." *New York Times*. May 19. https://www.nytimes.com/2014/05/20/upshot/asian-americans-have-had-the-sharpest-shift-toward-democrats.html.

Valentino, Nicholas A. and David O. Sears. 2005. "Old Times There Are Not Forgotten: Race and Partisan Realignment in the Contemporary South." *Journal of Politics*. 67: 731–761.

Vespa, Jonathan. 2018. *The Graying of America: More Adults Than Kids by 2035*. U.S. Census Bureau. https://www.census.gov/library/stories/2018/03/graying-america.html.

Vidal, D. Xavier Medina. 2017. "Immigration Politics and Group Consciousness for Newcomers to the South." *Politics, Groups, and Identities*. 5(4): 679–706.

White, Ismail and Chryl N. Laird. 2020. *Steadfast Democrats: How Social Forces Shape Black Political Behavior*. Princeton, NJ: Princeton University Press.

White, Steven. 2014. "The Heterogeneity of Southern White Distinctiveness." *American Politics Research*. 42(4): 551–578.

White, Steven. 2019. "Race, Religion, and Obama in Appalachia." *Social Science Quarterly*. 100(1): 38–59.

Williams, Daniel K. 2011. "Voting for God and the GOP: The Role of Evangelical Religion in the Emergence of the Republican South." In *Painting Dixie Red: When, Where, Why, and How the South Became Republican* edited by Glenn Feldman, pp. 21–37. Gainesville, FL: University of Florida Press.

Index

For the benefit of digital users, indexed terms that span two pages (e.g., 52–53) may, on occasion, appear on only one of those pages.

Tables and figures are indicated by *t* and *f* following the page number

1920 presidential election, 1
1928 presidential election, 1
1948 presidential election, 1, 22
1964 presidential election, 22
1968 presidential election, 111
1994 congressional election, 2, 33
1996 presidential election, 27–28
2000 presidential election, 2–5, 4*f*,
  21, 27–28
2004 presidential election, 2–3, 21, 73, 111
2008 presidential election, 2–3, 21, 68
2010 congressional elections, 7
2012 presidential election, 2–3, 5, 21
2014 congressional election, 2
2016 presidential election, 2–5, 4*f*, 21
2018 congressional election, 2–3, 21
2020 presidential election, 191

abortion, 29, 34, 45, 187–88
Abrams, Samuel T., 51
affective polarization, 16–17, 37–38, 40,
  43, 61–62
African Americans
  1996 presidential election and, 27–28
  2000 presidential election and, 27–28
  class differences among, 85
  conservatism among, 9–10,
    45–46, 112–13
  contact hypothesis dynamic, 45
  in the Deep South, 24–25, 64,
    114–15, 134
  Democratic Party voters among, 6, 8,
    9–10, 15, 16, 25–28, 34, 44, 59, 85,
    88–89, 112, 135, 136–37, 137*t*, 138,
    139–41, 144–45, 145*f*, 146–51,
    149*t*, 160, 178, 179, 182–83

disenfranchisement in the South
    (1877-1965) of, 21
  median period of residency in current
    city of, 89–90, 89*t*, 90*t*, 95*t*
  "movers" among, 89–92, 91*f*, 92*f*, 94*t*,
    96*t*, 97*t*
  Republican Party voters among, 1, 15,
    25, 85, 136–37, 137*t*, 145*f*,
    147–48
  in rural areas, 6
  threat perceptions among, 139–40,
    146–47, 177
  Voting Rights Act of 1965 and, 8, 24–26,
    41, 54, 134, 135
African American stayers
  African American non-stayers
    compared to, 142–59
  in communities experiencing
    population decline, 112, 147–48,
    149*t*, 150–51, 157*f*, 157, 160, 178,
    179, 183
  in communities experiencing
    population growth, 112, 141, 146,
    149*t*, 150–51, 157*f*, 157,
    160, 179
  Democratic Party voters and, 136–37,
    137*t*, 139, 144–45, 145*f*, 146–
    49, 149*t*, 150–51, 160, 177–78,
    179, 182–83
  gender effects on political beliefs
    among, 149*t*
  ideological beliefs among, 137–38,
    138*t*, 141, 144, 145, 148, 150–51,
    160, 179
  independent voters and, 136–37, 137*t*,
    145*f*, 147–48, 150–51

African American stayers (*cont.*)
median age among, 143, 149*t*, 151
median education levels among, 144*f*,
144, 149*t*
median family income
among, 143, 149*t*
movers' impact on, 146–51, 159
Republican Party voters and, 136–37,
137*t*, 145*f*, 147–48
threat perception among, 139,
146–47, 177
white stayers compared to,
142–43, 148–49
Alabama
2000 presidential election and, 4*f*
2016 presidential election and, 4*f*
2018 congressional elections
and, 2–3
Deep South and, 2, 4–5, 55–56,
133–34, 185–86
population growth in areas of, 55–56,
55*t*, 133–34
Republican Party and, 2, 4–5
retiree movers in, 169*t*
Allport, Gordon, 44–45
Appalachia
2010 congressional elections and, 7
author's personal experience in, 7,
10–11, 107
coal industry in, 42, 107, 108,
113–15, 116
Democratic Party and, 7, 108–9
population growth in some areas of, 108
population loss in, 10–11, 107,
108, 113–15
Republican Party and, 1–2, 5–6, 7, 73,
107, 108–9, 114–15, 116
threat perception in, 42, 116
Trump and, 7, 42, 107, 108–9,
114–15, 116
Arkansas
1928 presidential election and, 1
2000 presidential election and, 4*f*, 4–5
2016 presidential election and, 4*f*, 4–5
population decline in areas of, 56–57,
58*t*, 133–34, 181–82
population growth in areas of,
55*t*, 63–64

Republican Party and, 4–5, 72, 73
retiree movers, 168–69, 169*t*
Asheville (North Carolina), 14
Asian Americans
Democratic Party voters among, 88–89,
196–97n15
median period of residency in current
city of, 89–90, 89*t*, 90*t*, 95*t*
"movers" among, 89–92, 91*f*, 92*f*, 94*t*,
96*t*, 97*t*
Republican Party voters among, 25, 88–
89, 196–97n15

Baby Boomers, 36, 77, 161–62
Bexar County (Texas), 57*t*, 170
Bishop, Bill, 12–13, 28, 29–30, 72, 183
black belt hypothesis
conservative racial views among whites
and, 40–41, 68
Deep South and, 24–25, 64, 68,
114–15, 134, 181–82, 185,
193–94n10
group conflict theory and, 41
Key on the "hard core of the political
South" and, 134–35
local political contexts and, 26–28, 40–
41, 135, 180–81, 185
Republican Party strength among
Southern whites and, 7–8,
24–25, 26–28
Rim South and, 181–82
Bolivar County (Mississippi), 58*t*
Boucher, Rick, 7
Broward County (Florida), 57*t*, 169–71
Brown, David A., 5–6
Brown, Karen, 113–14
Brown, Thad A., 75, 84, 175–76
Brunswick County (North Carolina),
110–11, 162–63
Buchanan County (Virginia), 56–57, 58*t*,
113–15, 148–49
Buncombe County (North Carolina),
14, 162–63
Bush, George W., 44, 73, 108–9, 111

Campbell, Angus, 29, 74–75, 84, 103–4
Cary (North Carolina), 14, 31
Cedar Bluff (Virginia), 31, 107

class-based theories of Southern
    partisan change
conservative economic policies, 8–9
Democratic Party electoral
    performance and, 36, 62–63
Great Recession and, 35
income growth in the South and, 9, 10–
    11, 30, 36, 53–54, 76
potential relevance in future of,
    188–89
Reagan and, 7, 8–9, 23–24
Republican Party growth in the South
    and, 9, 10–11, 23–24, 30, 35–36,
    53–54, 62–63, 76
Rim South and, 4–5, 21
Clinton, Bill, 2, 107
Clinton, Hillary
Gore's election outcome (2000)
    compared to election outcome
    (2016) of, 4–5, 17
"movers" and, 102
Obama election outcome (2012)
    compared to election outcome
    (2016) of, 5
rural voters and, 60–61, 107
Texas and, 170
urban voters and, 60–61, 108–9
Virginia and, 73, 107, 108–9
Coahoma County (Mississippi), 58t
Collin County (Texas), 57t
contact hypothesis
communities experiencing population
    decline and, 116–17, 122–23
communities experiencing population
    growth and, 113, 122
homogeneous communities
    and, 42–43
increase in progressive political views
    and, 13, 16–17, 48, 113,
    136, 178
prejudice mitigation and, 44–45, 178
residential segregation and, 180–81
rural America and, 122–23
stayers of color and, 141
unequal effects among different racial
    groups and, 45, 178
COVID-19 pandemic, 20, 190–91
Cuban Americans, 88–89

cultural theories of Southern partisan
    change, 9–11, 28–30

Dallas County (Texas), 57t, 170
Danville County (Virginia), 58t
Dawson, Michael, 140
Deep South. *See also specific states*
African Americans in, 24–25, 64,
    114–15, 134
black belt hypothesis and, 24–25, 64,
    68, 114–15, 134, 181–82, 185,
    193–94n10
conservative racial views among whites
    in, 24–25, 134
definitions of, 185–86
Democratic Party and, 4–5
population decline in areas of, 18, 63–
    64, 133–34, 181–82, 184
population growth in areas of, 18, 55–
    56, 63–64, 133–34, 181–82, 184
presidential election of 1948 and, 22
Republican Party and, 2, 4–5, 65f, 65–
    67, 66f, 67f, 133, 134
Rim South compared to, 18–19, 55–56,
    63–68, 134, 181–82, 184
state legislatures in, 66f, 66–68, 67f
US House delegations from, 65f, 65–66
Democratic Party
1996 presidential election and, 27–28
2000 presidential election and, 2,
    4–5, 17
2008 presidential election and, 2–3, 21
2016 presidential election and, 2–3, 4f,
    4–5, 21
African American voters and, 6, 8, 9–10,
    15, 16, 25–28, 34, 44, 59, 85, 88–89,
    112, 135, 136–37, 137t, 138, 139–
    41, 144–45, 145f, 146–51, 149t,
    160, 178, 179, 182–83
Asian American voters and, 88–89,
    196–97n15
communities experiencing
    population decline and, 16, 125f,
    125–26, 183–84
communities experiencing population
    growth and, 4–5, 16–17, 17f, 18–
    19, 20, 24, 29–30, 31–32, 40, 46, 48,
    56–60, 58f, 60f, 62, 109, 111–12,

Democratic Party (*cont.*)
121–23, 125*f*, 125–26, 127–28, 136, 146, 150–51, 169–70, 179, 180
Dixiecrats and, 1, 22
improving performance in Southern states during twenty-first century of, 3, 11–12, 21, 22, 24–25, 30, 36, 47, 49, 73, 133
international migrants and, 87–88
Latino voters and, 15, 16, 34, 44, 85, 88–89, 112, 136–37, 137*t*, 139, 141, 152–53, 154–55, 156, 158–59, 160, 177–78, 179, 182–83
median age of supporters of, 11, 82, 94, 98–99, 105–6
median educational attainment of supporters of, 11, 36, 77, 84, 94–95, 98–99, 105–6, 144
median income levels among supporters of, 62–63, 70*t*, 84–85, 86–87, 95–98, 105–6
median period of residency in current city of members of, 99
migration patterns to the South and, 11–12, 33–34, 47–48, 49, 71, 72, 76
movers and, 12–13, 33, 39–40, 47, 74, 86–87, 98–102, 100*f*, 101*f*, 105–6, 109, 110, 111–12, 159, 162, 175–77, 179
New Deal and, 44, 84
people of color and, 16, 19–20, 36–37, 43, 44–46, 48, 59, 105–6
progressive civil rights policies supported by, 7–8, 34, 37, 69, 102–3, 135, 187–88
racial and ethnic diversity among supporters of, 36–37, 70*t*
racially conservative views among white supporters before 1965 and, 22, 25–26, 41, 69
Rim South and, 3–4, 21, 133
rural America and, 5–6, 53, 180
"Solid South" era (1877-1965) and, 1–2, 5–6, 21, 32, 47, 76, 184–85
unemployment levels and support for, 62, 70*t*
urban voters and, 5, 29–30, 53

white voters and, 15, 16, 85, 112, 136–37, 137*t*, 139, 146, 150, 182–83
Denton County (Texas), 57*t*
Dewey, Thomas, 1
Dixiecrats, 1, 22

Evangelical Christians, 9–11, 29, 30–31, 38

Fiorina, Morris, 51
Florida
2000 presidential election and, 4*f*, 4–5
2008 presidential election and, 2–3
2012 presidential election and, 2–3
2016 presidential election and, 2–3, 4*f*, 4–5
2018 congressional election, 2–3
Democratic Party in, 5, 72
Latinos in, 158–59
population growth in, 31, 55*t*, 56, 57*t*, 63–64, 133–34, 169, 181–82, 191
Republican Party in, 4–5, 169–70
retiree movers and, 162, 168–71, 169*t*
urbanization in, 5
Florida, Richard, 28–29
Fort Bend County (Texas), 57*t*

Gardner, John, 71
Generation X, 77
Generation Z, 36
geographic polarization in Southern states
Democratic Party electoral fortunes and, 3, 17–18, 73
migration patterns in Southern states and, 17–18
population growth patterns and, 40, 63–69, 184
Georgia
2000 presidential election and, 4*f*, 4–5
2016 presidential election and, 2–3, 4*f*, 4–5
2018 congressional election, 2–3
Deep South and, 2, 133, 185–86
Democratic Party and, 4–5, 72, 133
Latinos in, 158–59
population growth in, 55*t*, 56, 57*t*, 63–64, 133–34, 169, 181–82, 191

Republican Party and, 1–2
  retiree movers in, 168–69, 169*t*
gerrymandering, 3
Gervais, Bryan, 34
Gimpel, James G., 75
Goldwater, Barry, 22
Gore, Al, 2, 4–5, 17
Great Recession, 34–35, 189
Greenville (South Carolina), 31
Grossman, Matt, 187–88
group conflict theory, 115–16
Grundy (Virginia), 113–15
gun control, 34
Gwinnett County (Georgia), 57*t*

Harding, Warren G., 1
Harris County (Texas), 57*t*, 170
Henry County (Virginia), 58*t*
Hillsborough County (Florida), 57*t*
Hillygus, D. Sunshine, 33
Hispanics. *See* Latinos
Hood, M.V. III, 8, 23–26, 41, 54
Hoover, Herbert, 1
Hopkins, Daniel, 34, 135
Hopkins, Dave, 187–88
Horry County (South Carolina), 170
Humphrey, Hubert, 111
Hurricane Katrina (2005), 54, 55, 56–57,
  62–63, 128–29

independents
  affective polarization in declining
    communities and, 16–17
  African Americans and, 136–37, 137*t*,
    145*f*, 147–48, 150–51
  Democratic Party candidates
    supported by, 33
  Latino voters and, 136–37, 137*t*,
    152–53, 154
  movers who identify as, 33, 100*f*, 101*f*,
    101–2, 110
  race's impact on partisan alignment
    among, 38–39
  retiree movers and, 171*f*, 171–72
  white voters and, 38–39, 136–37, 137*t*

Jefferson County (Arkansas), 58*t*
Johnson, Lyndon, 187

Johnston, Richard, 35–36, 53–54
Jurjevich, Jason, 32–33, 74

Kerry, John, 108–9
Key, V.O.
  black belt hypothesis of, 7–8, 9, 24–25,
    26–27, 40–41, 54, 64, 68, 114–15,
    134, 180–82, 185, 193–94n10
  group conflict theory and, 41, 116
  Southern Politics in State and Nation
    and, 1, 6–7, 134–35
  Southern states defined by, 184–85, 186
Kidd, Quentin, 8, 23–26, 41, 54

Laird, Chryl N., 140
Lake County (Florida), 169–70
Latinos. *See also* Latino stayers
  class differences among, 85
  conservatism among, 45–46, 112–13
  contact hypothesis and, 45
  Democratic Party voters among,
    15, 16, 34, 44, 85, 88–89, 112,
    136–37, 137*t*, 139, 141, 152–53,
    154–55, 156, 158–59, 160, 177–78,
    179, 182–83
  diverse national origin identities
    among, 142
  ideological beliefs among, 137–38, 138*t*,
    152–53, 154–58, 155*f*, 156*t*, 160,
    178, 179
  independent voters among, 136–37,
    137*t*, 152–53, 154
  median period of residency in current
    city of, 89–90, 89*t*, 90*t*, 95*t*
  "movers" among, 89–93, 91*f*, 92*f*, 94*t*,
    96*t*, 97*t*
  Republican Party voters among, 25, 85,
    88–89, 136–37, 137*t*, 154–55, 156
  Trump and, 44
Latino stayers
  in communities experiencing
    population decline, 112, 141, 142,
    153, 154, 155*f*, 156, 156*t*, 157*f*, 160,
    178, 179
  in communities experiencing
    population growth, 112, 141–42,
    153–56, 155*f*, 157*f*, 158, 160,
    179, 183

Latino stayers (*cont.*)
  contact hypothesis and, 141, 154–55
  Democratic Party and, 112, 136–37,
    137*t*, 141, 152–53, 154–55, 156,
    160, 177–78, 179, 182–83
  gender effects on political beliefs
    among, 156*t*
  ideological beliefs among, 137–38, 138*t*,
    152–53, 154–58, 155*f*, 156*t*, 160,
    178, 179
  independent voters and, 136–37,
    137*t*, 154
  Latino non-stayers compared
    to, 151–53
  median age among, 151, 156*t*
  median education levels among,
    151, 156*t*
  median family income among, 156*t*
  median income levels among, 151
  movers' impact on, 153–59
  Republican Party and, 136–37, 137*t*,
    154–55, 156
  threat perception among, 141, 154, 177
Lee, Frances E., 15, 88–89
Lee County (Florida), 57*t*
Leflore County (Mississippi), 58*t*
LGBTQ community, 26, 29, 34, 37,
  45, 187–88
Louisiana
  2000 presidential election and, 4*f*, 4–5
  2016 presidential election and, 4*f*, 4–5
  Deep South and, 2, 185–86
  Democratic Party in, 21
  population decline in areas of, 56–57,
    58*t*, 133–34, 181–82, 201n28
  population growth in areas of,
    55–56, 55*t*
  Republican Party and, 2, 4–5
  retiree movers in, 169*t*
Lubbock (Texas), 31
Lublin, David, 8–9, 36, 53–54

Martinsville County (Virginia), 58*t*
Mason, Liliana, 44, 188
Maxwell, Angie, 9–10, 29
McKee, Seth C., 33
Mecklenburg County (North
  Carolina), 57*t*

Medicare, 165–66
Miami-Dade County (Florida), 169–70
Middle Eastern Americans
  median period of residency in current
    city of, 89–90, 89*t*, 90*t*, 95*t*
  "movers" among, 89*t*, 91*f*, 94*t*, 96*t*, 97*t*
migration patterns in Southern
    states. *See also* movers;
    population growth
  cultural explanations for, 28–30, 33
  Democratic Party's performance in the
    South and, 11–12, 33–34, 47–48,
    49, 71, 72, 76
  economic explanations for, 33–34, 143,
    159, 183–84
  educated professionals and, 28–29
  family-related explanations for,
    159, 183–84
  international migration and, 33–34,
    87–88, 98–99, 175
  inter-regional migration and, 33–34, 49,
    76, 98–99, 175–76
  intra-regional migration and, 12, 47,
    49, 69–70, 73–74, 76, 87, 88–89,
    98–99, 175, 176
  political explanations for, 183
  Southern partisan change and, 9, 11–12,
    30, 68, 74, 76, 175
  undocumented migration and, 87
Millennials, 36, 77
Mississippi
  2000 presidential election and, 4*f*, 4–5
  2016 presidential election and, 4*f*, 4–5
  Deep South and, 2, 133, 185–86
  Democratic Party and, 133
  population decline in areas of, 56–57,
    58*t*, 133–34, 181–82, 201n28
  population growth in areas of,
    55–56, 55*t*
  Republican Party and, 2, 4–5
  retiree movers in, 169*t*
Mississippi County (Arkansas), 58*t*
Monnat, Shannon, 5–6
Morris, Irwin L., 8, 23–26, 41, 54
movers. *See also* retiree movers
  Democratic Party growth during
    twenty-first century and, 12–13,
    33, 39–40, 47, 74, 86–87, 98–102,

100f, 101f, 105–6, 109, 110, 111–12, 159, 162, 175–77, 179
departure communities impacted by absence of, 121–22, 136, 176–77, 183
employment- and economic-related reasons motivating, 12–13, 75, 78
family-related reasons motivating, 12–13
housing-related reasons motivating, 12–13
independent party voters and, 33, 100f, 101f, 101–2, 110
inter-regional movers and, 79
intra-regional movers and, 39–40, 79
local moves and, 39
median age of, 12, 13, 33, 47, 74, 76–78, 79–82, 80f, 81f, 94, 94t, 96t, 97t, 98–99, 103–4, 105–6, 109, 110, 162, 176–77, 179, 181, 182–83
median educational attainment among, 12, 33, 74–75, 76–78, 82–84, 83f, 94–95, 94t, 96t, 97t, 98–99, 103–4, 105–6, 109, 162, 176–77, 179, 181, 182–83
median income levels among, 74–75, 77–78, 84–87, 94t, 95–98, 96t, 97t, 103–4, 176–77, 179
oil and gas industry and, 186
people of color as, 88–92, 91f, 92f
political culture in the home regions of, 71–72
political reasons motivating, 12–13, 39
progressive political views among, 12, 13, 17–18, 103, 104f, 105f, 109, 110, 159, 162, 176–77, 179, 180, 181, 182–83, 186
racial diversity levels among, 33, 87–93, 98, 105–6, 179
Republican Party growth during late twentieth century, 23, 32–33, 74, 75–76, 98–99, 100f, 101f, 104–5, 109, 175
stayers influenced by presence of, 12–13, 19–20, 46, 48, 73–74, 109–10,

111–12, 121–32, 136, 141, 146–51, 159, 176–77, 178, 180, 182–83
Myers, Adam, 48–49

Nadeau, Richard, 8–9
Native Americans
median period of residency in current city of, 89–90, 89t, 90t, 95t
"movers" among, 91f, 92f, 94t, 96t, 97t
New Deal, 44, 84
New Orleans (Louisiana). See Orleans Parish (Louisiana)
Northampton County (North Carolina), 148–49
North Carolina
2000 presidential election and, 4f, 4–5
2004 presidential election and, 111
2008 presidential election and, 2–3
2016 presidential election and, 4f, 4–5, 111
2018 gubernatorial election and, 2–3
African Americans in, 111
Democratic Party and, 4–5, 21, 72, 148–49
Latinos in, 158–59
majority-minority counties in, 148–49
population decline in parts of, 148–49
population growth in, 14, 55–56, 55t, 63–64, 111, 133–34, 169, 181, 191
Republican Party and, 1–2, 111
retiree movers and, 162–63, 169, 169t
tourism in, 110–11
urbanization in, 5
white voters in, 111

Obama, Barack, 2–3, 5, 22, 34, 37, 49, 68, 189
O'Neill, Tip, 185
Orange County (Florida), 57t
Orleans Parish (Louisiana), 52–53, 58t, 59, 62–63, 70t, 128–29

Palm Beach County (Florida), 57t, 169–70
people of color. See also African Americans; Asian Americans; Latinos; Native Americans
in areas facing population decline, 44
in areas with population growth, 44–45

people of color (*cont.*)
Democratic Party and, 16, 19–20, 36–
37, 43, 44–46, 48, 59, 105–6
as movers, 88–92, 91*f*, 92*f*
Republican Party's difficulty attracting
support from, 15, 36, 43
in rural areas, 6
as "stayers," 118–19, 118*t*, 119*t*
Tea Party views regarding, 37
threat perceptions among, 16–17, 19–
20, 45–46, 48
Pepper, Meredith, 123–24
Phillips County (Arkansas), 58*t*
Plane, David A., 32–33, 74
polarization. *See* affective polarization;
geographic polarization in
Southern states
population decline
affective polarization and, 16–17, 43
African American stayers in
communities with, 112, 147–48,
149*t*, 150–51, 157*f*, 157, 160, 178,
179, 183
author's categories for measuring, 125
contact hypothesis and, 116–17, 122–23
county-level data on, 56–57, 58*t*
decline of institutions in communities
facing, 113–14
Deep South areas and, 18, 63–64, 133–
34, 181–82, 184
Democratic Party's performance in
Southern states and regions
with higher levels of, 16, 125*f*,
125–26, 183–84
economic stagnation and, 14*f*, 14–15,
62, 113
ideological beliefs in areas with, 112,
121–22, 126–27, 127*f*, 130*t*,
131, 179
immigrants viewed as source of
problems in communities
facing, 116
independent voters in communities
experiencing, 125*f*
Latino stayers in communities with,
112, 141, 142, 153, 154, 155*f*, 156,
156*t*, 157*f*, 160, 178, 179

local problems attributed to national
causes by communities facing, 115
in majority minority communities,
16, 183–84
non-religious people viewed as source
of problems in communities
facing, 115, 116
people of color viewed as source of
problems in communities facing,
115, 116
Republican Party's performance in
Southern states and regions with
higher levels of, 17–18, 19, 40, 65*f*,
65–68, 66*f*, 67*f*, 111–12, 114–15,
116, 121–23, 125*f*, 179, 183–84
Rim South areas and, CROSS
in rural areas, 16, 34, 115
"stayers" in communities with, 19, 42,
112, 121–22, 125–27, 127*f*, 136,
139, 141, 142, 146, 147–49, 149*t*,
150–51, 153, 154, 155*f*, 156, 156*t*,
157*f*, 160, 178, 179, 183
Tea Party support in areas facing, 14–15
threat perception in communities
facing, 16–17, 45–46, 113, 115,
116, 122–23
white stayers in communities
experiencing, 19, 42, 122, 125–27,
127*f*, 136, 139, 146, 148–49, 157*f*,
157, 179, 183
population growth. *See also* migration
patterns in Southern states
2008 presidential election and, 68
African American stayers in
communities with, 112, 141,
146, 149*t*, 150–51, 157*f*, 157,
160, 179
author's categories for
measuring, 124–25
class-based theories of Southern
partisan change and, 24
contact hypothesis and, 113, 122
county-level data on, 56–57, 57*t*
Deep South areas and, 18, 55–56, 63–64,
133–34, 181–82, 184
Democratic Party performance in
Southern states and regions with
higher levels of, 4–5, 16–17, 17*f*,

18–19, 20, 24, 29–30, 31–32, 40, 46,
      48, 56–60, 58*f*, 60*f*, 62, 109, 111–
      12, 121–23, 125*f*, 125–26, 127–28,
      136, 146, 150–51, 169–70, 179, 180
   economic growth and, 62, 63, 113
   exit by community natives confronting
      changes from, 113, 122, 182–83
   Florida and, 31, 55*t*, 56, 57*t*, 63–64,
      133–34, 169, 181–82, 191
   geographic polarization and, 40,
      63–69, 184
   in Georgia, 55*t*, 56, 57*t*, 63–64, 133–34,
      169, 181–82, 191
   income growth and, 14*f*, 14–15
   independent voters in communities
      experiencing, 125*f*
   Latinos stayers in communities with,
      112, 141–42, 153–56, 155*f*, 157*f*,
      158, 160, 179, 183
   majority-minority communities and,
      59–60, 60*f*
   majority-white communities and, 59*f*, 59
   metropolitan areas and, 14
   in North Carolina, 14, 55–56, 55*t*, 63–
      64, 111, 133–34, 169, 181, 191
   progressive political views in areas with,
      16, 19, 20, 48, 63–64, 68, 112, 121–
      22, 127–28, 179, 181–82, 183–84
   racial diversity and, 68–69, 113
   Republican Party performance in
      Southern states and regions with
      higher levels of, 24, 29–30, 31–32,
      65*f*, 65–68, 66*f*, 67*f*, 125*f*
   Rim South areas and, 18, 55–56, 63–64,
      133–34, 181–82, 184
   in rural areas, 16
   smaller cities and, 14
   state-level data on, 55*t*, 56
   Texas and, 31, 55–56, 55*t*, 57*t*, 63–64,
      73, 133–34, 169, 181–82, 191
Porter, Eduardo, 113–15
Protestants, 36., *See also* Evangelical
      Christians

race-based theories of Southern
      partisan change
   black belt hypothesis and, 7–8, 9, 24–25,
      26–27, 40–41, 54, 64, 68,

114–15, 134, 180–82, 185,
      193–94n10
   class-based theories and criticisms
      of, 8–9
   Republican Party growth and,
      7–8, 30, 61
   Southern Strategy and, 7–8, 9–10,
      22, 26, 29
   Voting Rights Act and, 8, 54
reactionary Republicans, 19, 34, 36–37,
      43., *See also* Tea Party
Reagan, Ronald, 7, 8–9, 23–24, 35, 187
Reconstruction, 1, 21, 185
religiosity rates in the United States, 10–
      11, 30–31, 36
Republican Party
   1994 congressional elections and, 2
   abortion policy and, 34
   African American voters and, 1, 15, 25,
      85, 136–37, 137*t*, 145*f*, 147–48
   Appalachia and, 1–2, 5–6, 7, 73, 107,
      108–9, 114–15, 116
   Asian American voters and, 25, 88–89,
      196–97n15
   class-based theories of Southern
      partisan change and, 9, 10–11, 23–
      24, 30, 35–36, 53–54, 62–63, 76
   communities experiencing population
      growth and, 24, 29–30, 31–32, 65*f*,
      65–68, 66*f*, 67*f*, 125*f*
   communities facing population decline
      and, 17–18, 19, 40, 65*f*, 65–68, 66*f*,
      67*f*, 111–12, 114–15, 116, 121–23,
      125*f*, 179, 183–84
   conservative civil rights policies and,
      7–8, 102–3, 187–88
   COVID-19 pandemic and, 190–91
   Deep South and, 2, 4–5, 65*f*, 65–67, 66*f*,
      67*f*, 133, 134
   electoral fortunes in Southern states
      during 2010s for, 3
   Evangelical Christians and, 9–10, 38
   fiscal conservatism and, 23–24,
      34–35
   gender breakdown of supporters of,
      129, 130*t*
   Latino voters and, 25, 85, 88–89, 136–
      37, 137*t*, 154–55, 156

Republican Party (*cont.*)
  limited government philosophy and, 23–24, 187
  median age of supporters of, 11, 30–31, 77–78, 82, 94, 98–99, 104–5, 125–26, 129, 130*t*
  median educational attainment of supporters of, 9, 11, 23, 30–31, 77–78, 84, 94–95, 98–99, 104–5, 129, 130*t*
  median income levels among supporters of, 9, 23, 36, 53–54, 62–63, 77, 84–85, 86–87, 95–98, 104–5, 129, 130*t*
  median period of residency in current city of members of, 99
  migration patterns to the South and, 9, 11–12, 49, 71, 72, 74–75
  "movers" and twentieth-century growth in Southern states of, 23, 32–33, 74, 75–76, 98–99, 100*f*, 101*f*, 104–5, 109, 175
  people of color's disinclination to support, 15, 36, 43
  race-based theories of Southern partisan change and, 7–8, 30, 61
  racially conservative views among supporters of, 15, 22, 24–28, 34, 37, 41
  reactionary Republicans, 19, 34, 36–37, 43
  Reconstruction Era and, 1
  religiosity levels among supporters of, 36
  retiree movers and, 164, 166–67, 169–72, 171*f*, 173–74
  Rim South and, 1–2, 4–5, 21, 65*f*, 65–67, 66*f*, 67*f*
  rural voters and, 5–6, 11, 16, 29–30
  social conservatism and, 9–10
  Southern Strategy and, 7–8, 9–10, 22, 26, 29
  Tea Party and, 7, 14–15, 34, 36, 37
  unemployment levels and support for, 53–54
  white voters and, 11, 15–16, 17–18, 25–26, 30–31, 34, 36–37, 40, 42, 48, 61–63, 85, 88–89, 119, 122–23,
    125–26, 130*t*, 136–37, 137*t*, 138–39, 146, 148–49, 177, 179, 180–81, 183
retiree movers
  in Arkansas, 168–69, 169*t*
  definition of, 165–66
  Democratic Party and, 171*f*, 171–73
  in Florida, 162, 168–71, 169*t*
  gender breakdown among, 166, 171, 172–73, 173*t*
  geographic concentration of, 164–65, 167–71
  in Georgia, 168–69, 169*t*
  ideological beliefs among, 110, 163–65, 166–67, 169–70, 172*f*, 172–73, 173*t*, 179
  independent voters among, 171*f*, 171–72
  in Louisiana, 169*t*
  median age of, 110, 166, 172–73, 173*t*
  median education levels among, 166, 172–73, 173*t*
  median income of, 166, 172–73, 173*t*
  in Mississippi, 169*t*
  in North Carolina, 162–63, 169, 169*t*
  racial demographics among, 166
  Republican Party and, 164, 166–67, 169–72, 171*f*, 173–74
  retiree stayers compared to, 163–65, 166–67, 171*f*, 171–74, 172*f*, 179
  Social Security and, 165–66
  in South Carolina, 169*t*, 170
  in Tennessee, 168–69, 169*t*
  in Texas, 169–70, 169*t*
Rice, Tom W., 123–24
Rim South. *See also specific states*
  1928 presidential election and, 1
  Black Belt hypothesis and, 181–82
  class-based theories of southern partisan change and, 4–5, 21
  Deep South compared to, 18–19, 55–56, 63–68, 134, 181–82, 184
  Democratic Party and, 3–4, 21, 133
  economic growth in, 21
  population decline in areas of, 18, 63–64, 133–34, 181–82, 184
  population growth in areas of, 18, 55–56, 63–64, 133–34, 181–82, 184

Republican Party and, 1–2, 4–5, 21, 65*f*, 65–67, 66*f*, 67*f*
state legislatures in, 66*f*, 66–68, 67*f*
US House delegations from, 65*f*, 65–66
Rodden, Jonathan, 107–8
Roosevelt, Franklin D., 84, 187
Rozell, Mark J., 9–10
rural America
2016 presidential election and, 60–61
African Americans in, 6
contact hypothesis and, 122–23
Democratic Party and, 5–6, 53, 180
Great Plains and, 5–6
majority-minority communities in, 61
nationalist backlash against globalization in, 108
New England and, 5–6
people of color in, 6
population decline in, 16, 34, 115
population growth in parts of, 16
Republican Party and, 5–6, 11, 16, 29–30
suburbanization in, 6
Trump and, 5–6, 7, 60–61
whites in, 6, 16

Saint Bernard County (Louisiana), 58*t*
Scotland County (North Carolina), 148–49
segregation, 1, 180–81
Shafer, Byron E., 35–36, 53–54
Shields, Todd, 9–10, 29
Silent Generation, 36, 77, 162
Smith, Mark Caleb, 9–10
Social Security, 165–66
South Carolina
2000 presidential election and, 4*f*, 4–5
2016 presidential election and, 4*f*, 4–5
2018 congressional election, 2–3
Deep South and, 2, 185–86
Democratic Party and, 4–5
Latinos in, 158–59
population growth in, 55*t*, 63–64, 133–34, 181–82
Republican Party and, 2, 158–59, 170
retiree movers in, 169*t*, 170
tourism in, 110–11

Southern Politics in State and Nation (Key), 1, 6–7, 134–35
Southern Strategy, 7–8, 9–10, 22, 26, 29
Springer, Melanie, 185–86
stayers. *See also* African American stayers; Latino stayers; white stayers
in communities with population decline, 19, 42, 112, 121–22, 125–27, 127*f*, 136, 139, 141, 142, 146, 147–49, 149*t*, 150–51, 153, 154, 155*f*, 156, 156*t*, 157*f*, 160, 178, 179, 183
definition of, 117
Democratic Party and, 16, 99, 125–26, 178, 182–83
ideological beliefs among, 103, 104*f*, 111–12, 121–22, 125, 126, 182–83
local problems attributed to national causes by, 40, 115
median income levels among, 85–86
median time in residence in current cities among, 118–19, 118*t*, 119*t*
movers' influence on, 12–13, 19–20, 46, 48, 73–74, 109–10, 111–12, 121–32, 136, 141, 146–51, 159, 176–77, 178, 180, 182–83
people of color as, 118–19, 118*t*, 119*t*
perceptions of threats among, 14–15, 34, 40, 122–23, 139, 141, 146–47, 154, 177
Republican Party support and, 100*f*, 100–2, 101*f*, 111–12, 121–22, 177
Tea Party support among, 14–15
Trump and, 14–15, 102
Sunflower County (Mississippi), 58*t*

Tarrant County (Texas), 57*t*, 170
Tazewell County (Virginia), 30, 107, 108–9, 148–49
Tea Party, 7, 14–15, 34, 36, 37
Tennessee
1920 presidential election and, 1
2000 presidential election and, 4*f*, 4–5
2016 presidential election and, 4*f*, 4–5
Appalachia and, 73
Democratic Party in, 133
population decline in areas of, 133–34, 181–82

Tennessee (*cont.*)
    population growth in, 55*t*, 63–64
    Republican Party in, 1–2, 4–5, 72, 73
    retiree movers in, 168–69, 169*t*
    urbanization in, 5
Texas
    2000 presidential election and, 4*f*, 4–5
    2004 presidential election and, 73
    2016 presidential election and, 2–3, 4*f*,
        4–5, 73, 170
    2018 congressional election, 2–3
    Democratic Party and, 4–5, 72
    Latinos in, 158–59
    population growth in, 31, 55–56, 55*t*,
        57*t*, 63–64, 73, 133–34, 169,
        181–82, 191
    retiree movers in, 169–70, 169*t*
    urbanization in, 5
threat perception
    group conflict theory and, 115–16
    nationalized politics and, 41–42
    partisan change and, 138–39
    people of color and, 16–17, 19–20,
        45–46, 48
    political polarization and, 139
    population decline and, 16–17, 45–46,
        113, 115, 116, 122–23
    stayers and, 14–15, 34, 40, 122–23, 139,
        141, 146–47, 154, 177
    Trump supporters and, 14–15
    whites and, 14–15, 16–17, 19–20,
        41, 48
Thurmond, Strom, 1, 22
Travis County (Texas), 57*t*
Truman, Harry, 1, 22
Trump, Donald. *See also* 2016 presidential
        election
    Appalachia and, 7, 42, 107, 108–9,
        114–15, 116
    COVID-19 pandemic and, 191
    fiscal conservatism abandoned
        by, 23–24
    Latino voters and, 44
    out-group attacks by, 37
    perceptions of threat among supporters
        of, 14–15
    reactionary Republicans and, 34, 43
    rural voters and, 5–6, 7, 60–61

    stayers among the supporters of,
        14–15, 102
    Texas and, 73, 170
    urban voters and, 60–61

Union County (Arkansas), 58*t*
urban voters, 5, 29–30, 53, 60–61, 108–9
US House of Representatives, 1, 2–3, 7
US Senate, 1, 2

Virginia
    2000 presidential election and, 4*f*,
        4–5
    2008 presidential election and, 2–3
    2012 presidential election and, 2–3
    2016 presidential election and, 2–3, 4*f*,
        4–5, 114–15
    2018 congressional election, 2–3
    2019 state legislative election in,
        5, 21, 68
    Appalachia and, 73, 107, 113–15
    Democratic Party in, 2–3, 4–5, 21,
        72, 133
    population decline in areas of, 56–57,
        58*t*, 113–15, 148–49
    population growth in, 55*t*, 73,
        133–34, 191
    Republican Party in, 1–2, 114–15
Volcker, Paul, 187
Voting Rights Act (VRA)
    African American voter mobilization
        and, 8, 24–26, 41, 54, 134, 135
    race-based theories of Southern
        partisan change and, 8, 54
    white racial conservatives movement
        to Republican Party following, 22,
        24–26, 41, 54, 69, 134, 135

Wake County (North Carolina), 57*t*, 111
Wallace, George, 111
Wampler, William, 7
Washington County (Mississippi), 58*t*
White, Ismail, 140
white stayers
    African American stayers compared to,
        142–43, 148–49
    in communities experiencing
        population decline, 19, 42, 122,

125–27, 127*f*, 136, 139, 146, 148–
49, 157*f*, 157, 179, 183
in communities experiencing
population growth, 19, 112,
125–27, 127*f*, 136, 146, 150, 157*f*,
157, 179
Democratic Party and, 16, 112, 136–37,
137*t*, 139, 146, 150, 182–83
ideological beliefs among, 120*f*, 120,
122, 130*t*, 136–38, 138*t*, 177, 179
independent voters and, 136–37, 137*t*
median age among, 40, 119, 122, 137,
143, 151
median county income in communities
with, 121
median county population size in
communities with, 120–21
median education levels among, 40,
119, 122
median income levels among, 119
median time in residence in current
cities among, 118–19, 118*t*, 119*t*
movers' influence on, 121–32,
136–37, 159
otherizing of non-majority populations
by, 42–43
Republican Party and, 34, 40, 42, 119,
122–23, 125–26, 130*t*, 136–37,

137*t*, 139, 146, 148–49, 177,
179, 183
threat perceptions among, 34, 40, 122–
23, 139, 177
white movers compared to, 91*f*, 91–92
white non-stayers compared to,
119–21, 122
white voters. *See also* white stayers
class differences among, 85
contact hypothesis and, 45
Democratic Party and, 15, 16, 85,
112, 136–37, 137*t*, 139, 146,
150, 182–83
median period of residency in current
city of, 89–90, 89*t*, 90*t*
Republican Party and, 11, 15–16, 17–18,
25–26, 30–31, 34, 36–37, 40, 42,
48, 61–63, 85, 88–89, 119, 122–
23, 125–26, 130*t*, 136–37, 137*t*,
138–39, 146, 148–49, 177, 179,
180–81, 183
in rural areas, 6, 16
Tea Party and, 14–15
threat perceptions among, 14–15, 16–
17, 19–20, 41, 48
Winchester (Virginia), 108–9

Young, McKenzie, 33